CONTRASTS IN HEALTH STATUS

VOLUME 1

Infant Death: An Analysis by Maternal Risk and Health Care

DAVID M. KESSNER, *Project Director*
JAMES SINGER, *Staff Associate*
CAROLYN E. KALK, *Research Coordinator*
EDWARD R. SCHLESINGER, *Special Consultant*
Health Services Research Study

INSTITUTE OF MEDICINE
NATIONAL ACADEMY OF SCIENCES

Washington, D.C. 1973

Available from
Printing and Publishing Office, National Academy of Sciences,
2101 Constitution Avenue, N.W., Washington, D.C. 20418

LIBRARY OF CONGRESS CATALOGING IN PUBLICATION DATA

Institute of Medicine. Panel on Health Services Research.
    Infant death.

    (Its Contrasts in health status, v. 1)
    Includes bibliographical references.
    1. Infants—Mortality. 2. United States—Statistics, Medical. I. Kessner, David M.
II. Title. [DNLM: 1. Infant mortality—U.S. 2. Maternal health services—U.S. 3. Prenatal care. WQ175 I43 1973]
RJ60.U5157   362.1'9'82097471   73-8821
ISBN 0-309-02119-7

Printed in the United States of America

PANEL ON HEALTH SERVICES RESEARCH

SAMUEL M. NABRIT, *Chairman*, The Southern Fellowships Fund

KURT W. DEUSCHLE, Mount Sinai School of Medicine
AVEDIS DONABEDIAN, University of Michigan School of Public Health
LEONARD J. DUHL, University of California, Berkeley
RASHI FEIN, Harvard Medical School
CHARLES L. HUDSON, The Cleveland Clinic
ROBERT C. LONG, Louisville, Kentucky
DAVID MECHANIC, University of Wisconsin
CLYDE PHILLIPS, Cook County Hospital, Chicago, Illinois
NORA PIORE, Columbia University
ERNEST W. SAWARD, University of Rochester School of Medicine and
    Dentistry
JOHN B. TURNER, Case Western Reserve University
ADAM YARMOLINSKY, University of Massachusetts
ALONZO S. YERBY, Harvard School of Public Health

WALSH McDERMOTT, Chairman, Board on Medicine Cornell University
    Medical College (*ex officio*)
DAVID M. KESSNER, Institute of Medicine (*ex officio*)

PRINCIPAL CONSULTANTS

SPRAGUE H. GARDINER, Indiana University
SAMUEL W. GREENHOUSE, National Institutes of Health
ABRAHAM LILIENFELD, The Johns Hopkins University
SAM SHAPIRO, The Johns Hopkins University
WILLIAM A. SILVERMAN, Greenbrea, California
J. ROBERT WILLSON, University of Michigan

SPONSORS

Major support for this study was provided by the Carnegie Corporation of New York. The work was also supported by the Association for the Aid of Crippled Children and John Hancock Life Insurance Company.

iii

Contents

Foreword

Facts have their own eloquence; and this study is full of facts, full of eloquence. It is also a thorough and carefully modest study, unpretentious yet valuable and useful. No sweeping survey of a nation is to be found; no rhetoric clobbers the reader. Nevertheless, what these medical investigators did, they did with care and persistence. When it came time to draw conclusions, they, too, were formulated in such a way that large-scale generalizations were avoided and legitimate findings made plain and stressed. This is no poorly controlled, sprawling, overly ambitious study—designed as much for the next day's dramatic news story as for any legitimate research purpose. Rather, it represents a serious effort by medical scholars to determine the exact relationship between pregnancy and the availability and receipt of maternal health services.

This is a large and heterogeneous nation, not to be glibly compared with countries such as Sweden or Denmark. Nevertheless, as the authors note in this report, the infant mortality rate of the United States suffers in comparison to that of many of the West's industrial nations, a source of continuing concern both within and outside of the medical profession. Too often, serious political charges are made on the basis of those statistics; they are cited as "proof" that for all our wealth and power we are badly derelict in our social responsibilities toward one or another group of people. Meanwhile, quite justifiably, many demand more than accusations and condemnations. Such people are not necessarily coldhearted, unbelieving, or overly suspicious. They simply know that if something is to be done, information of the broadest and most precise kind will be needed. It is all

too easy these days to take up a given statistical fact (America's position *vis-à-vis* other nation's with respect to the survival of newborn
infants) and use it as a club against the entire society. We do things
wrong, we are indifferent or worse to the needs of others—and here,
right here, is the *proof.*

What, in fact, does this thoughtful and scrupulously methodical
study tell us? Nothing about the nation's political preferences or social policy; that is not what these researchers wanted to analyze. They
know their field of competence and have very much kept to it. But
what they have learned, they are not shy in disclosing, in a language
that is straightforward, unadorned, unmistakably clear, and to the
point: Women who are pregnant and who fail to receive the full advantages of contemporary medical knowledge have a far greater likelihood of losing their children than do those fortunate women who do
indeed visit obstetricians or other physicians during pregnancy and
thereby put themselves in a position to be helped through the various
crises and emergencies that may occur. Among New York City's pregnant women for 1968, for example, a number of infants died who
very definitely would have lived, given only a substantial and continuing medical relationship between their mothers and the various
health services that exist today in that city, among others. In other
words, such children were not the victims of a profession's intellectual or scientific inadequacies. They were not boys and girls born too
soon—because certain fatal diseases have yet to be understood and
made responsive to medical treatment. They were boys and girls who,
with their mothers, of course, needed only what millions of others received: adequate medical attention. Their deaths were, by and large,
utterly avoidable.

Nor can we ignore the obvious implications of this report: It is the
poor and, so often, the blacks and Puerto Ricans of New York City
who, for various reasons, fail to get adequate pre- and postpartum
medical care. I know from my own work in various parts of this
country how it has come about that specific mothers have failed to
receive such care. (In the rural South and Appalachia, I know mothers
who have never had their children delivered by a doctor, who have
never in their lives gone near a hospital.) Until now, however, I have
not been able to call upon a conscientious and meticulous study that
establishes, for at least one major American city (a proudly progres-
sive and enlightened one at that, possessed of major medical schools
and a number of fine hospitals), the exact state of affairs so far as the
connection between pregnancy and medical care—*and* does so in such

a way that the social and racial issues at stake are made thoroughly clear. This study, so modest in its aims, written in such clear, calm, and understated language, presents all the evidence one would think anyone needs to justify a vigorous extension of maternal health services to those segments of our population that are now, medically speaking so markedly removed from such services. It remains to be seen how quick this nation will be to respond to this evidence and, thereby, how many infants will one day live who might otherwise have died.

ROBERT COLES
Harvard University

Preface

This volume is the first report of the Institute of Medicine's study of Contrasts in Health Status. Begun in 1969 under the aegis of the former Board on Medicine of the National Academy of Sciences, the study was conceived to determine the differences in health status of distinct groups of persons in our population and, insofar as possible, to relate the differences to medical care, social, biologic, and behavioral characteristics.

In developing the study, we focused on the concept of using identifiable health conditions as indicators, or tracers, to isolate and analyze specific components of health status. The study reported in this first volume uses infant birth to examine differences in need for and receipt of health services by women during pregnancy where the ultimate outcome is the survival or death of the infant.

During the past two decades, the U.S. infant mortality rate has been compared frequently to the rates of foreign countries. The comparisons, which dramatize our relatively poor position among industrialized nations, are usually accompanied by proposals to alter or restructure our system of delivering health care. Such comparisons, however, are fraught with difficulties; it should be obvious, for example, that the way health services are provided is not the only difference between Sweden and the United States. A variety of factors, such as medical, demographic, social, economic, behavioral, and the delivery of health services, affect infant mortality.

In this study, we have attempted to relate medical care, social, and demographic characteristics of the study population. Our intent was to look at different groups of women, classified according to the risk they faced of losing their infant and assess the effect that health services may have had on ameliorating their risk. By using one year's birth and infant death records from a single large U.S. city, we felt we could minimize the changes over time in the demography and environment and the quality of the vital data—factors that often impair the validity of comparative infant death studies.

QUALITY OF DATA

For our study, we were fortunate to obtain access to vital-statistics data on 140,000 births in New York City for 1968. Because the data had been gathered, coded, and placed on computer tape by the city health department, we were able to devote our efforts to further refinement, analysis, and interpretation. The data available to us included information on the mother's race and nativity; mother's and father's education; time of first and number of subsequent prenatal-care visits; the hospital where the baby was born; the attendant at birth; specific medical information about the mother's health; the infant's health at birth; and selected details of pregnancy, labor, and childbirth. Further, individual death records are linked to birth records so that in the case of infant death, the condition of the infant at birth and the medical and social characteristics of its mother are readily determined.

Underregistration is minimal for live births and infant deaths in New York City. In contrast to those in some other jurisdictions, the vital records in New York are fairly well supervised. The primary limitations relate to the completeness and reliability of certain reported items. Demographic data such as age of mother, number of children born of this pregnancy, and birth order are completely and adequately reported, while the newer items of information including education of parents, date of first prenatal visit, and number of prenatal visits are not completely reported. Of greatest concern are those items of information that are clinical in nature.

After careful review of the available literature on the reliability of clinical vital statistics, we concluded that the underreporting of medical conditions, resulting in bias, would weaken the association between risk and outcome, rather than strengthen it. Thus, it would appear that data from this study would understate the relationship between risk and outcome, rather than exaggerate it.

These New York City data make it possible for the researcher to examine infant mortality among several distinct race–nativity groups: white native born, white foreign born, Puerto Rican, and black native born. It is also possible to combine factors and analyze pre-natal care and delivery by social, demographic, and medical character-istics. Because the data are case specific and linked to death records, the medical and social characteristics of each mother can be related to the survival or death of her infant. The mother's education, for example, can be related to the amount of prenatal care she received, the type of hospital services (private or ward) she had, and the birth weight and survival of her infant.

Owing to the scope of these vital data, we could classify mothers in four risk groups: one no-risk group and three at-risk groups based on social factors (educational attainment, number of previous chil-dren and age at pregnancy, and marital status); medical conditions that could be identified at the first prenatal visit or that developed during pregnancy or labor; and combined social and medical condi-tions. As a result, we were able to compare the pregnancies of women of comparable risk who received comparable health services or who received different levels of care and to analyze associations between health services and infant mortality in women of different risk.

LIMITATIONS OF DATA

It is important to clearly set forth the limitations of the study and the data. The study is not a controlled experiment where comparable pregnant women have been assigned different kinds of medical care, carefully followed during pregnancy, and the outcome of their preg-nancy measured. We have analyzed previously recorded data for associations between specific demographic, social, and medical-care characteristics and the outcome of pregnancy. These are not simple cause-and-effect relationships but very complex associations; rarely can a single social study, regardless of its design or quality of its data, indicate that the effect is the inevitable consequence of a cause or causes. In assessing the associations between health services and preg-nancy outcome, we controlled, to the extent possible, for important demographic, social, and medical-care characteristics. Yet the nature of the research problem and the available data imposed certain con-straints. In determining social risk, for example, we had to rely largely on education as a proxy for social and economic status. We had no direct measurement of how individual women viewed themselves, lived their lives, or felt about the value of or need for health care during pregnancy. When education was combined with age of the mother and the number of her previous pregnancies and marital status, however, we felt it was—with the exception of one group—a reasonable indicator of her social risk. The exception is the group of foreign-born mothers. From a 1-day survey, we learned that of 76 foreign-born mothers, 28 were born elsewhere in North America, 15 were born in South America, and 32 were born in Europe. We are not satisfied that their educational attainment in such varied countries of origin was adequately adjusted to reflect U.S. educational-attainment levels. Most likely, there are also important ethnic–cultural influences that are not reflected in our definition of social risk.

In measuring health services that the women received, we relied on three indicators: time of first prenatal visit to a physician, number of visits, and whether the baby was delivered in a hospital ward or private service. These indicators tell us nothing about the *content* of the care. The first two tell us only that the women received a certain amount of care but neither what it consisted of nor who provided it. The third indicator tells us something about the continuity of the care she received; if her baby was delivered on a private service, she probably had the same physician or association of physicians for all of her pregnancy care; if her baby was delivered on a ward service, the probability is high that her maternal care was fragmented. It should be noted that private service does *not* simply mean the services of private physicians who practice alone, although it probably includes many of them. It means, rather, that the patients were admitted under the name of a physician who could be practicing in a neighborhood health center, a prepaid group practice, a fee-for-service partnership, or any of the many other practice organizations found in medicine today.

When we classified health services, we named the three categories adequate, intermediate, and inadequate. We could have labeled them A, B, and C or X, Y, and Z. Regardless of the terms we chose, however, degrees of adequacy of care would be implicit in the ranking. We feel this is appropriate. The categories of care are based on professional medical standards; they imply qualitative differences.

Some of the limitations that we faced in interpreting the analyses in this volume are due to the study design, others to the nature of the data, and still others to the inherent difficulties of investigating a complex social–biologic phenomenon. For example, cost data on maternal services received by the women in the New York City study were not available.

The profusion of influences that impinge on an individual's health are often impossible to identify, let alone sort and measure. Maternal behavior, knowledge, family structure, cultural background, nutrition, biologic factors, economic status, and medical care inextricably intermingle in influencing the outcome of pregnancy. Mindful of these problems, the Panel on Health Services nevertheless felt that the study, despite its limitations, could advance understanding of the issues, raise further questions, and provide information relevant to public policy decisions.

EXTRAPOLATION OF THE DATA

The extent to which results of our study can be extrapolated to other cities, such as Detroit or Chicago, is a difficult question to answer. New York City, with its population of nearly 8 million, includes a variety of racial and ethnic groups of all social and economic classes. Insofar as other large urban areas fit that general description and the data are used appropriately, our conclusions may well apply. The applicability of the data to small towns, rural areas, or the United States as a whole should be made only with the greatest of caution.

ABORTION

The year of our New York City study, 1968, was 2 years before the state's abortion laws were liberalized to allow abortions on demand. Since the law was enacted, articles have appeared in the literature that suggest abortions may significantly reduce the infant death rate. We attempted to examine this contention from existing studies. We found that the studies generally lack adequate social data that would tell us more nearly which women in our study population would be likely candidates for abortion. Also, we found that the neonatal death rates—those most likely to be affected by abortions—have fluctuated so erratically in New York City over the past 11 years that attributing their reduction to an increase in abortions would indeed be hazardous. There is no question, however, that liberalized abortion laws have reduced maternal mortality.

MATERNAL HEALTH SERVICES

While we were analyzing the infant birth and death records, we felt it would be appropriate also to look at the overall organization and delivery of maternal and infant health services in the United States. We quickly learned, however, that this was a task too large and complex to be undertaken without severely overextending our study; the amount of new data and original investigation needed for such an undertaking is enormous. Yet, we felt specific projects designed to reduce infant death needed to be acknowledged and, at least, viewed from the standpoint of existing data and readily available information. For this part of the study, we selected several Maternity and Infant Care and neonatal intensive care projects. Unfortunately, they represent only a fraction of dollars spent and services provided that potentially affect the lives of infants. They are, however, organized attempts to improve care and reflect the nation's concern for prenatal, neonatal, and infant health.

ACKNOWLEDGMENTS

On behalf of my colleagues and myself, I want to acknowledge the many persons whose time and energy were devoted to organizing and executing this study. Without their perserverance, this report would not have been possible.

Helen C. Chase, staff associate (biostatistics), was responsible for organizing, planning, and coordinating the data processing and initial analyses. She also prepared a first draft of Chapters 2 and 3 and was especially helpful in compiling much of the background information on infant mortality found in Chapter 4.

We are especially grateful to the New York City Department of Health and Frieda Nelson, biostatistician, for making the data available.

Maureen Harris assisted in the analysis and organization of the data, and Maria Garst provided valuable secretarial assistance. Programming and computer services were provided by the Data Processing Unit of the National Academy of Sciences' Office of Scientific Personnel under the direction of Herbert Soldz. In particular, we would like to acknowledge Donna Yocum, Ingrid Meier, and Dharam Jain for their programming efforts.

The services of Barbara Smith, who provided the staff with the administrative support essential to completing this project, are gratefully acknowledged. Barbara L. Stewart deserves special mention for her meticulous preparation and proofreading of the final document.

In addition to the principal consultants and the staff members, many other colleagues have offered valuable suggestions and have given freely of their time. I wish to express my appreciation to all of these individuals for their continuing interest and support.

Nevertheless, the responsibility for insufficiencies or inaccuracies in the design and execution of this program rests solely with the Panel on Health Services Research and its primary staff.

DAVID M. KESSNER
Project Director
Health Services Research Study

Conclusions

Analyses of all births in New York City in 1968 were carried out to assess the associations between a three-factor maternal health services index, maternal risk, and pregnancy outcome. The analyses lead to the following conclusions:

The three-factor maternal health services index reflects a combination of the adequacy of prenatal and other health services delivered to the mother and the infant and the social, economic, and behavioral characteristics of the mother. The index does not provide information about the content of care delivered during the prenatal, obstetrical, postnatal, or interconceptional period. Nor does it provide information about behavioral factors that lead persons to seek and receive the care.

Generally, adequacy of care, as measured by this index, is strongly and consistently associated with infant birth weight and survival, an association that is pronounced throughout the entire first year of life. The findings indicate that if all women had the pregnancy outcome of those receiving adequate health services, the overall 1968 New York City infant mortality rate of 21.9 per 1,000 live births could have been reduced as much as 33 percent to 14.7 per 1,000. Implicit in these calculations is the assumption that the entire population of women would seek and receive the health services for whatever reasons—behavioral, social, and economic—as those identified by the index as having adequate care. In the total population, the death rate was more than two-and-one-half times higher for infants of mothers with inade-

1

quate care than it was for infants of mothers with adequate care. Mothers with intermediate care had a death rate among their infants that was 50 percent higher than the rate among infants of women with adequate care and about 100 percent lower than the rate among infants of women with inadequate care.

In each of four maternal risk groups and each of four ethnic groups, generally consistent trends are found between adequacy of care as measured by the index and infant birth weight and survival. For example, among the offspring of white native-born women with social risk and adequate care, the mortality rate was one half as high as among infants of mothers of the same ethnic and risk groups with inadequate care. Similarly, twice as many infants of Puerto Rican mothers at no risk with inadequate care weighed 2,500 grams or less at birth compared to infants of no-risk Puerto Rican mothers with adequate care.

The survival of infants of different ethnic groups varies widely. Infants born to white native-born women had a death rate of 15.2 per 1,000, while infants of black native-born women had a death rate of 35.7 per 1,000—almost two-and-one-half times higher. Among offspring of women who had no risks and received adequate care, the death rate among blacks was still 50 percent higher than the rate among whites. When women with adequate care and medical risks are compared, however, the rates for blacks and whites are similar. The impact of maternal health services on infant mortality in women with social risk, however, varied according to ethnic group. Among infants born to white women with social risks, adequate care compared to inadequate care was associated with an approximate 60 percent reduction in infant mortality; the rate for black infants, however, was reduced by less than 30 percent.

There is a consistent association between social classes as measured by the educational attainment of the mothers and infant birth weight and survival. The death rate among infants of all mothers with 1 year or more of college was less than one-half that among infants of mothers who did not complete high school.

Within categories of mothers' educational attainment, there are consistent trends relating the adequacy of care as measured by the health services index to infant survival. The offspring of all mothers with 1 year or more of college and adequate care had infant death rates one half as high as infants of college-educated mothers with inadequate care.

Assigning risk to women is a relatively simple and grossly discriminating method of predicting the chances of their infants' survival. Although women assigned to the no-risk category were not truly without risk (there were 783 deaths among the 64,613 live births in this group), there were 2,332 deaths—almost three times as many—in a similar size population of infants whose mothers were classified at risk for social, medical, or combined social–medical reasons. Overall, infant mortality increased progressively from among offspring of no-risk women to among offspring of social-risk women to among offspring of medical-risk women to among offspring of women with social–medical risks. More than 95 percent of the at-risk women could have been identified by minimal, easily obtained social and medical information during an initial prenatal examination.

There are major differences in the distribution of the risk categories according to the mothers' ethnic group. Almost three fourths of black native-born mothers were at some risk, while only slightly more than one third of white native-born mothers were at risk. The differences by ethnic group were most striking for the social risks. Among women with medical risks, more Puerto Rican and black mothers than white mothers were at risk, but the differences were less pronounced.

There is a gross misallocation of services by ethnic group and care when the risks of the women are taken into account. In the distribution of care by risk there was obvious misallocation: Among mothers with inadequate care, 70 percent were classified at social, medical, or combined social–medical risks, while among women with adequate care more than 60 percent were classified as without risk. In addition, among the 22,000 black and Puerto Rican mothers at social risk, less than 2 percent received health services that could be classified as adequate and more than 50 percent had inadequate care. Similarly, less than 10 percent of these mothers with medical risks alone had adequate care.

Data furnished by selected maternal and infant health projects suggest, in some instances, that these programs ease high infant death rates in the project areas. Descriptive reports of specific maternal and

infant health programs—such as the federally funded Maternity and
Infant Care (MIC) projects were analyzed. In many projects, however,
the absence of comparison groups made it difficult to separate the effects of MIC projects from a generally declining infant mortality rate.

*Assessment of the neonatal intensive care units (NICU's), based on
before-and-after data in specific hospitals, demonstrates a benefit
for a limited population of high-risk infants.* The high costs of operation and specialized staffing of these units, however, provide argu-
ments for regional NICU's tailored to meet the needs of large geographic areas.

In sum, the results of the analysis of the 140,000 births in New
York City clearly indicate that assigning risk categories to pregnant
women can be carried out with minimal information, that infants of
women in different risk groups do experience differences in survival,
and that the mother's receipt of health services is associated with the
survival of the infant. The data emphasize that not only are black and
Puerto Rican mothers subject to higher risk and their infants to higher
mortality but that there is a gross misallocation between risk and services particularly among black and Puerto Rican mothers. These findings alone call for concerted action in attacking blatant inequities.

   The implications of these conclusions for the organization and
delivery of health services are specified in a series of recommendations.

Recommendations

When this program was initiated, a large body of information relating maternal, demographic, and social characteristics to infant mortality was already available. There was considerably less information, and often conflicting opinions, on the association between health services and infant survival. The rationale for undertaking this study was our belief that new information relating maternal risk and care to the outcome of pregnancy could be developed by analyzing the New York City vital statistics and reviewing existing data on MIC projects and NICU's. It was apparent at the outset, however, that definitive answers to some critical questions could not be developed from either or both of these sources of data. Nonetheless, the panel and its consultants believed that a firmer basis for policy recommendations could be established.

While there is an inherent risk in generalizing from limited sources of information and while further research is needed to verify some of these findings and to clarify specific complex social–medical issues raised by these analyses, we feel specific recommendations directed to changing the delivery of services are in order. Further research can and should proceed, but changes in the delivery of maternal and infant health services can now be made in some clearly indicated areas without waiting for the results of new research.

The recommendations are divided into two major categories: changes in delivery of maternal and child health services and research in the delivery of maternal and child health services. Some of the recommendations derive from our interpretation of the results of analyses of the 1968 study of live births and infant deaths in New York

City. Other recommendations result from the review of existing MIC projects and NICU's. These recommendations are so indicated by references to specific supporting data in the text. Other recommendations stem from a large body of existing pertinent literature and the interpretation of this material by the Institute's Panel on Health Services Research and its staff, their consultants, and the Council of the Institute of Medicine.

In general, the health services recommendations relate to specific actions that can now be taken within the context of existing federal, state, and local programs for providing maternal and child health services or that could be incorporated into the present eclectic private system for maternal and child health care.

CHANGES IN THE DELIVERY OF MATERNAL AND INFANT HEALTH SERVICES

All pregnant women should be evaluated in the first trimester and classified by risks that could adversely affect the survival of their infants. Using the gross social and medical criteria from the New York City study's maternal risk categories, more than 95 percent of the women with risks can be identified during an initial evaluation. (For supporting data, see Table 3-5.) By identifying the at-risk woman early in her pregnancy, it will be feasible for her physician to establish a plan for maternal and infant care that is appropriate to her social, demographic, and medical characteristics. Identifying women who are at risk in the first trimester may not always be possible within the constraints of the present medical system; however, guidelines for establishing maternal risk categories will provide health professionals with a mechanism for incorporating this procedure into their medical practice routine. (For definitions of risk factors, see Table 2-3.) Professional obstetric associations have demonstrated an interest in refining the concept of maternal risk for pregnant women; they should also take the initiative in promulgating the use of risk classifications among the private health professionals who deliver obstetrical care.

Guidelines for prenatal, obstetrical, postnatal, and interconceptional care should be established that are appropriate for the management of different risk categories. The American College of Obstetricians and Gynecologists (ACOG) is now revising its 1964 standards for prenatal, obstetrical, postnatal, and interconceptional care. These standards should be developed so they are specific for each maternal risk group. The care criteria could then form the basis for a plan for minimal care that could be incorporated into federal, state, and local maternal health service programs and could be promulgated through the ACOG's members. Further, these management criteria could be used as objective standards in evaluating maternal health services.

The data analyses completed on the 1968 New York City cohort of live births and infant deaths lend support to the concept that prenatal health services do influence pregnancy outcome. (For supporting data, see Tables 1-2 and 1-4 and Figures 1-1 and 1-10.) The data also suggest that factors other than prenatal care—perhaps general medical care for the mother and infant, motivation to obtain health care, access to health care, and so on, also play a role in the more favorable pregnancy outcome associated with our index of inadequate health services. (For supporting data, see Chapter 1, p. 31.)

Thus, while the data cannot support a guarantee that adequate maternal health services will lower infant mortality by a given percentage, when they are taken together with the information available on neonatal intensive care units, they provide substantive information indicating that medical care does affect pregnancy outcome. (For supporting data, see Chapter 5, pp. 139–143.)

Health services programs that are responsible for a defined geographic area or population should identify all pregnant women in their jurisdiction. Delivery programs that can identify the population for whom they are responsible should initiate a concerted effort to register all pregnant women and classify them as to risk. This can be done now by programs such as MIC projects, Neighborhood Health Centers, Family Health Centers, and Migrant Health Centers. An initial medical and social history and physical examination would provide the information needed for gross identification of the no-risk and at-risk groups. The data analyses from the New York City study show that the risk categories used predict differences in pregnancy outcome for all ethnic groups. (For supporting data, see Table 1-4 and Figure 1-9.)

Categorical programs that deliver obstetric and infant services should be designed so that scientifically acceptable evaluations of their impact on infant survival can be made. It has been difficult (indeed, often impossible) to make reliable judgments of the effect of specific maternal and infant health delivery programs on the outcome of pregnancy. (For supporting data, see Chapter 5, p. 131*ff*.) While it would be arduous and costly to implement evaluation on a wide scale, programs with an existing data base could be used as sites for comparative studies. It is essential that selected maternal and infant care programs, as well as more broadly conceived community health projects, build an evaluation effort into the process of delivering service.

Updated federal regulations for the Maternity and Infant Care projects should be issued. MIC policies, published in 1964, have not been formally revised to reflect changes in the program required by the 1967 amendments to the Social Security Act. Revised policies should be issued. In keeping with the intent of the 1967 legislation, they should expand the program and require MIC projects to provide prenatal and postnatal care, family planning, and other services to any woman living in the project area without other eligibility or means test requirements. The policies should also require the projects to arrange for care for any woman in the project area who needs care and to whom the project cannot, for whatever reason, provide care. Further, when care is arranged for by the project, the project should assume responsibility for assuring that the care will meet the standards established for the project's own patients (Chapter 5).

It is clear that these recommendations concerning the delivery of maternal health services should not be undertaken without a concurrent reassessment of pertinent manpower and facility requirements. Although this study does not attempt to analyze health manpower roles or facilities in detail, pertinent existing literature has been reviewed, and we cannot avoid identifying need for changes in the organization of obstetric health services. The recommendations relating to facilities and manpower that follow have the unqualified support of a large body of expert professional judgment and can be instituted in the context of our present health services delivery system.

The delivery of special infant health services, particularly neonatal intensive care, should be regionalized. Available data support the contention that intensive care management of low-birth-weight infants organized regionally will result in reduction of infant mortality (Chapter 5, p. 143). Neonatal intensive care services require specially staffed and equipped, hospital-based facilities. Such special units should be developed on a centralized community or regional basis to avoid duplicating costly services and competing for scarce personnel.

Concurrent with the development of such services, a complementary effort to identify high-risk pregnancies should be undertaken. (A formal statement recommending centralized perinatal care was developed by the Committee on Maternal and Child Care of the American Medical Association and adopted by the American Medical Association, House of Delegates, in June 1971. It subsequently was endorsed by the American College of Obstetricians and Gynecologists, the American Academy of Pediatrics, and the American Academy of Family Physicians.)

Traditional obstetric and pediatric manpower roles should be redefined. The major national organizations of obstetricians and gynecologists, pediatricians, nurses, and nurse–midwives have addressed this issue. In a joint statement in 1971, the American College of Obstetricians and Gynecologists, the Nurses Association of the College, and the American College of Nurse–Midwives recommended the formation of "teams of physicians, nurse–midwives, obstetric registered nurses, and other health personnel." The composition of such maternal health teams would "be determined by local needs and circumstances," and they would be under the direction of qualified obstetrician–gynecologists:

In such medically directed teams, qualified nurse–midwives may assume responsibility for the complete care and management of uncomplicated maternity patients . . . obstetric registered nurses may assume responsibility for patient care and management according to their education, training, and experience, . . . [and] other health personnel who have been trained in specific areas of maternity care may participate in the team functions according to their abilities within the definitions of responsibility established by the team.

In addition, we believe that in defining new roles for health professionals in maternity care, it is crucial that comparative studies be designed to assess the kind of care the new professionals deliver, its cost, and its effect as compared with traditional services.

RESEARCH IN THE DELIVERY OF MATERNAL HEALTH SERVICES

Systematic analyses of pregnant women of different risk receiving varying levels of maternal health services should be carried out. It now seems clear that funds for health services research will be in short supply in the mid-1970's. To answer the important and complex questions raised by the analysis of the New York City data, however, further research must be carried out. These studies must be carefully designed so that the new information will clarify the critical social and health policy issues and establish a firm basis for determining maternal and infant health services priorities. From the results of our study, we have identified five major areas with pressing needs for carefully planned studies:

ROLE OF PATIENT SELF-SELECTION IN PREGNANCY OUTCOME

We are all aware that many different kinds of factors, such as biological, social, economic, behavioral, and medical care, influence an individual's health status. However, we cannot determine from the study of New York City births, for example, what the social, economic, and behavioral differences are between women classified at social risk who received adequate care and those of social risk who received inadequate care. Nor do we know with certainty whether there are differences between persons of various ethnic backgrounds and the severity and nature of their social risk. For example, we need to know if Puerto Rican and white native-born women at social risk should be categorized further so that the severity of the social risk can be identified and more appropriately addressed in each case. These are hard-to-fill gaps in our social–medical knowledge but ones that can be approached, if not bridged, with carefully designed research programs.

BETTER DEFINITION OF DELIVERED HEALTH SERVICES

It is necessary to clarify the relationship between categories of health services as used in this study—adequate, intermediate, and inadequate—and the actual content of delivered medical care. In attempting this, research should lead to more useful classifications of care, the identification of the important elements of care, and the ability to better define different levels of care. Implicit in this research objective is the need to study further the effect of different kinds of prenatal medical care on the outcome of pregnancy.

COST OF DELIVERING MATERNAL AND INFANT HEALTH SERVICES

The analyses in this report do not address the cost or cost effectiveness of delivering maternal and infant services. Indeed, it was virtually impossible to obtain cost data for categorical programs designed to give prenatal and infant care. In carrying out such studies, an effort to assess the direct and indirect benefits of such expenditure should be made. Of paramount importance is developing some measures of the present cost of delivering these services so that comparisons with new modes of delivery can be made.

REFINEMENT OF MATERNAL RISK MEASURES

To refine the risk categories used in the analysis of the New York City infant births and deaths, more detailed studies of the relationship between infant survival and maternal characteristics are required. From such new analyses, providers of obstetric services would be able to determine the risk faced by an individual female and direct her to appropriate services that decrease her chances of producing a low-birth-weight or nonviable infant. The risk scale would complement expanding efforts to identify and provide intensive neonatal care to those who are in greatest need of those services.

CONFIRMATION OF RESULTS OF NEW YORK CITY STUDY

Similar studies using existing vital statistics should be carried out for other U.S. populations to assess maternal risk, care, and pregnancy outcome in rural and other urban populations.

There are many alternative study designs that would probe these questions. We considered the ethical, logistic, and cost implications of six designs. Our conclusions are found in Appendix D.

Summary

In 1968, 142,017 live births were registered with the New York City health department. Of these children, 3,115 died the first year, resulting in an infant mortality rate of 21.9 per 1,000. More than 56 percent of the births were to white native- and foreign-born women, approximately 23 percent to black native-born mothers, and just under 16 percent to Puerto Rican women. The remaining 5 percent occurred among other race–nativity groups.

THE NEW YORK STUDY

This study focused on the relationships among the risk of the mother, the maternal health services she received, and the survival of her infant. (For definitions of risk and services, see Glossary.) Fifty-five percent of the mothers were considered to have one or more social, demographic, medical, or obstetric handicaps that could adversely influence the survival of their infants. The distribution of risks varied by race–nativity group. More than three fifths of the white native-born women were at no risk, while only about one fourth of the black native-born women were at no risk. Conversely, the percentage of black women at social risk was three times that of white native-born women at social risk. For the medical risks there was little difference in distribution by ethnic group.

Of all infant deaths, 75 percent were among offspring of the 55 percent of the mothers judged to be at risk. Approximately 95 percent of those mothers at risk had social, medical, or combined

13

social–medical conditions that could have been identified at the time of their first prenatal visit; infants born to this group of women accounted for 70 percent of the deaths.

Approximately 25 percent of the women received maternal health services judged adequate by a three-factor health services index: time of first visit for prenatal care, total number of visits, and type of hospital service where delivery took place. (For health service index definition, see Glossary.) The percentages of women receiving adequate and inadequate care varied greatly by race–nativity group. Among white native-born women, for example, 43.3 percent received adequate care and 16.1 percent inadequate, while 40.6 percent had intermediate care; among black native-born women, the distribution at the extremes was reversed—4.6 percent received adequate care, while 46.2 percent received inadequate care. Almost one half of the black women received health services graded as intermediate.

THE RESULTS

From the viewpoint of risk, mortality rates ranged from a low of 12.1 per 1,000 among infants of no-risk women to a high of 42.0 per 1,000 among infants of women at social and medical risk combined. Those whose mothers were at social or medical risk only had intermediate rates of 24.9 per 1,000 and 27.7 per 1,000, respectively. From the viewpoint of maternal care, the death rates varied from 13.3 per 1,000 live births for infants of mothers with adequate health care to 35.6 per 1,000 for infants of mothers with inadequate health care. Mothers who received intermediate care had a death rate of 18.5 per 1,000 among their infants. When risk and care are looked at simultaneously, the consistency of these findings becomes more apparent. Infant death rates in each risk category were lowest among infants whose mothers had adequate care, slightly higher if the mothers had intermediate care, and highest if the mothers had inadequate care. Generally, the same consistency was found for each ethnic group and for each risk category in each ethnic group.

When we contrasted risk and care across ethnic subpopulations, we found infant death rates varied more than ninefold, from a low of 7.4 per 1,000 for infants of white foreign-born mothers with adequate care and no risk to a high of 68.1 per 1,000 for infants of black native-born mothers with inadequate care and combined social and medical risk. For each ethnic group, offspring of women at no risk with adequate care had the lowest rates; however, infant death rates varied more than 400 percent even in the no-risk category between infants of no-risk white foreign-born women with adequate care and infants of no-risk black native-born women with inadequate care.

When we computed the relative risks of infant death for native-born white and black populations by care received, we generally found a greater risk of infant death for blacks, regardless of risk and adequacy of medical care. *With adequate care, however, there were smaller differences by ethnic group for those at no risk and essentially no difference for mothers at medical risk.* The most striking contrasts between the two ethnic groups were for mothers with social risk. For these handicaps, the differences by race were great; adequate medical care did not have as much impact in reducing mortality for black infants as it did for white infants.

The patterns for neonatal mortality rates were similar to the overall infant mortality rates. The same relationship between risk groups and outcome existed: The lowest rate was 9.1 per 1,000 for infants of the no-risk group and the highest was 32.7 per 1,000 for infants of the combined social and medical risk; the rates for infants of social and medical risk categories fell between the two extremes. There is a direct association between the three-factor health services index and neonatal mortality, with the rate of 11.1 per 1,000 for infants of women with adequate care and the rate of 26.4 per 1,000—a rate two-and-one-half times higher—for infants of women with inadequate care. *In sum, the associations between risk, care, and outcome are the same whether outcome is death during the first 28 days of life or death during the entire first year of life.*

For infants of white mothers, postneonatal deaths, or those occurring after 28 days and before 12 months of life, accounted for approximately 20 percent of the overall death rate; for infants of Puerto Rican and native-born black mothers, deaths in the postneonatal period constituted 25 to 29 percent, respectively, of the deaths during the first year of life. Postneonatal death rates for infants of Puerto Rican and black mothers were more than two and three times as high, respectively, as those for infants of white mothers. The trends in postneonatal deaths were consistent with the trends in infant and neonatal deaths; in many instances, however, differences by care and ethnic group for postneonatal rates are greater than are the differences for the other death rates. *The significance of this finding, because of the minimal impact of prenatal care on postneonatal death, is the strong suggestion that the three-factor health services in-*

dex measures a combination of factors that affect health care as well as prenatal care.

The highest relative risk of death among infant, neonatal, and post-neonatal rates is found for the postneonatal period among infants of black native-born women at social–medical risk with inadequate care. It is almost nine times higher than the relative risk for all infants of no-risk women who received adequate care and 45 times higher than the rate for infants of white foreign-born mothers at no risk with adequate care.

Infant mortality rates are related more closely to infant birth weight than to any other maternal or infant characteristic. The low-birth-weight infants (2,500 grams or less) made up 10 percent of all live births with proportions varying from 6.5 percent for white foreign-born mothers to 15.7 percent for black native-born mothers. Approximately 1.5 percent of all infants were in the weight range of 1,500 grams or less. Infant mortality in this lowest birth weight group was 609.5 per 1,000 compared to 55.4 per 1,000 among infants who weighed 1,501 to 2,500 grams and 8.4 per 1,000 among those who weighed more than 2,500 grams. Among those of optimal birth weight, 3,501 to 4,500 grams, the rate was only 5.8 per 1,000.

When the distribution of low-birth-weight infants is viewed in relation to risk category and type of care, the proportions of infants weighing less than 2,500 grams show trends similar to the death rates, indicating a direct relationship to risk and an inverse relationship to care. Thus, the lowest percentage (7.1) of low-birth-weight infants was born to no-risk women with about 11 percent born to women in each social and medical risk group and 15 percent born to women with combined social and medical risk. When care is considered, the lowest proportions, or 5.8 percent, are found in the no-risk adequate care group and the highest, or 19.6 percent, in the group at social–medical risk who received inadequate care. By ethnic group, the lowest rates were among infants of foreign-born white women and the highest among infants of native-born blacks.

As with infant, neonatal, and postneonatal mortality, a consistent inverse relationship exists between the medical care index and the percent of low-birth-weight infants; that is, low-birth-weight proportions increase as care declines from adequate to intermediate to inadequate. This holds true in each risk group also; the percentages increase from no risk to social risk to medical risk to combined social–medical risk.

In these analyses, the mother's educational attainment has served as an indicator of social status. As such, it is a proxy for a variety of components of the life style of the mother and those she will impose upon her newborn infant. While there is some question about the accuracy of educational attainment records for foreign-born mothers, it is important to note the trends in the relationship between mother's education and infant's birth weight. The trends differ by ethnic group. For black native-born women, for example, the higher the education, the higher the birth weight. For white native-born women, however, there is no clear relationship between mean birth weight and education. The strong relationship in native-born blacks between birth weight and education indicates that the life-style factors reflected by education play an important role in determining infant birth weight and, thus, survival in this population.

In contrast to the inconsistent education–birth weight relationship is the strikingly consistent relationship between the mother's education, care, and infant death. Infants of college-educated mothers with adequate care had a death rate of 10.1 per 1,000, while infants of college-educated mothers with inadequate care had a death rate of 22.0 per 1,000, more than twice as high. For infants of black native-born women with one or more years of college, there was a sixfold difference in death rates of 7.2 per 1,000 for those whose mothers had adequate care and 42.3 per 1,000 for those whose mothers had inadequate care.

Finally, we explored what the effect on infant mortality would have been if all pregnant women in the New York sample had had the pregnancy outcome of those with adequate care. These data indicate that the overall infant mortality rate would have been reduced 16 percent to 18.4 per 1,000 live births if mothers in each risk category had had the same pregnancy outcome as the other mothers in their ethnic group who had adequate care.

MATERNAL AND INFANT HEALTH SERVICES

We also attempted to assess, from currently available data, the effectiveness of maternal and infant health services. We found many gaps in the information needed for critical analysis. As one example, the federal–state medicaid programs, with rare exception, do not collect data on specific services purchased for mothers and infants although mothers and children make up more than half of those eligible for services under the $6.1 billion program.

We focused on two programs—MIC projects and NICU's—for which some descriptive data were available.

MATERNITY AND INFANT CARE PROJECTS

There were 56 MIC projects in operation by the end of fiscal year 1971. They reported 141,000 new maternity admissions and 42,600 new infant admissions during the preceeding 12 months; new family planning admissions totaled 130,000. Federal budget estimates indicate that services were provided to 144,000 mothers and 49,000 infants in fiscal year 1972, and services will be provided to 152,000 mothers and 53,000 infants in fiscal year 1973.

We reviewed descriptive reports furnished by five selected MIC projects: New York City, Providence, Chicago, Albuquerque, and Los Angeles. In many instances, data on comparison or control groups were inadequate or absent, and lack of such control data made it difficult to come to meaningful conclusions about the impact of the projects on infant death. Before-and-after data from selected projects, however, suggest that these programs may be reducing high infant mortality in some areas.

NEONATAL INTENSIVE CARE UNITS

A number of reports point to the effectiveness of NICU's in reducing infant mortality among high-risk newborn infants, especially when intensive neonatal care is preceded by intensive prenatal care, and strongly suggest that lowered neonatal mortality after intensive care is accompanied by more favorable long-term outcomes among surviving infants.

It is unclear, however, how many NICU's are operating in the United States at present. Neither the American Hospital Association, the American Academy of Pediatrics, or the American College of Obstetricians and Gynecologists maintains a registry. Apparently only eight of the NICU's receive direct federal project money.

As with the MIC projects, we reviewed descriptive reports furnished by five selected NICU's. Based on the before-and-after experience of the hospitals, it appears that the units can be expected to reduce mortality as well as morbidity among low-birth-weight infants from 40 to 70 percent. While the units did not report results for comparable weight groups of infants in all cases, all showed a consistent and striking decline in death rates.

Glossary

Brief definitions of the terms used in this report follow. For more complete definitions and technical details, see Chapter 2.

ETHNICITY See Race–Nativity.

FETAL PERIOD The period between conception and birth. The fetal period can be further broken down into *early* (less than 20 full weeks gestation), *intermediate* (20 to 27 weeks gestation), and *late* (28 weeks or longer).

HEALTH SERVICES All social, economic, environmental, and medical services that directly affect the health status of an individual.

HEALTH SERVICES INDEX A three-factor indicator of maternal health services. It is based on the time of first prenatal visit, number of prenatal visits, and hospital service, whether ward or private. (Private service, which means the woman was admitted to the hospital by a specified physician, is used as an indicator of the likelihood that the woman has a physician or group of physicians who have provided continuous care during pregnancy.) The index adjusts for length of gestation and is used to classify health services received by the woman as *adequate, intermediate,* and *inadequate.*

INFANT PERIOD The period from birth to 1 year of age. The infant period consists of the *neonatal period* (birth to 28 days of age) and the *postneonatal period* (age 28 days to 1 year).

MEDICAL CARE Specific preventive, diagnostic, and therapeutic services provided by medical professionals.

MEDICAL RISK Specific medical and obstetrical handicaps, such as diabetes and inadequate pelvis, that can influence the outcome of pregnancy.

RACE–NATIVITY The race of the infant as determined by maternal and paternal race and the mother's place of birth.

SOCIAL RISK Social and demographic factors, including mother's education, age, parity, and marital status, that may have an adverse effect on pregnancy outcome.

SOCIAL–MEDICAL RISK Two or more handicaps, at least one of which is social and at least one other of which is medical, faced by pregnant women.

19

ONE

An Analysis of
Live Births and
Infant Deaths:
New York City, 1968

In 1968, 142,017 live births were registered with the New York City
Department of Health. Total deaths, fetal and children under 1 year
of age, occurred at a rate of 132.9 per 1,000 fetal deaths and live
births. Of the live births, 3,115 died the first year, resulting in an infant mortality rate of 21.9 per 1,000. Approximately 47 percent of
the infant deaths took place during the first day of life, 70 percent
during the first week, and more than 75 percent during the first
month.

More than 56 percent of the births were to white native- and
foreign-born women, approximately 23 percent to black native-born
mothers, and just under 16 percent to Puerto Rican women. The remaining 5 percent were divided among a variety of race-nativity
groups and in these analyses are aggregated into a single category.

By type of risk, 55 percent of the mothers were considered to have
one or more social, demographic, or medical–obstetrical handicap
that could adversely influence the survival of the infant. (For risk
definitions, see Glossary or Chapter 2.) The distribution of maternal
risks varied widely by race–nativity group. More than three fifths of
the white native-born women were at no risk, while approximately
one fourth of the black native-born women were in the no-risk category. Conversely, there was a threefold difference in the percentage
of black women at social risk compared to that of white native-born
women. For the medical risks, there was little difference in the distribution by ethnic group. Of all infant deaths, 75 percent were
among offspring of the 55 percent of the mothers judged to be at

21

risk. Approximately 95 percent of those mothers at risk had social, medical, or combined social–medical conditions that could have been identified at the time of their first prenatal visit; infants born to this group of women accounted for 70 percent of all infant deaths.

Of the more than 140,000 pregnant women, approximately 25 percent received maternal health services judged adequate by a three-factor health services index: time of first visit for prenatal care, total number of visits, and type of hospital service where delivery took place. (For detailed description of three-factor index, see Chapter 2.) The percentages of women receiving adequate and inadequate care varied greatly by race–nativity group. Among white native-born women, for example, 43.3 percent received adequate care and 16.1 percent inadequate; among black native-born women, the distribution was reversed—4.6 percent received adequate care while 46.2 percent received inadequate care (Table 1-1). Slightly less than half of all women received health services graded as intermediate.

The analyses described in this chapter focus on the relationships between the mother's risk, maternal health services, and the outcome of the infant. These data are presented for the total population as well as for specific race–nativity groups. (A detailed description of the characteristics of the mothers, the live births, and the infant deaths is found in Chapter 3.)

RISK, CARE, AND INFANT MORTALITY

Infant mortality rates for the total population by risk category ranged from a low of 12.1 per 1,000 in no-risk women to a high of 42.0 per

TABLE 1-1 Distribution of Live Births by Three-Factor Health Services Index and Ethnic Group: New York City Live-Birth Cohort, 1968

Three-Factor Index	Total	White Native Born	White Foreign Born	Puerto Rican	Black Native Born	All Others
		Percent of Live Births				
Adequate	25.4	43.3	32.3	4.3	4.6	15.3
Intermediate	46.8	40.6	48.3	56.7	49.2	54.0
Inadequate	27.7	16.1	19.4	39.0	46.2	30.7
TOTAL	99.9	100.0	100.0	100.0	100.0	100.0
Number of live births	142,017	60,896	18,959	22,505	32,051	7,606

TABLE 1-2 Infant Mortality Rates by Risk Category, Three-Factor Health Services Index, and Ethnic Group: New York City Live-Birth Cohort, 1968

Risk Category and Three-Factor Index	Total	White Native Born	White Foreign Born	Puerto Rican	Black Native Born	All Others
			Deaths per 1,000 Live Births			
TOTAL	21.9	15.2	15.3	25.4	35.7	24.5
Adequate	13.3	12.6	12.9	18.8[a]	21.0	18.0
Intermediate	18.5	13.7	15.0	21.2	25.4	20.9
Inadequate	35.6	25.8	20.4	32.2	48.1	33.9
No risk	12.1	9.5	9.4	17.5	20.4	17.1
Adequate	8.7	8.6	7.4	12.2[a]	13.1[a]	8.2[a]
Intermediate	11.2	8.5	8.7	16.4	15.3	18.0
Inadequate	21.0	16.1	16.4	21.0	30.2	22.1[a]
Sociodemographic only	24.9	16.9	13.2	23.3	34.3	27.7
Adequate	12.3	9.7	9.2	14.1[a]	30.8[a]	31.8[a]
Intermediate	18.1	13.2	11.7	18.9	23.7	12.9
Inadequate	34.7	25.3	19.3	28.6	43.1	45.7[a]
Medical–obstetric only	27.7	24.4	26.3	28.5	41.7	21.1
Adequate	22.6	23.2	21.2	19.0[a]	18.5[a]	24.7[a]
Intermediate	24.2	20.9	33.3	20.9	30.6	17.2[a]
Inadequate	46.4	40.6	18.9[a]	48.2[a]	67.8	26.6[a]
Sociodemographic and medical–obstetric	42.0	36.9	26.5	38.1	54.2	40.6
Adequate	29.9	24.6	32.3[a]	53.1[a]	51.3[a]	35.1[a]
Intermediate	35.2	38.7	21.4	32.0	39.7	43.2[a]
Inadequate	55.1	50.8	32.2[a]	45.7	68.1	37.4[a]

[a] Rate based on 100–999 live births.

1,000 in those at combined social and medical risk. Intermediate rates were observed for the total population at social risk only, 24.9 per 1,000, and at medical risk only, 27.7 per 1,000 (Table 1-2). Without considering the mother's risk or ethnic group, infant death rates varied from 13.3 per 1,000 live births for all mothers with adequate health care to 35.6 per 1,000 for all mothers with inadequate health care. Those with intermediate care had an infant death rate of 18.5 per 1,000. Within each risk group these same relationships hold between care and infant death.

Figure 1-1 charts differences in infant death rates by risk group and care within each risk group. It displays a clear progression of increas-

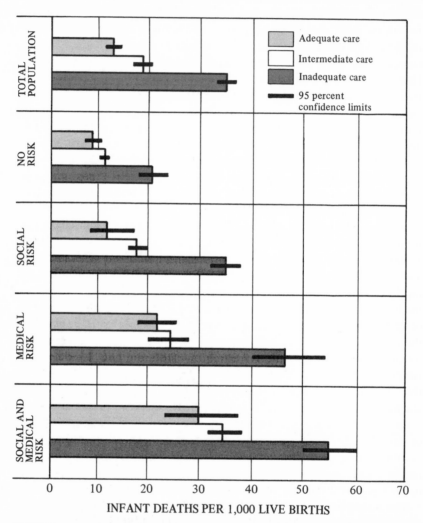

FIGURE 1-1 Infant mortality rates for all ethnic groups by risk category and three-factor health services index: New York City live-birth cohort, 1968. When the 95 percent confidence limits show that there is no overlap of the confidence intervals among groups, this suggests that the respective death rates are statistically significantly different. When the intervals do overlap, the rates are usually not significantly different, although in special circumstances this general statement is not valid. (See Chapter 2 for discussion.)

ing death rates by risk category from no risk, to social risk, to medical risk, to combined social–medical risk. Also, in each risk category, infant death rates are lowest in those with adequate care, slightly higher in those with intermediate care, and highest in those with inadequate care. Overall, these same findings were noted in each ethnic group. However, by ethnic group and within-risk and care-index categories, there are several inconsistencies. For the most part, these inconsistencies are observed for intermediate or inadequate care in specific ethnic–care–risk groups where the total number of births and deaths are quite small. The rates for these small populations tend to be unstable as indicated by their broad confidence limits. (For detailed confidence limits, see Appendix A, Table A-1.) There is, however, general consistency in the trends when the larger ethnic-specific risk and care groups are considered.

When individual risk, care, and ethnic subpopulations are contrasted, infant death rates varied more than ninefold: from a low of 7.4 per 1,000 for infants of white foreign-born mothers with adequate care and no risk to a high of 68.1 per 1,000 for infants of black native-born mothers with inadequate care and combined sociodemographic and medical risk. The lowest rates for each ethnic group were found for offspring of women at no risk with adequate care; however, even in the no-risk category, infant death rates varied more than 400 percent by care and ethnicity. Table 1-2 shows this fourfold difference between no-risk white foreign-born women with adequate care and no-risk black native-born women with inadequate care. The table also shows variations of a similar magnitude in infant death rates by care in each risk category. The highest infant mortality rates befall infants of women with both social and medical risks. The death rates in this combined risk category vary from less than 25 per 1,000 (white, native born, adequate care and white, foreign born, intermediate care) to 68.1 per 1,000 (black, native born, inadequate care).

The infant mortality rate, 8.7 per 1,000, for the total no-risk adequate-care population was used as a standard and given the value of 1.0. We then calculated relative risks for each risk, care, and ethnic group (Table 1-3). These calculations, based on Table 1-2, are simple ratios of the infant death rate for a specific risk, care, or ethnic group divided by the rate for the standard group. For example, the relative risk for the total population is determined by dividing the overall mortality rate of 21.9 by the mortality rate of 8.7 for all infants of no-risk mothers with adequate care, or 2.5. The relative risks, which range from 0.9 to 7.8, show more clearly the magnitude of the differences but reflect the same trends found in the infant mortality data. Similarly, they reflect the association of health services and infant mortality previously described for the total population, each risk category, and the various ethnic–care groups. Thus, the chance of dying in the first year of life was 7.8 times greater for infants of black native-born mothers at medical or combined medical–social risk who received *inadequate* care than it was for all infants of no-risk mothers who received *adequate* care. Infants of white foreign-born no-risk mothers with adequate care fared better than the standard popula-

TABLE 1-3 Relative Risks of Infant Mortality by Risk Category, Three-Factor Health Services Index, and Ethnic Group: New York City Live-Birth Cohort, 1968

Risk Category and Three-Factor Index	Total	White Native Born	White Foreign Born	Puerto Rican	Black Native Born	All Others
			Relative Risk[b]			
TOTAL	2.5	1.7	1.8	2.9	4.1	2.8
Adequate	1.5	1.4	1.5	2.2[a]	2.4	2.1
Intermediate	2.1	1.6	1.7	2.4	2.9	2.4
Inadequate	4.1	3.0	2.3	3.7	5.5	3.9
No risk	1.4	1.1	1.1	2.0	2.3	2.0
Adequate	1.0[b]	1.0	0.9	1.4[a]	1.5[a]	0.9[a]
Intermediate	1.3	1.0	1.0	1.9	1.8	2.1
Inadequate	2.4	1.9	1.9	2.4	3.5	2.5[a]
Sociodemographic only	2.9	1.9	1.5	2.7	3.9	3.2
Adequate	1.4	1.1	1.1	1.6[a]	3.5[a]	3.7[a]
Intermediate	2.1	1.5	1.3	2.2	2.7	1.5
Inadequate	4.0	2.9	2.2	3.3	5.0	5.3[a]
Medical–obstetric only	3.2	2.8	3.0	3.3	4.8	2.4
Adequate	2.6	2.7	2.4	2.2[a]	2.1[a]	2.8[a]
Intermediate	2.8	2.4	3.8	2.4	3.5	2.0[a]
Inadequate	5.3	4.7	2.2[a]	5.5[a]	7.8	3.1[a]
Sociodemographic and medical–obstetric	4.8	4.2	3.0	4.4	6.2	4.7
Adequate	3.4	2.8	3.7[a]	6.1[a]	5.9[a]	4.0[a]
Intermediate	4.0	4.4	2.5	3.7	4.6	5.0[a]
Inadequate	6.3	5.8	3.7[a]	5.3	7.8	4.3[a]

[a] Relative risk based on 100–999 live births.

[b] The standard used was the infant mortality rate for the total no-risk population with adequate care—8.7/1,000 live births.

tion; their relative risk was 0.9. Infants of white native-born mothers with a combined social–medical risk who received inadequate care had a relative risk 5.8 times that for all no-risk mothers with adequate care.

The relative risks of infant death for the native-born white and black populations by care received are contrasted in Figure 1-2. These data confirm a greater risk of infant death for blacks regardless of risk and adequacy of medical care, except that the relative risk in the small number of black women at medical risk with adequate care was slightly less than in comparable white native-born mothers. The most striking contrasts between the two ethnic groups were for mothers with social risk. For these handicaps, the differences by race were great; clearly, adequate health services as measured in this study did not have as much impact in reducing social risk for black infants as it did for white. On the other hand, the effect of health services in reducing mortality for black infants whose mothers had medical–obstetric risks was twice as large as that among white infants (Table 1-3).

RISK, CARE, AND NEONATAL MORTALITY

Maternal health services, particularly prenatal and obstetrical care, should have its greatest impact in reducing infant mortality during the neonatal period—the first 28 days of life. If this is the case and if the three-factor health services index reflects prenatal care only and not the broader factors included in maternal and child health services, there should be differences between the impact of care on neonatal and postneonatal mortality rates. To explore this issue, data were analyzed to evaluate the relationships between risk, care, and outcome, using neonatal and postneonatal death rates as outcome measures.

The patterns for neonatal mortality rates are almost identical to those described for total infant mortality rates (Table 1-4). For the whole population, the same relationship between risk groups and outcome is seen—the lowest rate, 9.1 per 1,000 in the no-risk group and the highest rate, 32,7 per 1,000 in the combined social and medical risk group with the rates for the separate social and medical risk categories between the two extremes. There is a direct relationship between the three-factor health services index and neonatal mortality. The rate for infants of women with inadequate care is 26.4 per 1,000, or about two-and-one-half times the 11.1 per 1,000 rate for infants of

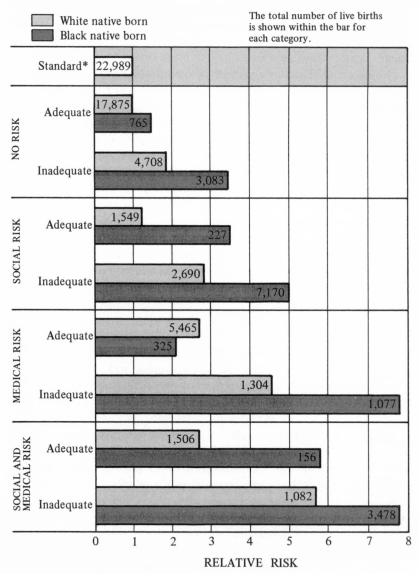

FIGURE 1-2   Relative risk of infant mortality by risk category and three-factor health services index for white native-born and black native-born mothers: New York City live-birth cohort, 1968.

*The standard population was the total population at no risk with adequate care. It has an infant mortality rate of 8.7 per 1,000 and was assigned a value of 1.0.

women with adequate care. Infants of women with intermediate care had a neonatal mortality of 13.9 per 1,000. In sum, the associations between risk, care, and outcome are the same whether outcome is death during the first 28 days of life or death during the first year.

Careful scrutiny of the neonatal death rates in each care group shows that differences by ethnic group remain when comparable care categories are contrasted (Figure 1-3). The neonatal death rate among infants of all white native-born mothers with adequate care, for example, is 10.4 per 1,000; the rate for children of all black native-born mothers with adequate care is 12.9 per 1,000; and among Puerto Rican children it is 17.8. The rate for blacks is 24 percent higher, and

TABLE 1-4 Neonatal Mortality Rates by Risk Category, Three-Factor Health Services Index, and Ethnic Group: New York City Live-Birth Cohort, 1968

Risk Category and Three-Factor Index	Total	White Native Born	White Foreign Born	Puerto Rican	Black Native Born	All Others
			Deaths per 1,000 Live Births			
TOTAL	16.7	12.2	12.4	19.1	25.4	19.3
Adequate	11.1	10.4	11.7	17.8^a	12.9	16.3
Intermediate	13.9	10.8	11.7	16.1	17.7	16.8
Inadequate	26.4	20.4	15.2	23.6	34.9	25.3
No risk	9.1	7.2	8.3	12.7	13.9	13.6
Adequate	6.7	6.4	7.1	12.2^a	7.8^a	8.2^a
Intermediate	8.3	6.3	7.4	12.2	9.6	15.6
Inadequate	15.5	13.0	13.4	13.6	22.1	13.5^a
Sociodemographic only	17.4	12.9	9.3	16.4	22.9	22.0
Adequate	10.8	9.7	8.3	14.1^a	13.2^a	31.8^a
Intermediate	12.2	10.0	7.4	13.6	14.9	10.1
Inadequate	24.3	18.2	13.9	19.6	29.8	35.2^a
Medical–obstetric only	23.3	21.1	21.8	23.4	33.4	20.3
Adequate	20.0	20.7	18.6	19.0^a	12.3^a	21.2^a
Intermediate	20.9	18.4	27.1	18.2	25.7	17.2^a
Inadequate	36.2	31.4	14.2^a	36.1^a	52.9	26.6^a
Sociodemographic and medical–obstetric	32.7	30.8	21.2	30.4	40.7	28.4
Adequate	25.5	21.2	29.0^a	44.2^a	38.5^a	26.3^a
Intermediate	26.8	30.3	17.1	24.8	29.8	29.2^a
Inadequate	43.1	45.3	22.5^a	37.3	51.2	27.4^a

^{a} Rate based on 100–999 live births.

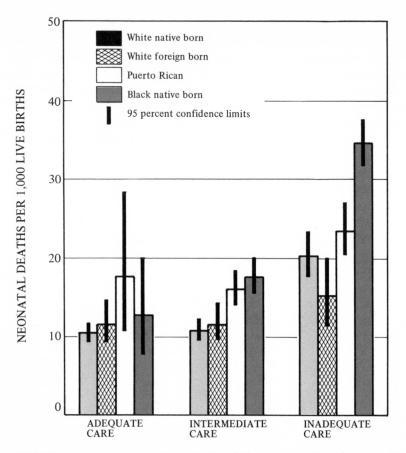

FIGURE 1-3   Neonatal mortality rates by ethnic group and three-factor health services index for total population of births: New York City live-birth cohort, 1968. When the 95 percent confidence limits show that there is no overlap of the confidence intervals among groups, this suggests that the respective death rates are statistically significantly different. When the intervals do overlap, the rates are usually not significantly different, although in special circumstances this general statement is not valid. (See Chapter 2 for discussion.)

the rate for Puerto Ricans is 71 percent higher than the rate for whites. Applying confidence limits to the rate for blacks, however, gives a range of 7.8 to 20.1; for the Puerto Ricans, it is 10.4 to 28.5. Such wide limits are due to the small number of blacks and Puerto Ricans who received adequate care. (An interpretation of these statistics is found in Chapter 2. See Chapter 3 for ethnic–care relationships;

see Appendix A, Table A-2, for confidence limits for each neonatal death rate by risk, care, and ethnicity.)

Similar neonatal mortality trends by ethnic group are displayed for infants of mothers with intermediate and inadequate care. Great variation is seen in the inadequate-care group, where the white native-born rates are approximately 15 percent lower than the Puerto Rican rates and 40 percent lower than the black native-born rates. As seen in Table 1-4, the association between care, ethnicity, and neonatal mortality is generally the same in individual risk categories as it is in the total population. Although the number of live births and deaths in some individual risk, care, and ethnic categories is small, and thus the confidence limits are broad, the trends are generally consistent.

Using the neonatal death rate for the no-risk adequate-care population as a standard, we calculated relative risks for neonatal death. The values are given in Table 1-5; they are similar to those for the infant death rates.

RISK, CARE, AND POSTNEONATAL MORTALITY

Among infants of white mothers, postneonatal deaths, or those occurring after 28 days and through the twelfth month, accounted for approximately 20 percent of the infant deaths; among infants of Puerto Rican and native-born black mothers, deaths in the postneonatal period comprised 25 and 29 percent, respectively, of the first-year deaths (Table 1-6). There were also major differences in the postneonatal death rates by ethnic group. Infants of Puerto Rican and black mothers had rates more than two and three times as high, respectively, as those for infants of white mothers.

The same relationships found for risk, care, and infant death and risk, care, and neonatal death also were found for postneonatal deaths. Despite the small numbers, the trends are consistent with the infant and neonatal mortality data. (See Appendix A, Table A-3, for confidence limits for postneonatal mortality rates.) In many instances, postneonatal rate differences by care and ethnic group show greater contrasts than do differences in the other death rates. *The significance of this finding, because of the probable minimal influence of prenatal care on postneonatal death, is the strong suggestion that the three-factor health services index reflects health services received by mother and child and specific prenatal medical care, as well as an array of other maternal social, behavioral, and economic characteristics.*

TABLE 1-5 Relative Risks of Neonatal Mortality by Risk Category, Three-Factor Health Services Index, and Ethnic Group: New York City Live-Birth Cohort, 1968

Risk Category and Three-Factor Index	Total	White Native Born	White Foreign Born	Puerto Rican	Black Native Born	All Others
			Relative Risk[b]			
TOTAL	2.5	1.8	1.9	2.9	3.8	2.9
Adequate	1.7	1.6	1.7	2.7[a]	1.9	2.4
Intermediate	2.1	1.6	1.7	2.4	2.6	2.5
Inadequate	3.9	3.0	2.3	3.5	5.2	3.8
No risk	1.4	1.1	1.2	1.9	2.1	2.0
Adequate	1.0[b]	1.0	1.1	1.8[a]	1.2[a]	1.2[a]
Intermediate	1.2	0.9	1.1	1.8	1.4	2.3
Inadequate	2.3	1.9	2.0	2.0	3.3	2.0[a]
Sociodemographic only	2.6	1.9	1.4	2.4	3.4	3.3
Adequate	1.6	1.4	1.2	2.1[a]	2.0[a]	4.7[a]
Intermediate	1.8	1.5	1.1	2.0	2.2	1.5
Inadequate	3.6	2.7	2.1	2.9	4.4	5.3[a]
Medical–obstetric only	3.5	3.1	3.3	3.5	5.0	3.0
Adequate	3.0	3.1	2.8	2.8[a]	1.8[a]	3.2[a]
Intermediate	3.1	2.7	4.0	2.7	3.8	2.6[a]
Inadequate	5.4	4.7	2.1[a]	5.4[a]	7.9	4.0[a]
Sociodemographic and medical–obstetric	4.9	4.6	3.2	4.5	6.1	4.2
Adequate	3.8	3.2	4.3[a]	6.6[a]	5.7[a]	3.9[a]
Intermediate	4.0	4.5	2.6	3.7	4.4	4.4[a]
Inadequate	6.4	6.8	3.4[a]	5.6	7.6	4.1[a]

[a] Relative risk based on 100–999 live births.

[b] The standard used was the neonatal mortality rate for the total no-risk population with adequate care—6.7/1,000 live births.

The relative risks for postneonatal death are shown in Table 1-7. Contrasting the relative risks between social and medical risk groups shows that social risk has more influence in the postneonatal period and that medical risk has more influence in the neonatal period, as one would expect. The highest relative risk among infant, neonatal, and postneonatal rates is found for the postneonatal period among infants of black native-born women at social–medical risk with inadequate care.* The value is 8.9; it indicates that the risk of losing an in-

*Excluding those categories for which there are less than 1,000 live births.

fant 1- to 12-months old was almost nine times higher for this group than for all no-risk women who received adequate care. And, when the risk of postneonatal death for these infants is compared to that for infants of white foreign-born mothers at no risk with adequate care, there is a staggering difference of more than 50-fold (Figure 1-4). Of less, but still significant, magnitude are the differences—6 and 13 times, respectively—between infants of white foreign-born mothers with no risk and adequate care and comparable groups of white and black infants of native-born mothers.

The infant, neonatal, and postneonatal relative risks by the inadequate versus adequate extremes of the care index are compared in

TABLE 1-6 Postneonatal Mortality Rates by Risk Category, Three-Factor Health Services Index, and Ethnic Group: New York City Live-Birth Cohort, 1968

Risk Category and Three-Factor Index	Total	White Native Born	White Foreign Born	Puerto Rican	Black Native Born	All Others
			Deaths per 1,000 Live Births			
TOTAL	5.3	3.0	3.0	6.3	10.2	5.1
Adequate	2.2	2.2	1.1	1.0[a]	8.1	1.7
Intermediate	4.6	2.9	3.3	5.1	7.7	4.1
Inadequate	9.2	5.3	5.2	8.7	13.2	8.6
No risk	3.0	2.3	1.2	4.9	6.5	3.6
Adequate	1.9	2.2	0.3	0.0[a]	5.2[a]	0.0[a]
Intermediate	2.9	2.2	1.3	4.2	5.7	2.4
Inadequate	5.5	3.2	3.0	7.3	8.1	8.6[a]
Sociodemographic only	7.5	3.9	3.8	6.9	11.4	5.7
Adequate	1.6	0.0	0.9	0.0[a]	17.6[a]	0.0[a]
Intermediate	5.8	3.2	4.3	5.3	8.8	2.8
Inadequate	10.4	7.1	5.4	8.9	13.2	10.6[a]
Medical–obstetric only	4.4	3.4	4.5	5.1	8.3	0.8
Adequate	2.7	2.6	2.5	0.0[a]	6.2[a]	3.5[a]
Intermediate	3.4	2.6	6.2	2.7	4.9	0.0[a]
Inadequate	10.2	9.2	4.7[a]	12.0[a]	14.9	0.0[a]
Sociodemographic and medical–obstetric	9.3	6.1	5.3	7.7	13.5	12.2
Adequate	4.4	3.3	3.2[a]	8.8[a]	12.8[a]	8.8[a]
Intermediate	8.4	8.4	4.3	7.2	9.9	13.9[a]
Inadequate	12.1	5.5	9.7[a]	8.3	17.0	10.0[a]

[a] Rate based on 100–999 live births.

TABLE 1-7   Relative Risks of Postneonatal Mortality by Risk Category, Three-Factor Health Services Index, and Ethnic Group: New York City Live-Birth Cohort, 1968

Risk Category and Three-Factor Index	Total	White Native Born	White Foreign Born	Puerto Rican	Black Native Born	All Others
			Relative Risk[b]			
TOTAL	2.8	1.6	1.6	3.3	5.4	2.7
Adequate	1.2	1.2	0.6	0.5^a	4.3	0.9
Intermediate	2.4	1.5	1.7	2.9	4.1	2.2
Inadequate	4.8	2.8	2.7	4.6	6.9	4.5
No risk	1.6	1.2	0.6	2.6	3.4	1.9
Adequate	1.0^b	1.2	0.2	0.0^a	2.7^a	0.0^a
Intermediate	1.5	1.2	0.7	2.2	3.0	1.3
Inadequate	2.9	1.7	1.6	3.8	4.3	4.5^a
Sociodemographic only	3.9	2.1	2.0	3.6	6.0	3.0
Adequate	0.8	0.0	0.5	0.0^a	9.3^a	0.0^a
Intermediate	3.1	1.7	2.3	2.8	4.6	1.5
Inadequate	5.5	3.7	2.8	4.7	6.9	5.6^a
Medical–obstetric only	2.3	1.8	2.4	2.7	4.4	0.4
Adequate	1.4	1.4	1.3	0.0^a	3.3^a	1.8^a
Intermediate	1.8	1.4	3.3	1.4	2.6	0.0^a
Inadequate	5.4	4.8	2.5^a	6.3^a	7.8	0.0^a
Sociodemographic and medical–obstetric	4.9	3.2	2.8	4.1	7.1	6.4
Adequate	2.3	1.7	1.7^a	4.6^a	6.7^a	4.6^a
Intermediate	4.4	4.4	2.3	3.8	5.2	7.3^a
Inadequate	6.4	2.9	5.1^a	4.4	8.9	5.3^a

[a] Relative risk based on 100–999 live births.

[b] The standard used was the postneonatal mortality rate for the total no-risk population with adequate care—1.9/1,000 live births.

Figure 1-5. These data demonstrate that the three proxies of care used in this study are associated with survival, regardless of time of infant death. The highest relative risk of infant death is found during the postneonatal period between infants whose mothers had inadequate care and infants whose mothers had adequate care. For example, there were no postneonatal deaths among 1,549 infants of white native-born mothers at social risk who received adequate care, but at a rate of 7.1 per 1,000 there were 19 deaths among 2,690 infants of similar mothers whose care was classified inadequate. Again, this strongly suggests that the three-factor care index reflects health services, of which prenatal care is only a part, received by women and their infants.

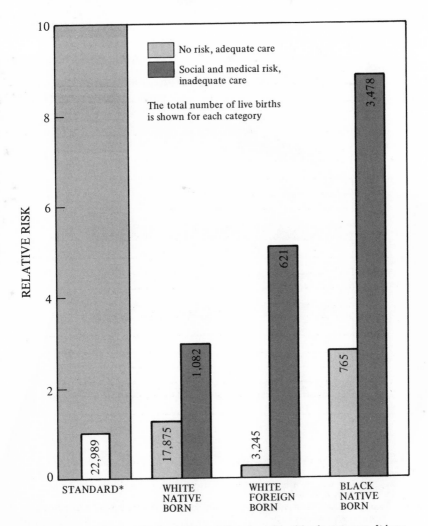

*The standard population was the total population at no risk with adequate care. It has a postneonatal mortality rate of 1.9 per 1,000 live births and was assigned a value of 1.0.

FIGURE 1-4 Contrasting relative risks of postneonatal mortality by ethnic group, risk, and three-factor health services index: New York City live-birth cohort, 1968.

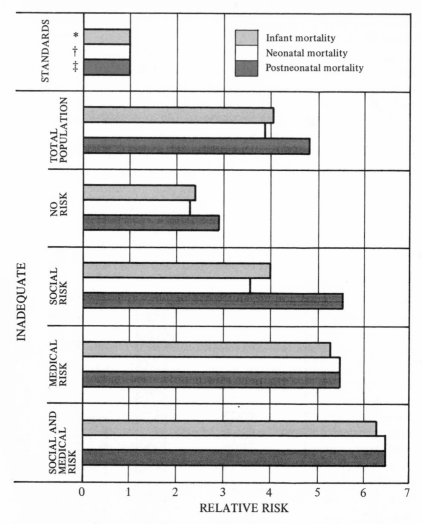

*The standard used was the infant mortality rate for the total no-risk population with adequate care—8.7/1,000 live births.
†The standard used was the neonatal mortality rate for the total no-risk population with adequate care—6.7/1,000 live births.
‡The standard used was the postneonatal mortality rate for the total no-risk population with adequate care—1.9/1,000 live births.

FIGURE 1-5   Relative risks of death for inadequate category of care by time of infant death for total, no-risk, and risk populations: New York City live-birth cohort, 1968.

CARE, RISK, AND BIRTH WEIGHT

Infant mortality rates are associated more closely to infant birth weight than to any other major maternal or infant characteristic. Low-birth-weight infants (2,500 grams or less) made up 10 percent of all live births with proportions varying from 6.5 percent among infants of white foreign-born mothers to 15.7 percent among infants of black native-born mothers. Approximately 1.5 percent of all infants weighed 1,500 grams or less, and the mortality rate among them was 609.5 per 1,000, compared to 55.4 per 1,000 among infants who weighed 1,501 to 2,500 grams and 8.4 per 1,000 among those who weighed more than 2,500 grams. Among those of optimal birth weight, 3,501 to 4,500 grams, the rate was only 5.8 per 1,000.

When the distribution of low-birth-weight infants is viewed in relation to risk category and type of care, a wide range in proportions is manifest (Table 1-8). In general, the proportions of infants weighing less than 2,500 grams by risk and care show trends similar to the death rates, indicating a direct relationship to risk and an inverse relationship to care. Thus, the lowest percentage by risk category, 7.1, of low-birth-weight infants is found in the no-risk group with about 11 percent in the social and medical risk groups and 15 percent in the combined social and medical risk group. When care is considered, the lowest proportions, 5.8 percent, are found in the no-risk adequate care group and the highest, 19.6 percent, in the group at social–medical risk who received inadequate care. Differences for ethnic groups were found by risk and care classifications. In general, the lowest rates are associated with foreign-born white women and the highest with native-born blacks (Table 1-8).

As with infant, neonatal, and postneonatal mortality, major differences are found in and between each care and risk category. The relationships between low birth weight, risk group, and care are illustrated in Figure 1-6. For the total population, a consistent inverse relationship exists between the medical-care index and the percent of low-birth-weight infants; that is, low-birth-weight proportions increase as care indices change from adequate to intermediate to inadequate. This holds true in each risk group also, with percentages of low-birth-weight infants increasing from no risk to combined social–medical risk.

In concert with the percentages of low-birth-weight infants, mean birth weights varied with the care and risk category of the mother. In

Figure 1-7, differences in mean birth weight between adequate and in-adequate care are shown for each risk group. Between the extremes, the differences vary from a low of 123 grams (about ¼ pound) for the no-risk group to a high of 262 grams (about ½ pound) for the social–medical risk group. In general, the strongest association be-tween care category and infant birth weight is found for those mothers who were at social risk or social–medical risk. (Mean birth weights and t-tests for each ethnic group by care and risk categories are found in Appendix A, Tables A-4 and A-5.)

TABLE 1-8   Proportion of Live Births Weighing 2,500 Grams or Less by Risk Category, Three-Factor Health Services Index, and Ethnic Group: New York City Live-Birth Cohort, 1968

Risk Category and Three-Factor Index	Total	White Native Born	White Foreign Born	Puerto Rican	Black Native Born	All Others
		Percent 2,500 Grams or Less[a]				
TOTAL	10.0	8.0	6.5	10.3	15.7	9.5
Adequate	7.1	7.1	5.6	7.6	11.1	8.7
Intermediate	8.9	7.5	6.2	8.8	13.0	8.4
Inadequate	14.4	11.6	8.6	12.7	19.1	11.8
No risk	7.1	6.4	5.5	8.1	11.0	7.7
Adequate	5.8	5.8	4.6	5.5	8.8	6.5
Intermediate	6.8	6.2	5.0	7.0	9.5	8.5
Inadequate	10.4	9.0	8.8	11.0	13.8	7.0
Sociodemographic only	11.6	10.1	5.4	10.6	15.4	11.0
Adequate	7.8	8.5	5.0	9.2	14.1	10.2
Intermediate	9.5	7.7	4.8	9.3	12.8	8.5
Inadequate	14.5	13.8	7.0	12.0	17.6	14.4
Medical–obstetric only	11.1	10.0	8.7	11.0	17.2	9.8
Adequate	9.7	9.8	8.3	9.5	11.4	11.7
Intermediate	10.2	9.5	9.1	8.8	14.4	7.7
Inadequate	16.2	12.9	8.7	16.3	23.8	12.9
Sociodemographic and medical–obstetric	15.1	12.9	9.1	12.4	21.5	11.2
Adequate	10.4	11.2	6.6	11.5	17.3	10.5
Intermediate	12.9	12.5	9.1	10.8	17.5	8.9
Inadequate	19.6	16.2	11.4	14.6	25.5	15.5

[a] Data missing on birth weight for 393 births.

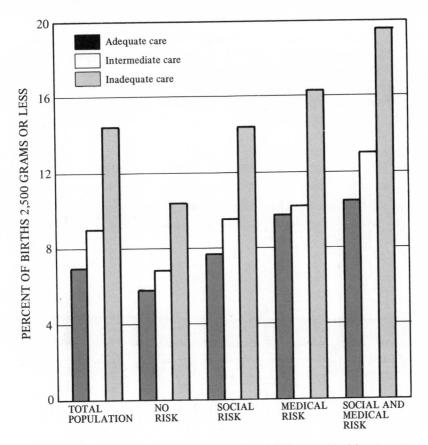

FIGURE 1-6 Proportion of live births less than 2,500 grams by risk category and three-factor health services index: New York City live-birth cohort, 1968.

MATERNAL EDUCATION AND OUTCOME

In these analyses, we used the mother's educational attainment as an indicator of her social status. As an indicator, education represents a variety of components: mother's health attitudes and practices, family income, and the situation in which her infant will be raised. The distribution of the mothers' education by ethnic group is shown in Table 1-9. There are marked variations in education attainment by ethnic group. While the comparability of educational classification for the foreign-born mothers must be questioned, there are nevertheless important trends in the relationship of the mother's education to

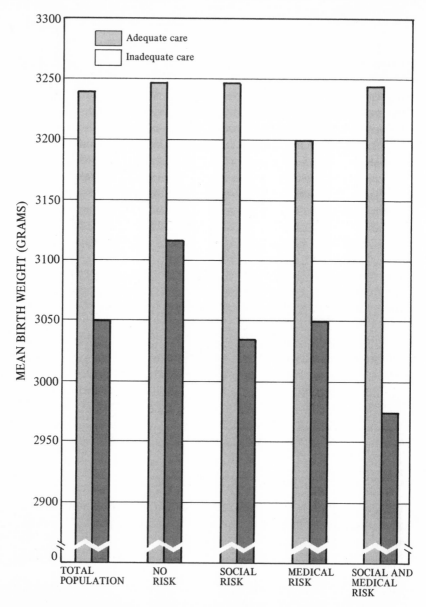

FIGURE 1-7   Mean birth weight (grams) by three-factor health services index for total, no-risk, and risk populations: New York City live-birth cohort, 1968.

TABLE 1-9 Distribution of Education of the Mother by Ethnic Group: New York City Live-Birth Cohort, 1968

Education of Mother	Total	White Native Born	White Foreign Born	Puerto Rican	Black Native Born	All Others
			Percent of Live Births			
None or elementary	13.1	2.3	26.0	36.7	8.5	19.2
High school, 1–3 years	22.5	13.6	12.9	34.9	37.6	17.8
High school, 4 years	41.7	51.2	37.9	20.4	41.8	36.9
College, 1–3 years	8.2	11.9	7.6	1.6	5.7	9.2
College, 4 years or more	9.6	17.1	9.1	0.5	1.9	10.8
Not stated	4.9	4.0	6.5	6.0	4.5	6.1
TOTAL	100.0	100.0	100.0	100.0	100.0	100.0
Number of live births	142,017	60,896	18,959	22,505	32,051	7,606

the infant's birth weight. Table 1-10 presents the distribution of low-weight births by mother's education and ethnic group. It is clear that for all ethnic groups, the proportions of low-weight births decline as educational level increases. The trends differ, however, for ethnic groups. There is a marked inverse relationship for black mothers and infants and an inconsistent relationship for white foreign-born mothers

TABLE 1-10 Proportion of Live Births Weighing 2,500 Grams or Less by Education of Mother and Ethnic Group: New York City Live-Birth Cohort, 1968

Education of Mother	Total	White Native Born	White Foreign Born	Puerto Rican	Black Native Born	All Others
			Percent 2,500 Grams or Less[a]			
None or elementary	10.2	10.3	5.7	10.4	17.9	10.1
High school, 1– 3 years	13.0	11.0	7.1	11.1	17.1	11.0
High school, 4 years	9.1	7.6	6.4	8.2	14.2	9.7
College, 1–3 years	8.5	7.6	6.8	8.6	13.9	7.1
College, 4 years or more	6.8	6.7	6.7	8.7	9.0	6.9
Not stated	11.4	8.2	7.8	13.1	18.7	10.5
TOTAL	10.0	8.0	6.5	10.3	15.7	9.5
Number of live births	142,017	60,896	18,959	22,505	32,051	7,606

[a] Data missing on birth weight for 393 births.

TABLE 1-11 Mean Birth Weight (Grams) by Education of Mother and Ethnic Group: New York City Live-Birth Cohort, 1968[a]

Education of Mother	Total	White Native Born	White Foreign Born	Puerto Rican	Black Native Born	All Others
None or elementary	3,164 ± 600	3,136 ± 609	3,330 ± 554	3,134 ± 576	2,975 ± 673	3,149 ± 592
High school, 1–3 years	3,083 ± 601	3,146 ± 574	3,270 ± 566	3,122 ± 573	2,975 ± 625	3,094 ± 597
High school, 4 years	3,185 ± 575	3,229 ± 551	3,298 ± 549	3,173 ± 546	3,034 ± 620	3,142 ± 578
College, 1–3 years	3,197 ± 561	3,225 ± 533	3,235 ± 543	3,170 ± 517	3,070 ± 650	3,178 ± 600
College, 4 or more years	3,215 ± 522	3,222 ± 516	3,230 ± 541	3,231 ± 484	3,158 ± 600	3,130 ± 483
Not stated	3,138 ± 616	3,207 ± 564	3,277 ± 572	3,080 ± 630	2,954 ± 681	3,133 ± 582
TOTAL	3,161 ± 582	3,213 ± 549	3,290 ± 554	3,136 ± 572	3,008 ± 632	3,136 ± 577

[a] For each education and ethnic group, the first figure is mean birth weight; the second figure is the standard deviation.

and infants. Among black mothers for whom education was stated, the percentage of low-weight infants varies from 17.9 for those with an elementary education or less to 9.0 for mothers with 4 years or more of college, a decline of almost one half. In comparable education groups of white native-born mothers, the proportion declined from 10.3 to 6.7, a decline of about one third.

These same relationships were examined for mean birth weight, and inconsistencies between the ethnic groups were again found (Table 1-11). For black native-born women, for example, there was a strong, direct relationship—the higher the education, the higher the birth weight—with a difference in mean birth weight of more than 180 grams (6 ounces) between infants born to women with an elementary education or less and those born to women with 4 years of college or more. For white foreign-born women, however, there was an apparent inverse relationship, with lower mean birth weights among the more educated groups; in white native-born women, there was an inconsistent relationship between education and mean birth weight. The strong and statistically significant association for native-born blacks between birth weight and education indicates that a variety of social factors, such as income, occupation, and attitude toward health care, play a major role in determining infant birth weight and, thus, infant survival. (Detailed mean birth-weight data and t-tests for ethnic groups by education are given in Appendix A, Tables A-6 and A-7.)

In contrast to inconsistent education–birth-weight relationships, is the striking consistency of relationship between mothers' education and infant death (Table 1-12). These data demonstrate an inverse relationship between education and infant mortality for each of the major ethnic groups. Infants of college-educated mothers experienced the lowest death rates, and infants of mothers with 1 to 3 years of high school experienced the highest. It is of interest that infants of women with no schooling or only elementary education had a lower mortality rate than those whose mothers began but did not complete high school. Of major importance, and true for each educational category, mothers with adequate care experience a lower infant death rate than do mothers with intermediate or inadequate care. Figure 1-8 shows that mothers with inadequate care, regardless of education, experience at least twice the infant mortality as do mothers with adequate care. College-educated mothers with adequate care had an infant death rate of 10.1 per 1,000 while college-educated mothers with inadequate care had an infant death rate of 22.0 per 1,000. For black

TABLE 1-12 Infant Mortality Rates by Education of Mother, Three-Factor Health Services Index, and Ethnic Group: New York City Live-Birth Cohort, 1968

Education of Mother and Three-Factor Index	Total	White Native Born	White Foreign Born	Puerto Rican	Black Native Born	All Others
			Deaths per 1,000 Live Births			
TOTAL	21.9	15.2	15.3	25.4	35.7	24.5
Adequate	13.3	12.6	12.9	18.8[a]	21.0	18.0
Intermediate	18.5	13.7	15.0	21.2	25.4	20.9
Inadequate	35.6	25.8	20.4	32.2	48.1	33.9
None, elementary	27.7	32.8	15.9	26.0	50.7	29.5
Adequate	16.9	10.3[a]	11.5[a]	37.9[a]	b	b
Intermediate	22.4	33.6[a]	14.5	21.0	39.4	20.7[a]
Inadequate	37.3	40.4[a]	22.3	32.0	60.5	43.7[a]
High school, 1–3 years	28.5	21.8	16.3	25.4	37.4	29.6
Adequate	20.4	17.9	12.1[a]	28.2[a]	36.6[a]	60.0[a]
Intermediate	21.1	18.5	13.7	20.4	24.5	26.3[a]
Inadequate	39.2	29.2	24.9[a]	32.6	49.1	28.5[a]
High school, 4 years	19.4	14.7	15.2	19.4	31.9	22.1
Adequate	13.7	13.4	13.9	10.6[a]	22.2[a]	10.3[a]
Intermediate	16.7	12.9	14.2	18.4	23.4	19.9
Inadequate	32.9	24.3	21.2	24.5	43.8	33.2[a]
College, 1 year or more	12.9	10.3	15.2	15.1[a]	25.3	17.7
Adequate	10.1	9.7	11.3	18.5[a]	7.2[a]	15.4[a]
Intermediate	12.9	9.5	19.0	16.8[a]	20.7	17.8[a]
Inadequate	22.0	16.0	16.4[a]	8.4[a]	42.3[a]	20.6[a]
Not stated	31.0	23.5	13.0	45.5	46.0	30.0[a]
Adequate	18.1	20.2[a]	15.9[a]	b	b	b
Intermediate	25.9	17.5	15.2[a]	40.1[a]	36.2[a]	20.9[a]
Inadequate	45.5	42.1[a]	3.8[a]	54.4[a]	54.2[a]	48.6[a]

[a] Rate based on 100–999 live births.

[b] Rate not computed; based on less than 100 live births.

native-born women with 1 or more years of college, there was a six-fold difference in infant death rates* between that for mothers with adequate care (7.2 per 1,000) and that for mothers with inadequate care (42.3 per 1,000). (For confidence limits on these data, see Appendix A, Table A-8.)

*Based on less than 1,000 live births.

SUMMARY

Data have been presented to explore associations among social and medical handicaps, or risks, of pregnant women, maternal health services, and pregnancy outcome. The 1968 New York City population of child-bearing women was divided into four risk categories by cri-

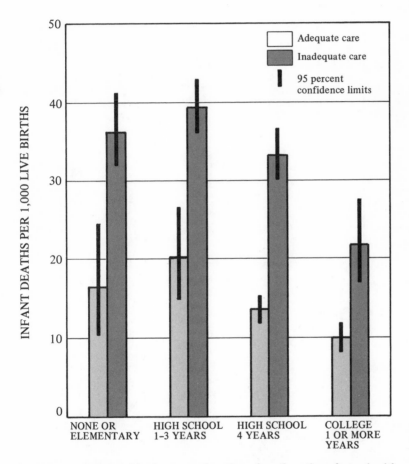

FIGURE 1-8 Relationships between education of mother, three-factor health services index and infant mortality: New York City live-birth cohort, 1968. When the 95 percent confidence limits show that there is no overlap of the confidence intervals among groups, this suggests that the respective death rates are statistically significantly different. When the intervals do overlap, the rates are usually not significantly different, although in special circumstances this general statement is not valid. (See Chapter 2 for discussion.)

teria based on available information about the women and best medical judgment. The risk categories proved to be discriminating in
separating the women into groups with clear differences in pregnancy
outcome. Figure 1-9 shows neonatal death rates are lowest for offspring of women in the no-risk category and progressively increase
for offspring whose mothers are in the social-risk, medical-risk, and
combined social–medical risk categories. The data suggest that the

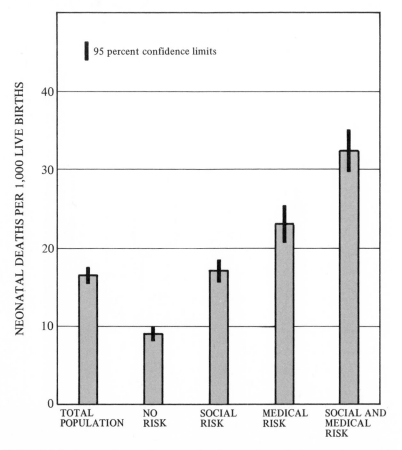

FIGURE 1-9 Neonatal mortality rates for the total population, no-risk, and risk
categories: New York City live-birth cohort, 1968. When the 95 percent confidence limits show that there is no overlap of the confidence intervals among
groups, this suggests that the respective death rates are statistically significantly
different. When the intervals do overlap, the rates are usually not significantly
different, although in special circumstances this general statement is not valid.
(See Chapter 2 for discussion.)

neonatal death rate for the no-risk group, 9.1 per 1,000, is truly different from that of any other risk group. The trends hold regardless of time of death or ethnic group.

For each risk and ethnic group, the three-factor health services index also discriminates differences in pregnancy outcome. Figure 1-10 displays neonatal death rates by contrasting care for the entire population and each risk group. These data demonstrate that neonatal

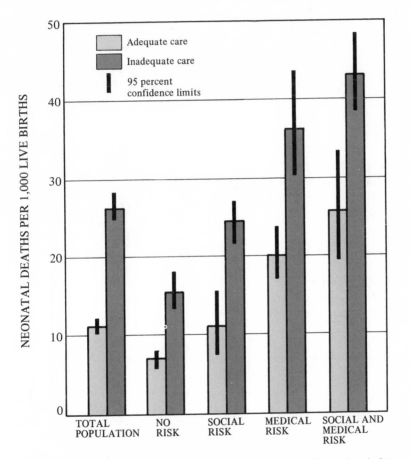

FIGURE 1-10 Neonatal mortality rates by three-factor health services index and risk category: New York City live-birth cohort, 1968. When the 95 percent confidence limits show that there is no overlap of the confidence intervals among groups, this suggests that the respective death rates are statistically significantly different. When the intervals do overlap, the rates are usually not significantly different, although in special circumstances this general statement is not valid. (See Chapter 2 for discussion.)

death rates vary consistently by the extremes of the care categories.

It is now possible, then, to explore a question implicit in these analyses: "What would be the impact on total infant mortality if all pregnant women had the same outcome as those who received 'adequate' care?" In answering the question, we must bear in mind that we found strong indications that the health services index reflects more than prenatal care. To an unmeasurable degree, it also reflects general medical care of both the mother and infant, attitudes toward health services, knowledge of health matters, and an array of other characteristics associated with people who receive adequate care. It is also clear, however, that categorical medical care reduces infant mortality and morbidity (see Chapter 5, neonatal intensive care units). How much of the reduction in infant mortality associated with our adequate-care index is due to actual medical care and how much is due to other maternal characteristics cannot be determined from the data. Behavior, knowledge, family structure, cultural background, nutrition, biologic factors, economic status, and medical care inextricably intermingle in influencing the outcome of pregnancy.

We can, however, use these data to project the impact on infant mortality if all the women had had the same pregnancy experience as those whose care met our three-factor criteria for adequacy. Such a projection requires that we adjust the rates for each of the four major ethnic groups in the four risk categories using the ethnic–risk–specific death rates for those women who had adequate care. Table 1-13 shows the results of this analysis for the four major ethnic groups. These data indicate that, if all mothers had had the same experience as the adequate-care mothers of their race and risk, the overall infant

TABLE 1-13   Infant Mortality Rates Adjusted for "Adequate Care" Index by Risk Category and Ethnic Group: New York City Live-Birth Cohort, 1968[a]

Ethnic Group	Number of Live Births	Deaths per 1,000 Live Births	
		Unadjusted	Adjusted
White native born	60,896	15.2	12.6
White foreign born	18,959	15.3	13.4
Puerto Rican	22,505	25.4	22.6
Black native born	32,051	35.7	29.3
TOTAL	134,411	21.8	18.4[b]

[a] Based on 134,411 live births. Excludes 7,606 live births from "all others" ethnic groups.
[b] Rate was calculated by adding expected deaths from each ethnic group and dividing by the total number of live births.

TABLE 1-14   Infant Mortality Rates Adjusted for "Adequate Care" Index by Risk Category Only: New York City Live-Birth Cohort, 1968

Risk Category	Number of Live Births	Deaths per 1,000 Live Births	
		Unadjusted	Adjusted
No risk	64,613	12.1	8.7
Social risk	36,351	24.9	12.3
Medical risk	20,685	27.7	22.6
Social and medical risk	20,368	42.0	29.9
TOTAL	142,017	21.9	14.7[a]

[a] Rate was calculated by adding expected deaths from each risk group and dividing by the total number of live births.

mortality rate would have been 16 percent lower, and approximately 460 additional infants would not have died in New York City in 1968.

A second approach is to assume that, within each risk group, it is possible to project the experience of mothers with adequate care, regardless of ethnicity, to those with inadequate or intermediate care. Such adjustments by risk group alone are presented in Table 1-14; they suggest that the overall infant mortality rate would have been reduced about one third, saving more than 1,000 infants. We have, of course, no precise way of knowing how many infant deaths adequate care can prevent. Adequate prenatal health services alone cannot address the social, economic, and cultural disabilities that befall pregnant women who now receive inadequate care. Our estimates of the impact of care, therefore, are only estimates—not guarantees.

TWO

Methodology: New York City Analysis

The data for these analyses were obtained from the 1968 standard certificates of birth, fetal death, and death maintained by the New York City health department. (For sample certificates, see Appendix B.) An important feature of this vital records system is the linkage of the death record for each infant to the birth record for the same infant. By linking the birth and death certificates, all characteristics on the birth records are available for analysis of infant deaths. The certificates were revised for 1968 to include education of the parents, date of first prenatal visit, and number of prenatal visits—information critical to this study. The fetal death and live-birth records of New York City are unique also in the amount of clinical information they contain including the mother's pre-existing medical conditions and complications of pregnancy and labor.

QUALITY OF DATA

Underregistration is minimal for live births and infant deaths in New York City. As a consequence, the infant mortality rates are considered reliable. Fetal deaths of 20 or more weeks of gestation are probably sufficiently registered to be useful, but those of lesser gestations are less adequately registered.[1]

COMPLETENESS OF DATA

Completeness of certain reported items is the primary limitation of the data. The vital records, in contrast to those in some other jurisdic-

50

tions, are fairly well controlled. They are checked by the five borough offices and again by the Bureau of Records and Statistics of the city department of health. When the records are coded, the health department directly communicates with hospitals to clarify missing and questionable items.

The rate for missing data for selected items on the fetal death and live-birth certificates is shown in Table 2-1. In some instances, the number for a particular item was very small. Demographic data such as age of mother, plurality, and birth order are considered to be adequately reported.[2] Only 27 of the 142,017 records, for example, were lacking information on mother's age. We allocated these records to the median age of mothers of the same race–nativity with the same birth order. If both the age of the mother and the number of births were unknown, the allocation was made solely on the basis of the median age of all mothers from the same race–nativity group. This technique avoided carrying a small group of cases as a separate category and, because very small numbers were involved, the aggregate statistics were not affected.

Newer items of information, including education of parents, date of first prenatal visit, and number of prenatal visits are not completely reported. Of greatest concern were those items of clinical information. In this analysis, clinical items are important because they determine the medical and obstetrical risks of each case. After careful review of the literature on the reliability of clinical vital statistics,[2-4] we concluded that the study could tolerate considerable underreporting of risk factors without biasing the results.

For fetal deaths, relatively little information was available for fetuses with gestation intervals of less than 20 weeks, due to a decision by the city health department not to code certain information for early fetal deaths. Also, incomplete entry of information on some of the records was a factor.

The certificate of fetal death is patterned after the certificate of live birth to permit the combination of their data for perinatal statistics. In comparison to live births, information on the fetal death certificates may be relatively incomplete for certain items, particularly those recently added to the document. For fetal deaths with gestation intervals of 20 or more weeks, for example, the education of the mother was missing from 38 percent of the records. Birth weight, although not a recent addition to the certificate, was missing from an equal proportion. As a result, the fetal death records were generally less useful for the study than the live birth and infant death records.

RELIABILITY OF DATA

A complete evaluation of each item of information on the tape disclosed occasional records with invalid code designations in a number of categories. We assumed these to be random errors and recoded them as unknown.

TABLE 2-1   Distribution of Missing Data for Selected Characteristics on Fetal Death and Live-Birth Certificates: New York City, 1968 Birth Cohort

	Fetal Death Certificates				Live-Birth Certificates	
	Gestation Less Than 20 Weeks and Not Stated		Gestation 20 Weeks or More			
Characteristic	Number	Percent	Number	Percent	Number	Percent
Certificates with one or more of the following items not stated	14,619	99.6	2,851	81.4	57,660	40.6
Age of mother[a]	0	0	0	0	0	0
Nativity of mother	322	2.2	54	1.5	104	0.1
Education of mother	7,239	49.3	1,330	38.0	6,897	4.9
Age of father	7,613	51.9	1,393	39.8	22,737	16.0
Nativity of father	6,345	43.2	1,088	31.1	17,052	12.0
Education of father	9,302	63.4	1,851	52.9	26,167	18.4
Total-birth order[b]	0	0	0	0	0	0
Birth weight	14,195	96.7	1,319	37.7	393	0.3
Gestation (weeks)	1,130	7.7	c	c	2,347	1.7
Interval to first prenatal visit	6,249	42.6	810	23.1	7,955	5.6
Number of prenatal visits	6,452	44.0	928	26.5	9,062	6.4
Congenital malformations	14,460	98.5	1,645	47.0	521	0.4
Apgar score						
1 minute	c	c	c	c	7,135	5.0
5 minutes	c	c	c	c	23,699	16.7
TOTAL CERTIFICATES	14,678		3,502		142,017	

[a] Certificates that failed to indicate age of mother were allocated on the basis of other information on the certificate.
[b] Certificates that indicated dashes or blanks for one or more of the components of previous pregnancy history were interpreted as zeros to derive birth order.
c Category not applicable.

It is apparent from studies done in the 1950's,[2,4] that recording of medical items on birth certificates is incomplete when compared with hospital records for the same infants. The conditions that were reported on the birth certificate, however, were accurate. Lilienfeld *et al.*[4] report that operative procedures such as episiotomy and use of forceps were reported on 94 percent of the birth certificates, while complications of pregnancy were reported on only 39 percent of the certificates.

Based on data reported from a study in the District of Columbia,[2] we made estimates of the percent of operative procedures and complications of pregnancy and labor that were correctly allocated. These data are presented in Table 2-2.

For each condition, the majority of the records would have been correctly allocated to at-risk and not-at-risk categories as defined in this study (see page 55 for definition). The proportion misallocated would be least for operative procedures (7 percent) and somewhat greater for complications related to pregnancy (19 percent) and labor (13 percent). All records for which there was no indication on the hospital record whether or not the condition was present or for which both records were positive but inconsistent, made up only 1 to 3 percent.

Data from the Washington, D.C., study also illustrate the relative degree of nonreported medical conditions on birth certificates as compared to hospital records. If the cases not reported on the birth certificates were highly biased in favor of either at-risk or not-at-risk groups, there would be added cause for concern for the present study. Such was not the case, however.

From the data, one can be reasonably confident that, although the recording of the medical and obstetric information was not perfect, it was adequate to provide contrasting groups of at-risk and not-at-risk cases. We recognize that there is underrecording of medical conditions; the mothers in our population classified as not-at-risk are a mixture of not-at-risk and at risk containing some mothers who were truly at risk but whose risk was not recorded. If there was no relationship between risk and outcome, such misallocations are unimportant because they will not bias the results. If there was a relationship between risk and outcome, diluting the group of not-at-risk records with some at-risk records will reduce any association between risk and outcome. Thus, any bias introduced by underreporting medical conditions would be in the direction of weakening the association between risk and outcome rather than strengthening it. The importance of this contamination depends on the frequency of the condition in the population and the degree of underreporting. In light of these

TABLE 2-2 Evaluation of Allocation of Birth Certificates Based on Matched
Hospital Records: Nine Hospitals in the District of Columbia, July–December
1952

| Allocation of Cases | Operative Procedures | | Complications | |
	Total	Excluding Forceps	Related to Pregnancy	Labor
			Percent	
Correctly allocated	90	97	79	84
Incorrectly allocated	7	2	19	13
Indeterminate	3	1	2	3
TOTAL	100	100	100	100

Source: National Office of Vital Statistics.[2]

studies, it appears that our data would understate the association between risk and outcome, rather than exaggerate it.

DEFINITIONS

ETHNIC GROUP

The ethnic classifications used in these analyses were based on categories constructed by the city health department before our study
began. They were derived by combining two characteristics: race of
the child and nativity of the mother. The race of the child was determined from the race of the parents. If both parents are of the same
race, the certificate was coded to that race. If either parent is black,
the certificate was coded to black. If either parent is white and the
other parent is of any nonwhite race other than black, the race of the
infant was coded to the nonwhite race. In rare instances when the
parents are of two different nonwhite races, the race of the child was
coded to that of the father.

The nativity of mother was coded to one of three groups: native
born (any place in the United States or its possessions, *except Puerto
Rico*), foreign born, or Puerto Rican. This classification differs from
traditional nativity groupings found in Census bureau publications in
which persons born in Puerto Rico are considered native born. Because of the concentration of Puerto Ricans in New York City, however, this procedure is a logical one.

RISK GROUP

We divided the population of mothers by the presence or absence of two kinds of maternal characteristics, social and medical, that could have an adverse effect on infant survival. The components of the risk categories and their frequencies are shown in Appendix B, Tables B-1 and B-2, including all of the social, medical, and obstetrical conditions reported on live-birth records and allocated according to the time when the risk could be identified. These classes were constructed for the present study in collaboration with obstetrical consultants.

The social risks are based on age of mother and total birth order* used together, education of mother, and legitimacy status. These determinations could all be made at the initial prenatal visit.

The medical risks are divided according to the earliest time at which they were judged to be identifiable: at first prenatal visit, during pregnancy, or during labor.

All women not classified in either the sociodemographic or medical–obstetric risk groups were labeled as not-at-risk.

Sociodemographic Risk Among characteristics identified on the vital records, age and education of mother, total birth order, and legitimacy status were selected as indicators of sociodemographic risks. In establishing criteria for the social-risk group, outside sources of information were used. Difference in the mortality rates between a group of at-risk births and the remainder of the cohort, which was defined to be not-at-risk, were analyzed. A series of alternative definitions were examined and analyzed by comparing ratios derived from the pooled variance of the infant mortality rates of the risk and nonrisk group divided by the difference between the means of the risk and nonrisk groups. These analyses provided a framework for selecting the alternative with the best contrast between the at-risk and not-at-risk groups based on their infant mortality experience. Risk categories defined by these criteria were used in the present study.

Age and Birth Order For the age of mother and birth order, unpublished data from the 1960 birth cohort for the United States were used; the data included fetal deaths with gestation intervals of 20

---

*Total birth order is the sum of the live births and fetal deaths that a mother has had including the birth being recorded. For example, if a mother has previously given birth to two live babies, either singly or as twins, and one dead baby, the next pregnancy is counted as number four in the total birth order.

weeks or more and live births. Four alternative combinations of maternal age and birth order were evaluated (Appendix B, Table B-3). The births that did not fall into these definitions were considered not-at-risk. The ratios described above of fetal deaths and infant deaths per 1,000 of the at-risk and not-at-risk groups in the four alternative classifications were close: 160.1, 163.0, 178.3, and 198.6, respectively. The third alternative was selected. These determinations were made without recourse to the infant mortality rates in the present study.

Educational Attainment   The education of the mother was used in preference to that of the father, or to a combination of the education for both parents, because on a large percentage of the records the education of the father was unspecified. The latter are presumably for illegitimate children for whom all information regarding the father is lacking. The same method was used to establish the education-risk categories as was used to establish the age and birth order risk categories. There are no national data relating infant mortality to education of mother. We used perinatal mortality data from a report of the North Carolina Board of Health[5] and examined four alternatives. The risk groups that were tested are as follows: I—8 years or less of education, II—11 years or less, III—12 years or less, IV—15 years or less. Using perinatal mortality rates, the ratios for the differences between at risk and not-at-risk were calculated as described for birth order and age. We selected the first alternative based on the comparative ratios. It should be noted, however, that this classification may not be appropriate for foreign educational systems. An effort was made to obtain data on the equivalent educational level of foreign-born women residing in New York City. Unfortunately, data were not readily available. The inappropriateness of this measure for foreign-born women may, in part, explain the unusual relations between infant mortality and education observed in the foreign-born white mothers.

Illegitimacy   The identification of illegitimate births was based on presumptive evidence. By law, no specific question on the certificate may ask whether an infant is illegitimate. The following criteria, however, have been established by the New York City health department to allocate births to the illegitimate group:

1. No name appears in the space provided for the name of the father. Such certificates generally lack all other information regarding the father as well.

2. The family name of the father differs from the family name of the child.

3. The family name of the child is the same as the maiden name of the mother.

4. The medical report contains an indication that the birth is out-of-wedlock.

5. The mother's address is a known shelter for unmarried mothers.

With regard to the second and third items, the certificates are queried before they are accepted as recorded. These criteria represent a definition of "presumed illegitimate birth," and all other births are presumed to be legitimate.

In all, the sociodemographic-risk groups included 56,719, or 39.9 percent, of the 142,017 infants in the live-birth cohort. Because of the possibility of multiple sociodemographic risks relating to the same birth, this number is less than the sum of all separate sociodemographic risks.

Medical and Obstetric Risks The construction of the risk categories for medical and obstetric factors was difficult. The coded medical data were reviewed and classified based on presumptions of an ability to detect the specified risk at critical points of time during pregnancy. The conditions were categorized into risks judged to be identifiable at first prenatal visit, during pregnancy, or immediately before labor or intrapartum.

Because of the form of the birth certificate and the way in which the information was recorded on it, we could not state precisely when the conditions were first noted. As an alternative, with the aid of the study's obstetrical consultants, the conditions were allocated to classes according to *when they should be detectable.* The results of the allocations, together with the frequencies in the present study are shown in Appendix B, Table B-2. In a few instances, conditions such as hypertensive disease or pelvic tumors were assigned to more than one risk group.

The first group includes such conditions as syphilis, tuberculosis, and malformed pelvis—risks that should be identifiable at the first prenatal visit. A mother was also allocated to this risk group if the birth certificate showed a death among her previously live-born infants, a previous fetal death irrespective of the gestation interval, or a previous delivery within a year. In the live-birth cohort of 142,017 infants, there were 5,447 whose birth certificates showed a sibling death. Records with previous fetal deaths were higher: 16,492 records showed one or more early fetal deaths (gestation interval of less than 20 weeks) and 4,240 records with one or more fetal deaths with longer gestation intervals. The number of records that indicated a previous delivery took place within a year was 3,665. Compared to some of the other medical–obstetric risks, the number of women with previous infant or fetal deaths or who had delivered within a year was relatively large; they constituted as much as half of the mothers at medical–obstetric risk.

The second group of risks included conditions, such as pre-eclampsia, pyelonephritis, and first-trimester German measles, that should be identifiable during pregnancy. The third group of risks included conditions identifiable immediately before labor or intrapartum. These included ruptured uterus, placenta praevia, fetal distress, and premature birth.

THREE-FACTOR HEALTH SERVICES INDEX

We formulated a composite description of maternal health services based on three items of information on the birth certificate: time of the first prenatal visit, number of prenatal visits, and type of hospital service. Type of hospital service was further divided into private service (that is, the woman was admitted and cared for by her personal physician) and general service (she was cared for by house staff). Because of some connotations surrounding the term "private service," it is important to stress that we use it to refer to neither the mode of practice of the personal physician nor the woman's accommodations in the hospital. Rather, we use it as an indication of the continuity of her care regardless of the physician who delivered her baby or whether she was housed in a one-person room or a four-person room.

Clearly, this index of health care is a proxy description of the services utilized by the mother. For simplicity, we divided it into adequate, intermediate, and inadequate classes as defined in Table 2-3. The classes are in accord with recommendations for prenatal care set forth by the American College of Obstetricians and Gynecologists[6] and the World Health Organization.[7]

The length of gestation was taken into account in structuring the index of care. A mother who delivered at 28 weeks gestation, for example, was not expected to have had as many prenatal visits as one who carried to term. For 1.7 percent of the live births for which gestation was not recorded, the three-factor index could not be calculated. Also, the maximum number of visits was limited to nine as these data had been coded with nine, indicating nine or more visits. We treated those for whom the number of visits was not coded (6.4 percent of the live births) as if they had made no visits. Similarly, if the time of the first visit was not coded (5.6 percent of the live births), the women were grouped in the late-care and no-care category.

OUTCOME MEASURES

Death Rates and Ratios　In this report, we have used the term "rate" for describing relationships to the entire at-risk population and the term "ratio" for describing relationships to selected segments of the population. For example, the fetal death *rate* is the number of fetal deaths per 1,000 live births *and* fetal deaths, while the fetal death

TABLE 2-3　Three-Factor Health Services Index Controlled for Gestation and Based upon Number of Prenatal Visits, Interval to First Prenatal Visit, and Type of Hospital Service

Medical Care Index	Gestation (weeks)		Number of Prenatal Visits
Adequate[a]	13 or less	and	1 or more or not stated
	14–17	and	2 or more
	18–21	and	3 or more
	22–25	and	4 or more
	26–29	and	5 or more
	30–31	and	6 or more
	32–33	and	7 or more
	34–35	and	8 or more
	36 or more	and	9 or more
Inadequate[b]	14–21[c]	and	0 or not stated
	22–29	and	1 or less or not stated
	30–31	and	2 or less or not stated
	32–33	and	3 or less or not stated
	34 or more	and	4 or less or not stated
Intermediate	All combinations other than specified above		

[a] In addition to the specific number of visits indicated for adequate care, the interval to the first prenatal visit had to be 13 weeks or less (first trimester), and the delivery must have taken place on a private obstetrical service.
[b] In addition to the specific number of visits indicated for inadequate care, all women who started their prenatal care during the third trimester (28 weeks or later) were considered inadequate.
[c] For this gestation group, care was considered inadequate if the time of the first visit was not stated.

ratio is the number of fetal deaths per 1,000 live births *only*. Further, the rates and ratios are expressed in five age-of-offspring categories as follows:

- Fetal—the period between conception and birth. The fetal period is further broken down into *early* (less than 20 full weeks gestation), *intermediate* (20 to 27 weeks), and *late* (28 weeks or longer). Official U.S. data do not record deaths of fetuses of less than 20 weeks gestation; New York City data, however, do.
  - Infant—the period from birth to 1 year of age
  - Neonatal—the period from birth to 28 days of age
  - Postneonatal—the period from age 28 days to age 1 year

Gestation The accuracy of weeks-of-gestation data found on vital records is suspect. There is often a predominance of gestations at 36 and 40 weeks.[1] This peaking is avoided when gestation is calculated from the first day of the last menstrual period.[8,9] The gestation intervals in the present study were based on the date of onset of the last normal menstrual period. The computation of the gestation interval was done by the computer and was deemed adequate for the present study. The data, however, are subject to errors in patient recall; in transferring data to vital records; and in punching, verification, and computation.

Birth Weight Weight was originally punched in pounds and ounces or grams with a key to indicate the scale. If weight was given in pounds and ounces, it was converted to ounces and multiplied by 28.35 to convert to grams. The birth weight in grams was then grouped in 500-gram intervals.

Apgar Scores The Apgar score is based on five vital signs graded at birth[12]: heart rate, respiratory effort, reflex irritability, muscle tone, and color. Each sign is given a score of 0, 1, or 2, with a maximum total score of 10. Testing is usually done 1 and 5 minutes after birth. When scores are taken under carefully controlled conditions, low scores are associated with neonatal mortality, particularly during the first 2 days of life, low birth weight, and neurological abnormalities at 1 year of age.[10,11] Ideally, the scoring should be done by a trained impartial observer, not necessarily a professional.

The 1-minute and 5-minute Apgar scores were added to the confidential medical report of the 1968 New York City live-birth certificates. These 1-minute and 5-minute scores were reported on 95.0 percent and 83.3 percent, respectively, of live-birth certificates. There is no information, however, about how carefully the time was observed or the quality of the scoring.

Apgar, the originator of the score, has indicated some of its limitations.[12] She has pointed out that, of the five signs, color is probably the most difficult to judge because of differences in skin pigmentation among different ethnic groups. Also, when observations are made by many different observers, the quality of the information is poorer than it would be from controlled studies.

Congenital Malformations The live-birth certificate requires reporting of congenital malformations. Such reporting, however, varies with the recorder's ability to detect malformations at birth, the severity of the malformation, and the diligence of those who transfer the information to the vital records. Several studies have attempted to analyze the completeness of such recording[2,4,13] and have found consistently incomplete recording of congenital malformations. Minor anomalies, such as birthmarks, which occur frequently but are relatively unimportant, are often omitted from the record; severe malformations, such as anencephaly, are recorded more completely.

A number of investigators have tried to estimate the occurrence of congenital malformations or have compared the routine reporting of congenital malformations on birth records and hospital records.[3,14-20] Based on these studies, one may conclude that congenital malformations of all degrees of severity probably occur in less than 8 percent of live births. Congenital malformations are also underreported on the confidential medical report on the birth certificates.[2,4,13,21] This underreporting is attributable to two causes: Some malformations are not readily identifiable at birth, and there is a failure to report some minor malformations such as birthmarks. Compared to mortality and birth weight, malformations were probably less completely reported although those reported were likely to have been reported correctly.

STATISTICAL TECHNIQUES

CONFIDENCE LIMITS

For selected mortality rates, 95 percent confidence limits were calculated by a method that assumes a Poisson-distributed variable. The tabular values and method of calculating the limits are described by Haenszel, Loveland, and Sirken.[22]

All comparisons between two groups or two subgroups are made on the basis of separately computed confidence intervals. That is, a 95 percent confidence interval is computed for one population mean, and another separate interval is obtained for the other mean. Clearly, this is not an exact procedure for assessing the statistical significance of the difference between two means. In most instances, however, it will lead to correct conclusions. When the 95 percent confidence intervals do not overlap, the obvious conclusion is that there is a statistically significant difference between the two means; it is rare that a different conclusion would be drawn if the exact procedure for assessing the difference between the means was used. The situation is, however, somewhat different when the confidence intervals overlap; here the implication is that the two means do not differ significantly. It should be noted that nontrivial and not-unusual examples can be devised to demonstrate that the exact procedure for assessing the difference between the means could lead in this instance to the opposite conclusion; that is, it is possible that situations could arise in which there is a significant difference between the means although two 95 percent confidence limits overlap.*

RELATIVE RISK

In an epidemiologic cohort study, the general question to be tested is whether individuals exposed to a factor have higher rates of the disease under study than those who are not exposed. In our infant mortality analyses, the analogous question is whether women who are exposed to different levels of medical care have different infant mortality rates. To measure the excess risk (increased infant mortality) of *nonexposure* to medical care, the risk to mothers with adequate care was taken as a standard; the risk to mothers with other levels of care was expressed in relation to the standard. The ratio, then, defines *relative risk*. Measures of risk are discussed by Clark and MacMahon.[24]

ADJUSTED RATES

A critical factor in calculating adjusted rates is the selection of a standard population or a standard set of rates for comparison. The selected standards should not be too divergent from the group under study. In the present study, the data are presented to a large extent

*S. Greenhouse, personal communication, February 1973.

in terms of mother's risk and race–nativity; it is proper, then, to adjust rates in risk and race–nativity specific groups; that is, the standards for adjusting the overall infant mortality rate for adequacy of care were the infant mortality rates for adequate care, specific for each risk group and each race–nativity group within each risk group.

STEPWISE MULTIPLE LINEAR REGRESSION

We used a multiple linear regression utility program developed by the Office of Scientific Personnel of the National Academy of Sciences (NAS). The NAS freely adapted the program from the procedures described by Efroymson.[25]

We performed two sets of analyses. In one, infant survival or death was the dependent variable; in the other, percent low-birth-weight infants was the dependent variable. When the dependent variable was infant survival or death, and birth weight was included as one of a series of independent variables, birth weight alone predicts survival almost as accurately as birth weight plus six other independent variables. Thus the multiple correlation coefficient for birth weight of 2,500 grams or less was 0.5128. This value was increased to 0.5140 by adding the six other variables. Similarly, birth weight of 2,500 grams or less accounts for 26.3 percent of the variance in survival ($R^2 = 0.263$) and the R^2 for birth weight plus six additional independent variables was 0.264. When this analysis was done, *excluding* birth weight as an independent variable, the multiple correlation coefficient is only 0.0905 and the R^2 is 0.0082. Thus, less than 1 percent of the variance in survival is accounted for by social, medical care, and medical-risk factors when birth weight is eliminated as an independent variable.

When percent birth weight of less than 2,500 grams is the dependent variable, gestation is the independent variable that accounts for more than 96 percent of the variance among 10 variables. For example, the total R^2 for gestation less than 38 weeks was 0.1771, while the total R^2 for all 10 independent variables was 0.1832. Again, when gestation was removed as an independent variable, a combination of social, demographic, medical care, and medical historical factors achieve a total multiple correlation coefficient of 0.1222 and a R^2 of 0.0149. Excluding gestation as an independent variable, less than 2 percent of the variance in the percent low birth weight is explained.

These linear regression analyses are not presented in detail as part of the major findings of this study because they do not contribute to our further understanding of the complex relationships among maternal, social, and medical characteristics; medical care delivery factors; and outcome measured as infant survival or death or as proportion at low birth weight.

REFERENCES

1. Chase HC: The current status of fetal death registration in the United States. Am J Public Health 56:1734–1744, 1966
2. Oppenheimer E, Schwartz S, Russell AL, et al: Evaluation of obstetric and related data recorded on vital records: District of Columbia, 1952. Vital Statistics Reports. U.S. Department of Health, Education, and Welfare, National Office of Vital Statistics, Selected Studies 45:359–416, 1957
3. Gentry JT, Parkhurst E, Bulin GV: An epidemiological study of congenital malformations in New York State. Am J Public Health 49:497–513, 1959
4. Lilienfeld AM, Parkhurst E, Patton R, et al: Accuracy of supplemental medical information on birth certificates. Public Health Rep 66:191–198, 1951
5. North Carolina State Board of Health: Perinatal statistics, 1968. Public Health Statistics Section of the North Carolina State Board of Health, Raleigh, North Carolina (photo offset, no publication date)
6. American College of Obstetricians and Gynecologists: Manual of standards in obstetric-gynecologic practice. Second edition. Chicago, 1965
7. World Health Organization Technical Report Series, No. 51 and 115: Committee on maternal and child health. First and second reports. Washington, D.C.
8. Hamnes LM, Treloar AE: Gestational interval from vital records. Am J Public Health 60:1496–1505, 1970
9. California' Health: San Diego reports on trial revision of the birth certificate. 13:141–143, 1956. California State Department of Public Health, Berkeley, California
10. Drage JS, Kennedy C, Schwarz BK: The Apgar score as an index of neonatal mortality. Obstet Gynecol 24:222–230, 1964
11. Drage JS, Berendes H: Apgar scores and outcome of the newborn. Pediatr Clin North Am 13:635–643, 1966
12. Apgar V: A proposal for a new method of evaluation of the newborn infant. Curr Res Anesth Analg 32:260–267, 1953
13. Mackeprang M, Hay S, Lunde AS: Completeness and accuracy of reporting of malformations on birth certificates. HSMHA Health Rep 87:43–49, 1972
14. Ivy RH: Congenital anomalies as recorded on birth certificates in the Division of Vital Statistics of the Pennsylvania Department of Health, for the period 1951–1955 inclusive. Plast Reconstr Surg 20:400–411, 1957
15. Babbott JG, Ingalls TH: Field studies of selected congenital malformations occurring in Pennsylvania. Am J Public Health 52:2009–2017, 1962
16. Bock HB, Zimmerman JH: Study of selected congenital anomalies in Pennsylvania. Public Health Rep 82:446–450, 1967
17. Silberg SL, Marienfeld CH, Wright H, et al: Surveillance of congenital anomalies in Missouri 1953–1964. Arch Environ Health 13:641–644, 1966

18. Ingalls TH, Klingberg MA: Implications of epidemic embryopathy for public health. Am J Public Health 55:200–208, 1965
19. Hendricks CH: Congenital malformations. Analysis of the 1953 Ohio records. Obstet Gynecol 6:592–598, 1955
20. McIntosh R, Merrett KK, Richards MR, et al: Incidence of congenital malformations—a study of 5,964 pregnancies. Pediatrics 14:505–520, 1954
21. Milham S: Underreporting of incidence of cleft lip and palate. Am J Dis Child 106:185–188, 1963
22. Haenszel WU, Loveland DB, Sirken MG: Lung-cancer mortality as related to residence and smoking histories. I. White males. J Natl Cancer Inst 28:947–1001, 1962
23. MacMahon B: Epidemiologic methods. Preventive medicine. Edited by DW Clark and B MacMahon. Boston, Little, Brown and Company, 1967, pp 97–98
24. Efroymson MA: Multiple regression analysis. Mathematical methods for digital computers. Edited by A Ralston and HS Wilf. New York, John Wiley & Sons, Inc, 1960, pp 191–203

THREE

Description of the Population: New York City Analysis

This analysis is based on the cohort of live births and fetal deaths for 1968 registered with the New York City Department of Health (Table 3-1).

RACE-NATIVITY

We used two characteristics recorded on the New York City birth certificate to classify the population by ethnic group: race of the child and nativity of the mother. The distribution of live births by ethnic groups is shown in Table 3-2.

AGE OF MOTHER

There were marked variations in the maternal age distribution among the ethnic groups (Table 3-3). White foreign-born and Chinese and Japanese mothers generally were older than the white native-born mothers. Puerto Rican and black mothers were youngest, with 17.8 and 26.4 percent, respectively, of the live births to mothers under 20 years of age. This rate is two to three times the proportions for births among white native-born and foreign-born mothers of the same age. The largest proportion of live births, 34.2 percent, were to mothers 20 to 24 years of age, with another 29.4 percent of the infants born

TABLE 3-1 New York City Live-Birth and Fetal
Death Cohorts, 1968

	Number
Fetal deaths	18,180
Gestation less than 20 weeks	13,548
Gestation 20–27 weeks	1,737
Gestation 28 weeks or more	1,765
Gestation unknown	1,130
Live births	142,017
Survivors	138,902
Infant deaths	3,115

TABLE 3-2 Distribution of Live Births by Ethnic Group, New York City Live-
Birth Cohort, 1968

Ethnic Group	Number	Percent
White		
Native born	60,896	42.9
Foreign born	18,959	13.3
Puerto Rican	22,505	15.8
Black		
Native born	32,051	22.6
Foreign born	4,405	3.1
Puerto Rican	1,126	0.8
Chinese	1,257	0.9
Japanese	265	0.2
Other	553	0.4
TOTAL	142,017	100.0

to mothers 25 to 29 years of age. Thus, 63.6 percent of all live births
were to mothers in their third decade of life.

TOTAL BIRTH ORDER

More than one third, or 36.5 percent, of all the births were first
births; approximately one fourth, or 26.2 percent, were second births,
while 12.5 percent were fifth or higher births (Table 3-4).

We found expected differences in birth order by ethnic group.
White native-born and white foreign-born mothers had higher propor-

TABLE 3-3 Distribution of Mother's Age by Ethnic Group: New York City Live-Birth Cohort, 1968

Age of Mother (years)	Total	White Native Born	White Foreign Born	Puerto Rican	Black Native Born	All Others
			Percent of Live Births			
Less than 15	0.3	0.1	0.0	0.2	1.0	0.1
15–19	13.2	8.2	5.1	17.6	25.4	8.4
20–24	34.2	34.7	28.7	39.7	34.3	28.1
25–29	29.4	34.4	32.2	24.3	21.6	31.5
30–34	14.4	14.2	21.2	11.8	11.1	19.7
35–39	6.6	6.6	10.0	4.9	5.1	9.6
40 and over	1.8	1.8	2.7	1.4	1.5	2.5
TOTAL	100.0	100.0	100.0	100.0	100.0	100.0
Number of live births	142,017	60,896	18,959	22,505	32,051	7,606

tions in the lower birth orders, and Puerto Ricans and black mothers had higher proportions in the higher orders.

EDUCATION OF MOTHER AND FATHER

The variation among ethnic groups by the mother's educational level was marked (Table 3-5). Proportionately, thirty-four times as many white native-born as Puerto Rican mothers had 4 or more years of college, while four times as many black as white native-born mothers had only an elementary school education or less. Patterns for educational attainment of the fathers are shown in Table 3-6. In general, the level is higher than for the mothers with approximately one-and-one-half times as many fathers with 4 years or more of college. (Education, however, was not stated for 18.4 percent of the fathers compared with "not stated for" slightly less than 5 percent of mothers.)

ILLEGITIMACY

Of all live births, 18.5 percent, or more than 26,000, were coded by the health department as illegitimate. Illegitimacy by ethnic group is shown in Table 3-7. The differences document a wide range of rates

TABLE 3-4 Distribution of Total Birth Order by Ethnic Group: New York City Live-Birth Cohort, 1968

Total Birth Order	Total	White Native Born	White Foreign Born	Puerto Rican	Black Native Born	All Others
		Percent of Live Births				
First	36.5	39.5	36.8	30.4	34.7	37.7
Second	26.2	28.3	28.6	23.7	22.8	25.5
Third	15.9	15.8	16.8	17.0	14.8	15.3
Fourth	8.8	7.9	8.5	10.6	9.5	8.9
Fifth	5.0	3.9	4.1	6.5	6.6	5.2
Sixth or higher	7.5	4.6	5.1	11.8	11.5	7.5
TOTAL	100.0	100.0	100.0	100.0	100.0	100.0
Number of live births	142,017	60,896	18,959	22,505	32,051	7,606

TABLE 3-5 Distribution of Mother's Education by Ethnic Group: New York City Live-Birth Cohort, 1968

Education of Mother	Total	White Native Born	White Foreign Born	Puerto Rican	Black Native Born	All Others
		Percent of Live Births				
None or elementary	13.1	2.3	26.0	36.7	8.5	19.2
High school, 1–3 years	22.5	13.6	12.9	34.9	37.6	17.8
High school, 4 years	41.7	51.2	37.9	20.4	41.8	36.9
College, 1–3 years	8.2	11.9	7.6	1.6	5.7	9.2
College, 4 or more years	9.6	17.1	9.1	0.5	1.9	10.8
Not stated	4.9	4.0	6.5	6.0	4.5	6.1
TOTAL	100.0	100.0	100.0	100.0	100.0	100.0
Number of live births	142,017	60,896	18,959	22,505	32,051	7,606

from a low of 5.1 percent of infants of white foreign-born mothers to a high of 45 percent of infants of black native-born women. Table 3-8 contrasts the differences in neonatal death rates for legitimate and illegitimate infants by the age and ethnicity of the mother. The overall rates and the rates for most mother's age groups are higher for illegitimate infants than for legitimate infants, with the striking exception of the rates in the mother's age group of 17 years and younger. The

TABLE 3-6 Distribution of Father's Education by Ethnic Group: New York City Live-Birth Cohort, 1968

Education of Father	Total	White Native Born	White Foreign Born	Puerto Rican	Black Native Born	All Others
			Percent of Live Births			
None or elementary	10.4	2.7	21.6	27.7	5.8	13.2
High school, 1–3 years	14.9	10.6	9.7	27.6	17.7	11.8
High school, 4 years	33.3	40.3	34.2	17.7	31.4	30.1
College, 1–3 years	7.9	11.8	7.6	1.9	4.8	8.5
College, 4 or more years	15.0	26.1	16.2	0.9	2.6	17.5
Not stated	18.4	8.6	10.7	24.2	37.6	18.9
TOTAL	100.0	100.0	100.0	100.0	100.0	100.0
Number of live births	142,017	60,896	18,959	22,505	32,051	7,606

death rate among illegitimate infants of white native-born mothers, for example, is nearly 20 percent lower than among their legitimate counterparts; for infants of black native-born mothers, the corresponding difference is 16 percent. One explanation for the better survival rates among illegitimate infants of younger women may be in the social status of the mothers. It does not seem too unlikely that unmarried women 17 years and younger come from families of higher status generally than do married women 17 years and younger.

RISK CATEGORIES

More than one half of the infants of the mothers were judged to be at sociodemographic, medical–obstetric, or combined sociodemographic–medical risk. The distribution of risks by ethnic group is shown in Table 3-9.

At-risk proportions vary from 37.7 percent in white native born to 73.3 percent in black native born. Within the sociodemographic-risk groups, the range is even broader; black women have more than three times the portion of risks as white native born in this group. A much narrower range is found in the medical–obstetric category; the expected variation is found in the combined social and medical risk category.

Table 3-10 details the distribution of risk categories and their component parts by ethnic group. Because one mother can be at risk for multiple causes, such as age and education, in a single risk group, the sum of the percentages for the parts is greater than the total.

In the sociodemographic category, the relationships of ethnic group to individual social and demographic variables mirror the ethnic distributions previously discussed for these factors. There is a relatively narrow range by ethnic group in the medical–obstetric category— 25.7 percent in white native-born to 32.4 percent in Puerto Rican mothers. Within the component parts of this risk group, however, twice as many black mothers as white had conditions identifiable during pregnancy. Considering both sociodemographic and medical–obstetric risks identifiable at the first prenatal visit, more than 95 percent of the at-risk population could have been identified during an initial prenatal evaluation.

The average number of risks per mother was based on a consideration of the distribution of all recorded risks. These data are reported by ethnic group in Table 3-11. They show major differences between white native-born, Puerto Rican, and black mothers.

MEDICAL CARE

TIME OF FIRST PRENATAL VISIT

Of the cohort, 3.3 percent of the mothers had no prenatal care. By ethnic group, the proportion varied from 1.5 percent in white native born to 6.4 percent in black native born (Table 3-12).

TABLE 3-7 Distribution of Illegitimate Births by Ethnic Group: New York City Live-Birth Cohort, 1968

Legitimacy	Total	White Native Born	White Foreign Born	Puerto Rican	Black Native Born	All Others
		Percent of Live Births				
In wedlock	81.5	93.8	94.9	75.1	54.7	81.2
Out-of-wedlock	18.5	6.2	5.1	24.9	45.3	18.8
TOTAL	100.0	100.0	100.0	100.0	100.0	100.0
Number of live births	142,017	60,896	18,959	22,505	32,051	7,606

More than half of the white group started prenatal care in the first trimester, while only one sixth of the Puerto Ricans and blacks had early care. Conversely, the proportion of black mothers receiving late care was three times that of white native-born mothers receiving late care.

NUMBER OF PRENATAL VISITS

The pattern is similar for the number of prenatal visits (Table 3-13). Less than one third of the blacks had nine or more visits, while just

TABLE 3-8   Neonatal Death Rates by Ethnic Group, Legitimacy Status, and Age of Mother: New York City Live-Birth Cohort, 1968

Mother's Age (years) and Child's Legitimacy Status	Total	White Native Born	White Foreign Born	Puerto Rican	Black Native Born	All Others
			Deaths per 1,000 Live Births			
TOTAL	16.7	12.2	12.4	19.1	25.4	19.3
Legitimate	14.6	11.4	12.0	18.1	23.0	18.3
Illegitimate	25.7	23.1	19.5^a	22.1	28.4	23.7
17 and under						
Total	23.6	19.9	5.8^a	22.1	26.3	25.9^a
Legitimate	23.6	22.1^a	0.0^a	22.2	30.4	42.3^a
Illegitimate	23.6	17.7^a	b	21.8^a	25.5	16.4
18–19						
Total	20.3	15.6	11.2^a	20.8	25.0	19.8^a
Legitimate	16.8	13.9	10.0^a	23.4	16.5	17.9^a
Illegitimate	25.9	21.3^a	18.9^a	14.1^a	30.9	22.9^a
20–29						
Total	15.5	11.1	11.6	18.6	25.3	17.9
Legitimate	13.6	10.4	11.1	17.1	23.2	16.6
Illegitimate	26.5	26.5	21.3^a	23.5	28.7	23.6^a
30–34						
Total	15.9	12.0	13.2	18.8	24.4	20.0
Legitimate	14.9	11.8	12.9	16.4	24.5	19.6
Illegitimate	24.3	20.8^a	20.3^a	27.3^a	24.2	22.5
35 and older						
Total	19.0	16.2	15.8	19.0	27.2	23.8
Legitimate	18.0	16.1	16.1	19.2	24.1	22.0^a
Illegitimate	26.7	19.4^a	8.8^a	18.2^a	34.7^a	32.9^a

^{a}Rate based on 100–999 live births.
^{b}Rate not computed; based on less than 100 live births.

TABLE 3-9 Distribution of Risk Category by Ethnic Group: New York City Live-Birth Cohort, 1968

Risk Category	Total	White Native Born	White Foreign Born	Puerto Rican	Black Native Born	All Others
		Percent of Live Births				
Infants not-at-risk	45.5	62.3	44.7	29.1	26.7	40.7
Infants at risk	54.5	37.7	55.3	70.9	73.3	59.3
Sociodemographic risk only	25.6	12.1	26.1	38.5	41.5	27.5
Medical–obstetric risk only	14.6	18.1	15.3	10.5	10.1	15.6
Sociodemographic and medical–obstetric risk	14.3	7.6	13.9	21.9	21.7	16.2
TOTAL	100.0	100.0	100.0	100.0	100.0	100.0
Number of live births	142,017	60,896	18,959	22,505	32,051	7,606

TABLE 3-10 Distribution of Component Parts of Risk Category by Ethnic Group: New York City Live-Birth Cohort, 1968

Risk Category	Total	White Native Born	White Foreign Born	Puerto Rican	Black Native Born	All Others
		Percent of Live Births				
Infants with no risk	45.5	62.3	44.7	29.1	26.7	40.7
All infants at risk	54.5	37.7	55.3	70.9	73.3	59.3
Infants with sociodemographic risks	39.9	19.6	40.0	60.4	63.2	43.7
Age of mother/birth order	19.8	13.0	16.7	27.6	28.9	19.6
Education of mother	13.2	2.3	26.0	36.7	8.5	19.2
Illegitimacy	18.5	6.2	5.1	24.9	45.3	18.8
Infants with medical–obstetric risks	28.9	25.7	29.2	32.4	31.8	31.8
Identifiable at first prenatal visit	24.3	21.6	25.0	27.3	26.2	26.9
Identifiable during pregnancy	4.2	3.1	3.3	4.7	6.3	4.3
Identifiable at labor	5.5	5.5	6.1	6.4	4.4	5.6
TOTAL	100.0	100.0	100.0	100.0	100.0	100.0
Number of live births	142,017	60,896	18,959	22,505	32,051	7,606

over half of the native-born and foreign-born whites had this intensity of care. By proportions, more than three times as many black as white native-born mothers had only one to four prenatal visits.

HOSPITAL AND SERVICE

Virtually all of the infants—99.9 percent—were delivered in a hospital: 70 percent in voluntary institutions, 20 percent in municipal hospitals, and the rest in proprietary hospitals.

The cohort was divided almost equally between infants delivered on a private service and infants delivered on a general service: 53.8

TABLE 3-11   Average Number of Risks per Mother by Ethnic Group: New York City Live-Birth Cohort, 1968

Ethnic Group	Average Number of Risks per Mother
White native born	1.5
White foreign born	2.7
Puerto Rican	3.6
Black native born	3.2
All others	2.7
TOTAL	2.4

TABLE 3-12   Distribution of Interval to First Prenatal Visit by Ethnic Group: New York City Live-Birth Cohort, 1968

Interval to First Prenatal Visit	Total	White Native Born	White Foreign Born	Puerto Rican	Black Native Born	All Others
			Percent of Live Births			
Early care (13 weeks or less)	41.8	62.6	50.1	18.2	16.6	30.8
Midcare (14–27 weeks)	36.2	25.0	34.6	50.8	46.4	44.2
Late care (28 weeks or later)	13.0	7.1	10.1	18.5	21.7	15.1
No care	3.3	1.5	1.7	5.3	6.4	3.5
Not stated	5.6	3.7	3.5	7.3	9.0	6.4
TOTAL	100.0	100.0	100.0	100.0	100.0	100.0
Number of live births	142,017	60,896	18,959	22,505	32,051	7,606

percent and 44.2 percent, respectively (Table 3-14). Approximately 2,200 deliveries, or 1.6 percent, were by nurse–midwives.

THREE-FACTOR HEALTH SERVICES INDEX

Based on the three proxies of care—time of first prenatal visit, number of visits (adjusted for length of gestation), and hospital service—a composite health services index was constructed (see Chapter 2, page 58 for definition). In combination, the descriptors of prenatal and intrapartum care highlight the pattern of health services received by the various ethnic groups (Table 3-15). As one would anticipate, the trends for the composite index are similar to those for the component parts.

In all, only one fourth of the mothers received adequate care, slightly less than one half received intermediate care, and more than one fourth received inadequate care. The differences by ethnic group were large. Proportionately, 10 times as many white native-born as Puerto Rican or black mothers received adequate care, while the proportion of white mothers receiving inadequate care was more than one-half less than that of either of the two minority groups.

The relation of care and risk categories for each ethnic group are also presented in Table 3-15. In the total population, more than one third of those not-at-risk received adequate care, while less than one tenth at social risk received such care. For those at medical risk, more than one third had adequate care compared to one eighth for those

TABLE 3-13   Distribution of Number of Prenatal Visits by Ethnic Group: New York City Live-Birth Cohort, 1968

Number of Prenatal Visits	Total	White Native Born	White Foreign Born	Puerto Rican	Black Native Born	All Others
			Percent of Live Births			
9 or more visits	44.2	57.6	51.9	30.0	25.3	40.2
5–8 visits	32.7	29.5	33.3	37.2	34.7	34.6
1–4 visits	13.3	7.1	9.4	19.4	23.2	14.2
No visits	3.3	1.5	1.7	5.3	6.4	3.5
Not stated	6.4	4.3	3.8	8.1	10.4	7.5
TOTAL	100.0	100.0	100.0	100.0	100.0	100.0
Number of live births	142,017	60,896	18,959	22,505	32,051	7,606

classified as combined social and medical risk. There were major differences by ethnic group. Thus, over 20 percent of the white native and foreign born at social risk had adequate care, while less than 2 percent of Puerto Rican and black native-born mothers of the same risk group had adequate care. Proportionately, five times as many white mothers at medical risk had adequate care compared to the Puerto Rican and black mothers. These data also show that almost two thirds of the mothers with adequate care were not-at-risk, while more than two thirds of the mothers with inadequate care were at risk.

FETAL AND INFANT DEATHS

Losses associated with 1968 births included 18,180 fetal deaths and 3,115 infant deaths, for a combined rate of 132.9 per 1,000 fetal deaths and live births.

The distribution of infant deaths by time of death demonstrates the expected pattern (Table 3-16). Nearly 50 percent of the deaths occurred during the first day of life, almost 70 percent during the first week of life, and more than three fourths during the first month.

ETHNIC GROUP

Infant mortality rates among the major ethnic groups ranged from 15.2 per 1,000 live births for white infants to 35.7 for the black in-

TABLE 3-14   Distribution of Type of Hospital and Service by Ethnic Group: New York City Live-Birth Cohort, 1968

Type of Hospital and Service	Total	White Native Born	White Foreign Born	Puerto Rican	Black Native Born	All Others
			Percent of Live Births			
Proprietary, private service	9.5	13.7	16.2	2.3	3.5	4.9
Voluntary, private service	44.3	69.9	55.1	12.1	13.2	38.4
Voluntary, general service	25.0	10.8	17.8	45.3	41.2	28.6
Municipal, general service	19.2	3.8	10.1	38.3	39.1	25.3
Other and nonhospital	2.0	1.8	0.8	2.0	3.1	2.9
TOTAL	100.0	100.0	100.0	100.0	100.0	100.0
Number of live births	142,017	60,896	18,959	22,505	32,051	7,606

TABLE 3-15 Distribution of Three-Factor Health Services Index by Risk
Category and Ethnic Group: New York City Live-Birth Cohort, 1968

| Ethnic Group/ Three-Factor Health Services Index | Risk Category | | | | |
	No Risk	Socio-demographic	Medical– Obstetric	Socio-demographic and Medical– Obstetric	Total
ALL ETHNIC GROUPS					
All care groups					
Number	64,613	36,351	20,685	20,368	142,017
Percent	100.0	100.0	100.0	100.0	100.0
Adequate					
Number	22,989	3,162	7,465	2,509	36,125
Percent	35.6	8.7	36.1	12.3	25.4
Intermediate					
Number	29,626	17,157	9,489	10,241	66,513
Percent	45.9	47.2	45.9	50.3	46.8
Inadequate					
Number	11,998	16,032	3,731	7,618	39,379
Percent	18.5	44.1	18.0	37.4	27.7
WHITE NATIVE BORN					
All care groups					
Number	37,921	7,353	11,018	4,604	60,896
Percent	100.0	100.0	100.0	100.0	100.0
Adequate					
Number	17,875	1,549	5,465	1,506	26,395
Percent	47.1	21.0	49.6	32.7	43.3
Intermediate					
Number	15,338	3,114	4,249	2,016	24,717
Percent	40.5	42.4	38.6	43.8	40.6
Inadequate					
Number	4,708	2,690	1,304	1,082	9,784
Percent	12.4	36.6	11.8	23.5	16.1
WHITE FOREIGN BORN					
All care groups					
Number	8,483	4,941	2,894	2,641	18,959
Percent	100.0	100.0	100.0	100.0	100.0
Adequate					
Number	3,245	1,087	1,181	620	6,133
Percent	38.2	22.0	48.8	23.5	32.3
Intermediate					
Number	3,898	2,561	1,290	1,400	9,149
Percent	46.0	51.8	44.6	53.0	48.3
Inadequate					
Number	1,340	1,293	423	621	3,677
Percent	15.8	26.2	14.6	23.5	19.4

TABLE 3-15 (continued)

	Risk Category				
Ethnic Group/ Three-Factor Health Services Index	No Risk	Socio- demographic	Medical– Obstetric	Socio- demographic and Medical– Obstetric	Total
PUERTO RICAN					
All care groups					
Number	6,556	8,661	2,355	4,933	22,505
Percent	100.0	100.0	100.0	100.0	100.0
Adequate					
Number	491	142	211	113	957
Percent	7.5	1.6	9.0	2.3	4.3
Intermediate					
Number	4,013	4,493	1,480	2,784	12,770
Percent	61.2	51.9	62.8	56.4	56.7
Inadequate					
Number	2,052	4,026	664	2,036	8,778
Percent	31.3	46.5	28.2	41.3	39.0
BLACK NATIVE BORN					
All care groups					
Number	8,558	13,302	3,234	6,957	32,051
Percent	100.0	100.0	100.0	100.0	100.0
Adequate					
Number	765	227	325	156	1,473
Percent	9.0	1.7	10.0	2.2	4.6
Intermediate					
Number	4,710	5,905	1,832	3,323	15,770
Percent	55.0	44.4	56.7	47.8	49.2
Inadequate					
Number	3,083	7,170	1,077	3,478	14,808
Percent	36.0	53.9	33.3	50.0	46.2
ALL OTHERS					
All care groups					
Number	3,095	2,094	1,184	1,233	7,606
Percent	100.0	100.0	100.0	100.0	100.0
Adequate					
Number	613	157	283	114	1,167
Percent	19.8	7.5	23.9	9.3	15.3
Intermediate					
Number	1,667	1,084	638	718	4,107
Percent	53.9	51.8	53.9	58.2	54.0
Inadequate					
Number	815	853	263	401	2,332
Percent	26.3	40.7	22.2	32.5	30.7

fants with native-born mothers (Table 3-17). In these ethnic groups, there was a twofold range in neonatal death rates, but the greatest contrasts occurred in postneonatal death rates: 3.0 per 1,000 for white infants and 10.2 per 1,000 for black infants with native-born mothers.

AGE OF MOTHER

The highest overall loss rates, including early, intermediate, and late fetal deaths, occurred among infants of women aged 40 and older (Table 3-18). Infant mortality rates appear to be highest for the small number of women less than 15 years of age and for those aged 15 to 19 years and lowest for women 25 to 29 years of age.

TOTAL BIRTH ORDER

Table 3-19 shows that infant mortality rates by total birth order increased from low-order to high-order births. The rate is lowest among first-born children (18.0 per 1,000 live births), while the rate is almost doubled for infants sixth or higher in birth order. The same trends of increasing infant mortality with increasing birth order are apparent within specific maternal age groups; the highest rates are found among offspring of the small 15- to 19-year-old group having their fourth child and lowest among offspring of women aged 25 to 34 years having their second child.

TABLE 3-16 Distribution of Infant Deaths and Infant Mortality Rates by Age at Death: New York City Live-Birth Cohort, 1968

Age at Death	Number of Infant Deaths	Percent of Infant Deaths	Mortality Rate per 1,000 Live Births
Under 1 year	3,115	100.0	21.9
Under 28 days	2,368	76.0	16.7
Under 7 days	2,171	69.7	15.3
Under 1 day	1,452	46.6	10.2
1–6 days	719	23.1	5.1
7–13 days	96	3.1	0.7
14–20 days	52	1.7	0.4
21–27 days	49	1.6	0.4
28 days–11 months	747	24.0	5.3

TABLE 3-17   Infant Mortality Rates by Race–Nativity Group and Age at Death: New York City Live-Birth Cohort, 1968

Race of Child and Nativity of Mother	Number of Live Births	Number of Deaths			Mortality Rate (per 1,000 live births)		
		Infant	Neonatal	Post-neonatal	Infant	Neonatal	Post-neonatal
TOTAL	142,017	3,115	2,368	747	21.9	16.7	5.3
White							
Native born	60,896	923	741	182	15.2	12.2	3.0
Foreign born	18,959	291	235	56	15.3	12.4	3.0
Puerto Rican	22,505	572	430	142	25.4	19.1	6.3
Black							
Native born	32,051	1,143	815	328	35.7	25.4	10.2
Foreign born	4,405	118	97	21	26.8	22.0	4.8
Puerto Rican	1,126	33	24	9	29.3	21.3	8.0
Chinese	1,257	18	15	3	14.3	11.9	2.4
Japanese	265	6	5	1	22.6[a]	18.9[a]	3.8[a]
All others	553	11	6	5	19.9[a]	10.9[a]	9.0[a]

[a] Rate based on 100–999 live births.

EDUCATION OF MOTHER

For approximately 4,000 mothers who had postgraduate college education, the infant mortality rate was 7.6 per 1,000 live births. This contrasts with rates of 27.7 for those with elementary and 28.5 for those with incomplete high school education (Table 3-20). The interrelationships of mother's education, ethnicity, and age and total birth order are shown in Table 3-21. The trends shown in Table 3-20 are again demonstrated for each of the variables by education of the mother. Thus, for 13,000 mothers with 4 years or more of college, infant death rates varied from 9.1 per 1,000 in first-order births to 24.4 per 1,000 in sixth- or higher-order births. The lowest rates by education and maternal age were in women 25 to 29 years of age with 4 years or more of college.

BIRTH WEIGHT

The distribution by birth weight of the live-born cohort showed the expected black–white differences (Table 3-22). The percentage of low-birth-weight infants (2,500 grams or less) varied by ethnic group from 15.7 percent among native-born blacks to a surprisingly low rate of 6.5 percent among foreign-born whites. The predominant weight group was 3,001 to 3,500 grams, and it included 39.6 percent of the live births, with another 44.9 percent within 500 grams on either side of this weight class. In all, 84.5 percent of the live births weighed between 2,501 and 4,000 grams at birth, and 89.8 percent weighed 2,501 grams or more.

Mean birth weights varied considerably by ethnic group. As seen in Table 3-23, foreign-born white mothers had the heaviest babies and native-born blacks the lightest (foreign-born black mothers' babies were heavier than those of their native black counterparts). The statistical significance of the differences in mean birth weight by ethnic group is shown in Table 3-24.

TABLE 3-18   Infant Loss by Age of Mother and Time of Infant Death: New York City Live-Birth and Fetal Death Cohorts, 1968

Age of Mother (years)	Rate per 1,000			
	Total Loss[a]	Early Fetal Deaths[b]	Intermediate/Late Fetal Deaths[c]	Infant Mortality[d]
Under 15	136.4[e]	59.9[e]	39.6[e]	43.5[e]
15–19	120.6	70.2	24.5	30.5
20–24	119.2	81.1	20.0	21.9
25–29	122.4	86.5	21.2	18.5
30–34	148.6	106.1	28.6	19.5
35–39	190.3	137.4	38.9	23.3
40 and older	269.4	209.9	49.5	27.0
TOTAL	132.9	91.6	24.1	21.9

[a] All fetal deaths and deaths under 1 year of age. Rate per 1,000 live births and all fetal deaths.

[b] Fetal deaths with gestation periods of 19 completed weeks or less and gestation not stated. Rate per 1,000 live births and all fetal deaths.

[c] Fetal deaths with gestation periods of 20 completed weeks or more. Rate per 1,000 live births and intermediate and late fetal deaths.

[d] Deaths under 1 year of age. Rate per 1,000 live births.

[e] Rate based on 100–999 live births.

TABLE 3-19 Infant Mortality Rates by Age of Mother, Ethnic Group, and Total Birth Order: New York City Live-Birth Cohort, 1968

Ethnic Group and Total Birth Order	Total	Age of Mother (years)							
		Under 15	15–19	20–24	25–29	30–34	35–39	40–44	45 or over
Number of live births	142,017	437	18,728	48,631	41,812	20,409	9,410	2,444	146
				Deaths per 1,000 Live Births					
Ethnic group									
White native born	15.2	a	22.7	14.6	12.9	14.0	19.8	24.2[b]	
White foreign born	15.3	a	16.4[b]	13.0	14.2	16.4	19.0	27.1[b]	
White Puerto Rican	25.4	a	29.0	26.6	22.7	22.9	22.5	22.4[b]	
Black native born	35.7	42.6[b]	37.0[b]	36.4	35.0	31.7	34.3	36.3[b]	
All others	24.5	a	39.3[b]	22.5	20.4	24.6	30.1[b]	26.2[b]	
Total birth order									
First	18.0	44.6[b]	24.1	15.6	14.2	18.2	17.3[b]	30.0[b]	
Second	20.7	a	49.5	21.2	14.1	14.0	16.3	25.2[b]	
Third	22.7	a	37.3[b]	31.9	17.1	15.6	21.7	13.4[b]	
Fourth	28.0	c	62.2[b]	39.9	24.6	22.1	22.0	36.4[b]	
Fifth	27.0	c	a	38.3	29.8	20.9	20.0	31.6[b]	
Sixth or higher	33.1	c	a	53.3[b]	39.3	28.9	28.9	26.9	
TOTAL	21.9	43.5[a]	30.5	21.9	18.5	19.5	23.3	25.8	47.9[a]

[a] Rate not computed; based on less than 100 live births.
[b] Rate based on 100–999 live births.
[c] No live births.

82

BIRTH WEIGHT

Differences in mortality by infant birth weight were very great (Table 3.25). Among infants weighing 2,500 grams or less, the mortality rate was 140.5 per 1,000, or 17 times the infant mortality rate (8.4 per 1,000) among infants who weighed more than 2,500 grams. Regardless of ethnic group or level of education, mortality among low-birth-weight infants, as displayed in Table 3-26, remained exceedingly high.

Nearly 90 percent of the infants weighed more than 2,500 grams. Their mortality rate varied from 5.9 per 1,000 for white infants with foreign-born mothers to 13.5 per 1,000 for black infants. By mothers' education, the rates declined from 11.8 per 1,000 for infants of mothers with an elementary school education or less to 4.6 per 1,000 for infants of those with 4 years or more of college. Infants who weighed 2,500 grams or more and were born to white native-born mothers with 4 or more years of college had a strikingly low mortality rate of 3.7 per 1,000.

Mortality among babies who weighed 2,501 grams or more at birth was inversely related to mothers' educational level with the notable exception of the white foreign-born group. Among infants of white foreign-born mothers, there was virtually no difference by education of the mother—7.6 per 1,000 for those whose mothers had only an elementary education and 5.0 for those whose mothers had 4 or

TABLE 3-20 Infant Mortality Rates by Education of Mother: New York City Live-Birth Cohort, 1968

| Education of Mother | Number | | Deaths per 1,000 Live Births |
	Live Births	Infant Deaths	
None, elementary	18,734	519	27.7
High school	91,120	2,056	22.6
1–3 years	31,955	910	28.5
4 years	59,164	1,146	19.4
College	21,303	296	13.9
1–3 years	11,577	176	15.2
4 years	9,726	120	12.3
Postgraduate	3,964	30	7.6
Not stated	6,896	214	31.0
TOTAL	142,017	3,115	21.9

TABLE 3-21   Infant Mortality Rates by Education of Mother, Age of Mother, Birth Order, and Ethnic Group: New York City Live-Birth Cohort, 1968

Age of Mother, Total Birth Order, and Ethnic Group	Total	Education of Mother				
		None or Elemen-tary	High School (years)		College (years)	
			1–3	4	1–3	4 or more	Not Stated
			Deaths per 1,000 Live Births				
Age of mother (years)							
Under 15	43.5[a]	50.5[a]	32.8[a]	b	b	c	b
15–19	30.5	33.5	31.8	25.1	22.6[a]	b	38.5[a]
20–24	21.9	27.7	27.4	19.0	17.0	12.9	32.8
25–29	18.5	24.4	25.7	18.5	12.5	8.4	27.3
30–34	19.5	25.6	26.7	17.2	14.4	12.3	26.3[a]
35 or over	24.1	27.3	29.5	22.5	17.0[a]	16.1	31.5[a]
TOTAL	21.9	27.7	28.5	19.4	15.2	11.0	31.0
Total birth order							
First	18.0	21.7	23.1	16.4	16.8	9.1	27.7
Second	20.7	27.3	29.0	19.5	12.0	10.4	21.6
Third	22.7	28.6	30.0	19.3	14.6	12.9	31.3
Fourth	28.0	31.4	33.5	24.4	16.0[a]	15.1[a]	46.2[a]
Fifth	27.0	35.0	26.4	23.4	17.1[a]	21.1[a]	41.1[a]
Sixth or higher	33.1	31.4	38.6	28.2	20.4[a]	24.4[a]	49.2[a]
TOTAL	21.9	27.7	28.5	19.4	15.2	11.0	31.0
Ethnic group							
White native born	15.2	32.8	21.8	14.7	11.6	9.4	23.5
White foreign born	15.3	15.9	16.3	15.2	16.7	14.0	13.0
Puerto Rican	25.4	26.0	25.4	19.4	16.6[a]	9.6[a]	45.5
Black native born	35.7	50.7	37.4	31.9	24.0	29.1[a]	46.0
All others	24.5	29.5	29.6	22.1	25.6[a]	10.9[a]	30.0[a]
TOTAL	21.9	27.7	28.5	19.4	15.2	11.0	31.0

[a] Rate is based on 100–999 live births.
[b] Rate not computed; based on less than 100 live births.
[c] No live births.

more years of college. This is in contrast to the white native-born group, in which the range in infant death rates between infants of mothers with elementary and college education was 15.5 to 3.7 per 1,000. There were relatively few Puerto Rican and black infants whose mothers had college educations; consequently, the infant mortality rates are indicated as relatively unstable or not shown at all. In blacks, nevertheless, these data show a strong relationship between infant mortality and education when birth weight is considered. Black infants weighing 2,501 grams or more whose mothers had 1 to 3 years of college had less than one-third the mortality (5.6 per 1,000) of black infants whose mothers had an elementary education (19.7 per 1,000).

In the low-birth-weight infants, a similar but less striking inverse relation exists between mothers' education and infant mortality. For the white native-born mothers, the infant mortality rates in the infants less than 2,500 grams were 183.1 per 1,000 and 85.8 per 1,000 for the elementary and 4 years or more college group, respectively. It should be noted, however, that these rates are based on less than 1,000 live births.

TABLE 3-22 Distribution of Birth Weight by Ethnic Group: New York City Live-Birth Cohort, 1968

Birth Weight (grams)	Total	White Native Born	White Foreign Born	Puerto Rican	Black Native Born	All Others
		Percent of Live Births				
2,500 or less	10.0	8.0	6.5	10.3	15.7	9.5
2,501 or more	89.8	91.8	93.3	89.4	84.0	90.2
1,000 or less	0.8	0.4	0.5	0.7	1.5	1.1
1,001–1,500	0.8	0.5	0.5	0.8	1.5	0.6
1,501–2,000	1.8	1.3	1.1	2.0	3.0	1.8
2,001–2,500	6.6	5.7	4.4	6.8	9.8	6.0
2,501–3,000	23.9	22.7	18.4	25.2	28.4	24.9
3,001–3,500	39.6	40.6	40.3	40.1	36.6	41.8
3,501–4,000	21.0	22.6	27.0	19.5	15.8	19.2
4,001–4,500	4.5	5.1	6.6	4.0	2.7	3.6
4,501–5,000	0.6	0.7	0.9	0.5	0.4	0.6
5,001 or more	0.1	0.1	0.1	0.1	0.1	0.1
Not stated	0.3	0.3	0.2	0.3	0.3	0.2
TOTAL	100.0	100.0	100.0	100.0	100.0	100.0
Number of live births	142,017	60,896	18,959	22,505	32,051	7,606

TABLE 3-23 Mean Birth Weight (Grams) by Ethnic Group: New York City Live-Birth Cohort, 1968

Ethnic Group	All Live Births			Single Births			Plural Births		
	Number of Live Births	Mean Birth Weight	Standard Deviation	Number of Live Births	Mean Birth Weight	Standard Deviation	Number of Live Births	Mean Birth Weight	Standard Deviation
White									
Native born	60,743	3,213	549.4	59,565	3,230	534.0	1,178	2,364	638.7
Puerto Rican	22,430	3,136	571.5	21,984	3,154	552.8	446	2,215	710.3
Foreign born	18,918	3,290	553.6	18,480	3,311	533.2	438	2,409	670.1
Black									
Native born	31,950	3,007	633.2	31,236	3,026	616.7	714	2,177	737.5
Puerto Rican	1,123	3,071	605.2	1,095	3,094	585.2	28	2,167	788.9
Foreign born	4,402	3,153	603.6	4,269	3,178	584.1	133	2,348	668.6
Chinese	1,256	3,146	465.1	1,242	3,156	456.4	14	2,286	439.5
Japanese	264	3,110	543.5	262	3,116	541.7	2	2,367	100.4
All others	545	3,116	571.3	534	3,136	550.4	11	2,165	767.8
Total number of births	142,017			139,041			2,976		
Total birth weight stated	141,631	3,161	582.3	138,667	3,179	565.8	2,964	2,299	685.9

86

GESTATION

The distribution of infants by gestation interval and ethnic group is shown in Table 3-27. The pattern by ethnic group is similar to other characteristics we have presented. The lowest proportion, 5.2 percent, of gestations of less than 36 weeks was among white native-born mothers and the highest, 14.5 percent, was among black native-born mothers.

When gestation is cross-tabulated with birth weight and ethnic group, Puerto Rican mothers with 35 weeks gestation or less had the lowest proportion of low-birth-weight infants and white native-born mothers with the same gestation period had the highest proportion of low-birth-weight infants. For gestation intervals of 36 weeks and greater, white native- and foreign-born mothers had the lowest proportions of low-birth-weight infants (Table 3-28).

As expected, high infant mortality rates were associated with low gestation intervals (Table 3-29). As noted in the birth weight analyses, the mortality rates for gestation intervals of less than 35 weeks were higher for infants of the white native-born group than for infants of black native-born mothers, regardless of birth weight. In the longest gestation-interval groups, 36 to 39 and 40 to 43 weeks, however, infant mortality was twice as high for black infants as for those with white native-born mothers. These groups also include 87.9 percent of all live births. The lowest infant mortality rate observed by gestation was 4.7 per 1,000 for infants of white native-born mothers when the infants weighed 2,501 grams or more and the mothers completed 40 to 43 weeks of gestation.

A detailed breakdown of the two major gestational groups by optimal birth weight intervals and ethnic group demonstrates again that extraordinarily low infant death rates are obtainable. Table 3-30 shows that for the white native-born and foreign-born mothers, infant deaths occurred at rates of approximately 4 per 1,000 when gestation was 40 to 43 weeks and the infant's birth weight was 3,001 to 4,000 grams; in this instance, infants of white foreign-born mothers were observed to have the extraordinarily low rate of 2.9 per 1,000. Similar trends were seen for blacks and Puerto Ricans where the rates were as low as 6 per 1,000 for the higher birth weight and longer gestational period.

TABLE 3-24 T-Test Values for Significance of Differences in Mean Birth Weight by Ethnic Group: New York City Live-Birth Cohort, 1968

Ethnic Group	White		Black			Chinese	Japanese	All Others
	Puerto Rican	Foreign Born	Native Born	Puerto Rican	Foreign Born			
ALL LIVE BIRTHS								
White								
Native born	−17.81**	16.84**	−57.33**	−8.57**	−7.00**	−4.28**	−3.04**	−4.10**
Puerto Rican		−27.77**	−24.20**	−3.69**	1.78	0.64	−0.73	−0.80
Foreign born			−50.99**	−12.82**	−14.59**	−9.01**	−5.25**	−7.24**
Black								
Native born				3.31**	14.35**	7.69**	2.63**	3.98**
Puerto Rican					−4.04**	3.42**	0.96	1.45
Foreign born						−0.35	−1.12	−1.34
Chinese							−1.11	−1.18
Japanese								0.14
SINGLE BIRTHS								
White								
Native born	−17.72**	18.08**	−56.61**	−8.32**	−6.12**	−4.84**	−3.45**	−4.06**
Puerto Rican		−28.86**	−24.57**	−3.51**	2.50*	0.09	−1.13	0.78
Foreign born			−52.23**	−13.01**	−14.46**	−10.02**	−5.89**	−7.49**

Black							
Native born		−4.05**	3.57**	15.11**	7.31**	2.33**	4.06**
Puerto Rican				−4.22**	2.86**	0.54	1.37
Foreign born					−1.21	−1.67	−1.58
Chinese						−1.25	−0.81
Japanese							0.48
PLURAL BIRTHS							
White							
Native born	1.23	−5.82**	−1.61	−0.27	−0.45	0.01	−1.03
Puerto Rican	−4.16**	−0.88	−0.35	1.91	0.37	0.30	−0.23
Foreign born		−5.36**	−1.85	−0.92	−0.68	−0.09	−1.19
Black							
Native born			−0.07	2.49*	0.55	0.36	−0.05
Puerto Rican				−1.30	0.59	0.40	−0.01
Foreign born					−0.34	0.04	−0.86
Chinese						0.25	−0.50
Japanese							−0.36

*Statistically significant at 5% level.
**Statistically significant at 1% level.

APGAR SCORE

The percentage distributions of the Apgar scores by ethnic group are displayed in Table 3-31. The scores cluster around 9 and 10 and proportionately almost twice as many infants of black and Puerto Rican mothers have 1 to 3 1-minute scores as do infants of white native-born mothers. Despite the cautions previously raised about Apgar scoring, infant mortality did vary inversely with the rating (Table 3-32). Differences in infant mortality were clear when the extremes of the Apgar score were compared; on the 1-minute score the death rates varied from a high of 360.1 per 1,000 for infants with a 1 to 3 score to approximately 8.0 per 1,000 for those with a score of 9 or 10. The same trends are shown for the 5-minute Apgar score.

CONGENITAL MALFORMATIONS

Malformations and birth injuries were recorded for 1.4 percent of the live births. The distribution did not vary greatly by ethnic group.

TABLE 3-25 Live Births, Infant Deaths, and Infant Mortality Rates by Birth Weight: New York City Live-Birth Cohort, 1968

Birth Weight (grams)	Number of Live Births	Number of Infant Deaths	Mortality Rate per 1,000 Live Births
2,500 or less	14,160	1,990	140.5
2,501 or more	127,464	1,073	8.4
1,000 or less	1,067	904	847.2
1,001–1,500	1,112	422	379.5
1,501–2,000	2,556	335	131.1
2,001–2,500	9,425	329	34.9
2,501–3,000	33,977	412	12.1
3,001–3,500	56,290	435	7.7
3,501–4,000	29,783	167	5.6
4,001–4,500	6,380	41	6.4
4,501–5,000	902	13	14.4[a]
5,001 or more	132	5	37.9[a]
Not stated	393	52	132.3[a]
TOTAL	142,017	3,115	21.9

[a] Based on 100–999 live births.

TABLE 3-26 Infant Mortality Rates by Birth Weight, Race–Nativity Group, and Education of Mother: New York City Live-Birth Cohort, 1968

| Birth Weight and Race–Nativity Group | Total | Education of Mother (years) | | | | | |
| | | None, Elementary School | High School | | College | | Not Stated |
			1–3	4	1–3	4 or More	
TOTAL	21.9	27.7	28.5	19.4	15.2	11.0	31.0
White native born	15.2	32.8	21.8	14.7	11.6	9.4	23.5
White foreign born	15.3	15.9	16.3	15.2	16.7	14.0	13.0
Puerto Rican	25.4	26.0	25.4	19.4	16.6[a]	9.6[a]	45.5
Black native born	35.7	50.7	37.4	31.9	24.0	29.1[a]	46.0
All others	24.5	29.5	29.6	22.1	25.6[a]	10.9[a]	30.0[a]
TOTAL 2,500 GRAMS OR LESS	140.5	163.7	139.7	138.9	119.4[a]	96.2[a]	179.2[a]
White native born	116.7	183.1[a]	120.6[a]	120.7	93.9[a]	85.8[a]	176.8[a]
White foreign born	149.6	150.5[a]	161.8[a]	155.8[a]	[b]	139.1[a]	[b]
Puerto Rican	152.4	151.9[a]	139.9[a]	155.1[a]	[b]	[b]	234.3[a]
Black native born	150.5	186.5[a]	139.7	151.5	137.3[a]	[b]	171.0[a]
All others	178.2[a]	163.3[a]	229.7[a]	157.5[a]	[b]	[b]	[b]
TOTAL 2,501 GRAMS OR LESS	8.4	11.8	11.6	7.0	5.4	4.6	10.4
White native born	6.1	15.5	9.4	5.8	4.8	3.7	8.6
White foreign born	5.9	7.6	5.3	5.2	6.7	5.0	4.4
Puerto Rican	10.5	11.3	10.8	7.2	12.2[a]	[b]	16.6
Black native born	13.5	19.7	16.0	11.1	5.6	16.0[a]	13.2
All others	7.7	13.0	5.0	7.1	4.6[a]	5.2[a]	12.2[a]

[a] Based on 100–999 live births.
[b] Rate not computed; based on less than 100 live births.

Overall, however, malformations and birth injuries accounted for 9.2 percent of the infant deaths. The infant mortality rate was 140.5 per 1,000 for the live births who had a recorded malformation or birth injury. It varied from a low of 95.3 per 1,000 in infants of black native-born mothers to 179.0 per 1,000 in infants of white foreign-born mothers (Table 3-33).

TABLE 3-27   Distribution of Gestation Interval by Ethnic Group: New York City Live-Birth Cohort, 1968

Weeks of Gestation	Total	White Native Born	White Foreign Born	Puerto Rican	Black Native Born	All Others
		Percent of Live Births				
Less than 20	0.1	0.0	0.0	0.1	0.3	0.1
20–27	0.9	0.5	0.5	1.1	1.9	1.2
28–31	1.5	0.9	1.1	1.9	2.7	1.6
32–35	6.1	3.8	4.5	8.3	9.6	6.6
36–39	47.8	48.4	48.1	44.7	47.7	51.1
40–43	40.1	43.9	43.1	38.7	33.2	35.5
44 or more	1.9	1.5	1.6	2.7	2.1	1.6
Not stated	1.7	1.0	1.0	2.6	2.5	2.3
TOTAL	100.0	100.0	100.0	100.0	100.0	100.0
Number of live births	142,017	60,896	18,959	22,505	32,051	7,606

TABLE 3-28   Distribution of Gestation Interval by Ethnic Group for Infants of Birth Weight 2,500 Grams or Less: New York City Live-Birth Cohort, 1968

Weeks of Gestation	Total	White Native Born	White Foreign Born	Puerto Rican	Black Native Born	All Others
		Percent of Live Births 2,500 Grams or Less				
32 or less	71.0	77.5	74.3	60.8	71.5	68.5
32–35	38.9	46.8	38.0	27.8	41.0	31.1
36–39	8.3	7.5	5.2	8.9	11.6	7.2
40–43	3.6	2.8	2.0	4.2	6.3	4.0
44 or more	5.9	5.1	3.6	5.6	8.3	5.6
Not stated	16.1	14.9	11.6	14.3	20.0	13.1
Total number live births less than 2,500 grams	14,148	4,856	1,225	2,315	5,040	712
Percent 2,500 grams or less of total live births	10.0	8.0	6.5	10.3	15.7	9.5

TABLE 3-29 Infant Mortality Rates by Ethnic Group, Birth Weight, and Gestation Interval: New York City Live-Birth Cohort, 1968

Birth Weight and Ethnic Group	Total	Gestation (completed weeks)							
		Less Than 20	20–27	28–31	32–35	36–39	40–43	44 or More	Not Stated
Number of live births	142,017	152	1,333	2,199	8,616	67,815	56,917	2,638	2,347
					Deaths per 1,000 Live Births				
ALL LIVE BIRTHS			3,684						
White native born	15.2		375.0[a]		66.4	8.1	5.9	17.2[a]	40.7[a]
White foreign born	15.3		374.6[a]		37.4[a]	7.5	7.3	13.1[a]	47.6[a]
Puerto Rican	25.4		319.7[a]		39.8	13.9	10.7	18.1[a]	48.1[a]
Black native born	35.7		355.0[a]		40.7	16.9	14.2	11.9[a]	59.2[a]
All others	24.5		411.0[a]		40.1[a]	9.0	10.4	24.2[a]	56.8[a]
TOTAL	21.9	736.8[a] {	583.6	} 195.1	47.1	10.9	8.6	15.9	50.7
		358.0							
2,500 GRAMS OR LESS									
White native born	116.7		460.8[a]		110.7	34.5	45.9[a]	b	b
White foreign born	149.6		495.7[a]		83.1[a]	34.0[a]	87.0[a]	b	b
Puerto Rican	152.4		493.0[a]		104.7[a]	52.8[a]	49.5[a]	b	b
Black native born	150.5		468.5		69.9	49.5	43.3[a]	b	185.2[a]
All others	178.2[a]		573.3[a]		109.7[a]	39.1[a]	64.8[a]	b	b
TOTAL	140.5		479.0		91.7	42.3	49.9	83.9[a]	206.3[a]
2,501 GRAMS OR MORE									
White native born	6.1		52.1[a]		24.4	5.9	4.7	13.7[a]	14.2[a]
White foreign born	5.9		b		9.4[a]	5.8	5.8	10.2[a]	0.0[a]
Puerto Rican	10.5		44.1[a]		15.0	10.0	8.7	10.5[a]	22.6[a]
Black native born	13.5		44.2[a]		18.9	12.5	12.2	9.7[a]	22.3[a]
All others	7.7		b		5.8[a]	6.7	8.1	17.2[a]	6.9[a]
TOTAL	8.4		42.3		17.4	8.0	7.0	11.7	17.2

[a] Rate is based on 100–999 live births.
[b] Rate not computed; based on less than 100 live births.

93

TABLE 3-30   Infant Mortality Rates for Gestation Intervals 36–39 and 40–43 Weeks and Birth Weight 2,501 Grams or More, by Ethnic Group: New York City Live-Birth Cohort, 1968

| | Gestation Interval | | | | | |
| | 36–39 Weeks | | | 40–43 Weeks | | |
Ethnic Group	2,501–3,000 Grams	3,001–3,500 Grams	3,501–4,000 Grams	2,501–3,000 Grams	3,001–3,500 Grams	3,501–4,000 Grams
	Deaths per 1,000 Live Births					
White native born	7.9	5.3	4.6	7.6	4.9	3.0
White foreign born	10.4	4.3	2.9	11.5	5.9	3.2
Puerto Rican	14.2	8.2	8.1	10.8	9.1	6.0
Black native born	15.1	10.5	13.0	14.2	12.9	7.9
All others	10.6	5.2	4.7	9.6	7.7	8.4
TOTAL	11.1	6.6	6.3	10.3	7.3	4.4

TABLE 3-31   Distribution of 1- and 5-Minute Apgar Scores by Ethnic Group: New York City Live-Birth Cohort, 1968

	Total	White Native Born	White Foreign Born	Puerto Rican	Black Native Born	All Others
Number of live births	142,017	60,896	18,959	22,505	32,051	7,606
	Percent of Live Births					
Apgar score (1 minute)						
1–3	1.8	1.2	1.5	2.2	2.6	2.3
4–6	5.2	4.2	4.5	5.7	6.7	6.4
7–8	19.4	18.6	19.7	20.8	19.6	20.0
9	34.9	36.5	34.6	35.4	31.8	35.0
10	33.7	34.9	35.2	30.4	33.6	31.6
Not scored	5.0	4.6	4.5	5.5	5.8	4.8
TOTAL	100.0	100.0	100.0	100.0	100.0	100.0
Apgar score (5 minute)						
1–3	0.7	0.5	0.6	0.8	1.0	0.9
4–6	1.0	0.8	0.7	1.1	1.5	1.3
7–8	3.5	2.6	3.0	4.2	4.7	4.1
9	10.3	9.8	9.2	11.8	10.6	11.3
10	67.9	70.4	71.0	64.6	64.1	65.3
Not scored	16.7	15.9	15.5	17.6	18.1	17.1
TOTAL	100.0	100.0	100.0	100.0	100.0	100.0

TABLE 3-32 Infant Mortality Rates by 1-Minute and 5-Minute Apgar Scores and Ethnic Group: New York City Live-Birth Cohort, 1968

	Total	White Native Born	White Foreign Born	Puerto Rican	Black Native Born	All Others
Number of live births	142,017	60,896	18,959	22,505	32,051	7,606
		Deaths per 1,000 Live Births				
Apgar score (1 minute)						
1–3	360.1	333.3[a]	298.9[a]	332.7[a]	407.4[a]	424.4[a]
4–6	77.3	77.0	58.3[a]	70.1	92.1	66.1[a]
7–8	16.4	11.9	15.2	19.7	23.1	15.1
9	8.2	5.4	4.9	10.4	15.3	6.8
10	8.4	6.3	5.8	10.8	12.5	8.8
Not scored	51.9	31.4	34.1[a]	52.9	90.5	51.8[a]
TOTAL	21.9	15.2	15.3	25.4	35.7	24.5
Apgar score (5 minute)						
1–3	565.3[a]	508.6[a]	523.8[a]	552.3[a]	611.3[a]	b
4–6	269.2	279.2[a]	230.2[a]	265.6[a]	275.4[a]	b
7–8	62.2	63.2	60.7[a]	59.9[a]	66.7	45.5[a]
9	15.9	11.7	10.4	21.1	22.3	15.1[a]
10	8.3	5.7	5.6	10.1	14.3	7.9
Not scored	35.8	23.6	25.5	38.7	59.6	36.1
TOTAL	21.9	15.2	15.3	25.4	35.7	24.5

[a] Rate based on 100–999 live births.
[b] Rate not computed; based on less than 100 live births.

TABLE 3-33 Live Births and Infant Deaths and Infant Mortality Rates for Malformations and Birth Injuries by Ethnic Group: New York City Live-Birth Cohort, 1968

	Total	White Native Born	White Foreign Born	Puerto Rican	Black Native Born	All Others
Number of live births with malformations or injuries	2,036	738	257	367	556	118
Number of infant deaths with malformations or injuries	286	122	46	47	53	18
Infant mortality rates among live births with malformations or injuries	140.5	165.3[a]	179.0[a]	128.1[a]	95.3[a]	152.5[a]

[a] Rate based on 100–999 live births.

FOUR

A Selected Review
of the Epidemiology
# of Infant Mortality

Generally, epidemiologic studies of infant mortality consider factors
that fall into two broad categories: biologic and sociodemographic.
This chapter presents a survey of apparent relationships between infant mortality and selected sociodemographic characteristics reported
in the literature and summarizes some of the more prominent characteristics of fetal and infant mortality in the United States. The attempt
here is to provide a background for understanding infant mortality in
its broadest context; that is, its association with characteristics that
describe the population of mothers and infants.

Although more recent national data are available than those of
1968 data that we present here, 1968 is the most recent year for
which complete vital statistics are available. We also felt it was appropriate to use that year's data to enhance our analyses of the 1968
New York City live-birth cohort. While the infant death rate in 1968
was 22.3 per 1,000 live births, the rate has declined since then. In
1969, the rate was 21.5 per 1,000.[1] Provisional data for 1970 and
1971 indicate the rate dropped still further to 20.2 and 19.6, respectively, while provisional monthly data, for the first 5 months of 1972,
show a further rate decline to 18.9.[2]

In the United States, the 1968 death rate per 1,000 estimated population in the first year of life was 22.3. It was exceeded only by the
death rates of persons aged 65 years or older.[3] There were 76,263
deaths of persons under 1 year of age and 55,293 registered deaths of
fetuses with gestations of 20 or more completed weeks, for a combined
loss of 131,556 infants before birth and during the first year of life.

The fetal death ratio and neonatal and postneonatal death rates
have declined from 1942 to 1968, dropping at a fairly rapid pace un-

til the mid-1950's when they appeared to level off (Figure 4-1). In general, declines occurred in each death period, but the greatest relative decline was in the postneonatal period; fetal death ratios declined 38 percent, neonatal mortality rates declined 37 percent, and postneonatal mortality rates declined 61 percent. The greater decline in the postneonatal rate probably reflects improved environmental and socioeconomic conditions and control of major infectious and communicable diseases, which were significant causes of death among children in earlier decades. Fetal and neonatal mortality have been more resistant to improvement. There has been relatively less success in preventing premature birth and congenital malformations and in reducing mortality associated with placental complications, respiratory problems, and congenital malformations.

Because of the more rapid decline in postneonatal mortality between 1942 and 1968, fetal and neonatal mortality, which accounted for 78 percent of the infant loss in 1942, accounted for 84.8 percent of the loss in 1968.

The pattern of infant death is consistent throughout the first year of life: the closer to birth, the higher the rate. In 1968, infant mortality varied widely from 16.1 per 1,000 live births in the first four weeks of life to 0.2 per 1,000 in the twelfth month of life—about an 80-fold difference (Appendix C, Table C-1). On an hour-by-hour basis, the relative risk in the first hour of life is about 9,000 times the risk during any hour of the twelfth month.

Variation within the neonatal period is also great: The rate in the first hour of life is more than five times the rate in the remaining hours of the first day, and the rate in the first week of life is about 40 times the rate in the fourth week.

MATERNAL AGE

In this country, the great majority of infants are born to mothers within a relatively narrow age range. More than one third, for example, are born to mothers 20 to 24 years of age and another one fourth are born to mothers 25 to 29 years of age (Table 4-1). A significant trend toward younger maternal age occurred between 1960 and 1968. Fetal mortality is lowest among offspring of mothers in the 20- to 24-year-age group, neonatal mortality is lowest among offspring of mothers in the 25- to 29-year-age group, and postneonatal mortality is lowest among infants of mothers 30 to 34 years old (Figure 4-2 and Table C-2).

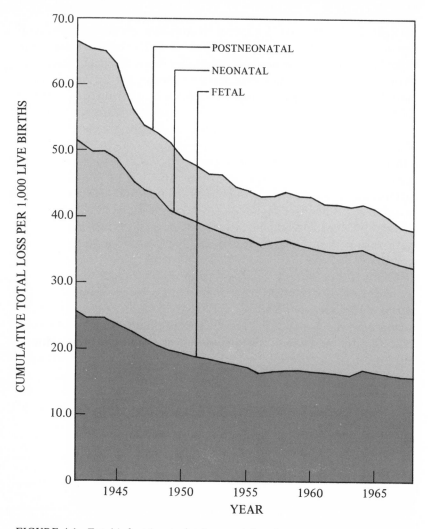

FIGURE 4-1   Total infant loss in fetal, neonatal, and postneonatal periods:
United States, 1942–1968. Fetal deaths include only those for which the period
of gestation was given as 20 complete weeks or more or was not stated. (See Appendix C, Table C-4.)

BIRTH ORDER

Between 1960 and 1968, a major shift toward a smaller average family size occurred. In 1968, nearly two thirds of all live-born infants in the United States were first or second births and only 7 percent were a sixth or higher birth (Table 4-2). Fetal, neonatal, and postneonatal mortality rates are higher at the higher birth orders (Figure 4-3 and Table C-3).

The higher mortality among offspring of mothers under 15 years of age is not evident for first births in general: Only fetal mortality is higher for first births. With this one exception, first-born infants apparently have no added risk over other infants. Similar mortality patterns are found for birth-order groups in individual maternal age groups. For fetal mortality, for example, optimum rates are among second births for all mothers 15 years of age and older. For young mothers, however, the higher the birth order, the higher the fetal mortality, while for older mothers, the highest rates are among their first born. This may reflect, among other things, two different phenomena: low socioeconomic status of young mothers and biologic factors in older mothers.

Infant mortality patterns by maternal age and birth order are similar to fetal mortality patterns by maternal age and birth order. Mortality is usually higher in high birth orders regardless of maternal age; among infants of mothers over 25 years of age, first births have higher

TABLE 4-1   Percent Distribution of Live Births by Age of Mother: 1960 and 1968, United States

Age of Mother (years)	Percent of Live Births	
	1960	1968
Under 15	0.2	0.3
15–19	13.8	16.9
20–24	33.5	37.3
25–29	25.7	25.8
30–34	16.2	12.0
35–39	8.5	5.9
40–44	2.2	1.7
45 and over	0.1	0.1
TOTAL	100.2	100.0

Source: U.S. Department of Health, Education, and Welfare.[4,5]

mortality than second births. Lowest rates by mother's age in years
and birth order are as follows: 15 to 19, first birth; 20 to 24, second
birth; 25 to 29, third birth; 30 to 34, fourth birth; 35 to 39, fifth
birth; and 40 to 44, sixth birth.

High birth orders are more common among rural women and urban
women of lower socioeconomic status. These two population groups,
however, have certain maternal-age characteristics as well. Women in

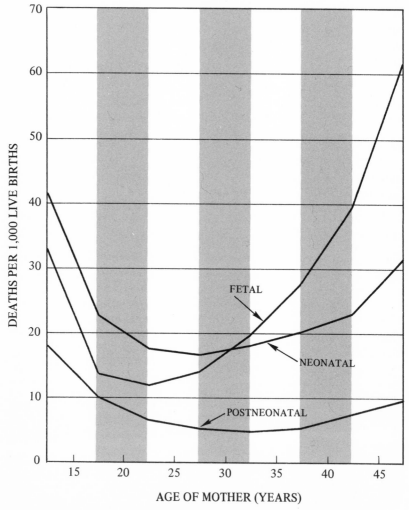

FIGURE 4-2   Fetal death ratios and neonatal and postneonatal mortality rates
by age of mother: United States, 1960 live-birth cohort. (See Appendix C,
Table C-2.)

rural and lower socioeconomic groups, for example, tend to have more children, start childbearing earlier, and continue childbearing later than women in higher socioeconomic groups. Thus, higher fetal and infant mortality rates for higher birth orders and older maternal ages may reflect both biologic and socioeconomic conditions.

Although infant mortality is high among infants born to mothers under age 15 and over age 44 and among infants who are sixth or higher in order of birth, the effect of these disadvantageous factors on the overall infant mortality rate is not very great because the proportion of births in these categories is relatively small. Table 4-3 compares the U.S. experience in 1960 two ways: First, births and deaths among infants born to mothers under age 15 and over age 44 are omitted; second, sixth and higher birth orders are omitted.

RACE

About 83 percent of all U.S. births are white infants. Of the remaining 17 percent, about 90 percent are blacks; the rest are American Indians, Orientals, and others. Thus, in the following statistics, data for nonwhites are essentially data for blacks.

TRENDS

Fetal and infant mortality rates among nonwhite infants have been consistently higher than among white infants since the inception of

TABLE 4-2 Percent Distribution of Live Births by Birth Order: 1960 and 1968, United States

	Percent of Live Births	
Total Birth Order	1960	1968
First	25.3	37.5
Second	23.7	26.2
Third	18.9	15.4
Fourth	12.6	8.8
Fifth	7.6	4.9
Sixth	11.8	7.2
TOTAL	99.9	100.0

Source: U.S. Department of Health, Education, and Welfare.[4,5]

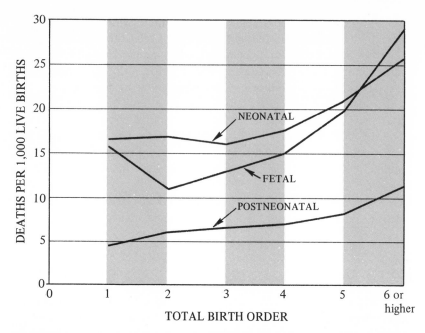

FIGURE 4-3   Fetal death ratios and neonatal and postneonatal mortality rates
by total birth order: United States, 1960 live-birth cohort. (See Appendix C,
Table C-3.)

TABLE 4-3   Total Death Rates and Ratios: Maternal Age 15–44 and Birth
Orders 1–5: 1960, United States

Rate (ratio)	1960 Actual	Mothers 15–44 Years Only	Birth Orders 1–5 Only
White			
Perinatal death ratio	31.0	30.9	29.2
Fetal death ratio	14.1	14.1	13.0
Infant mortality rate	22.2	22.1	21.2
Neonatal mortality rate	16.9	16.8	16.2
Postneonatal mortality rate	5.3	5.3	5.0
Nonwhite			
Perinatal death ratio	53.5	53.2	49.5
Fetal death ratio	26.8	26.6	23.4
Infant mortality rate	41.4	41.3	39.9
Neonatal mortality rate	26.7	26.6	26.1
Postneonatal mortality rate	14.7	14.7	13.8

Source: U.S. Department of Health, Education, and Welfare.[6]

TABLE 4-4 The Ratios of Nonwhite to White Mortality by Time of Death: 1968, United States

Rate (ratio)	Ratio Nonwhite to White Mortality
Fetal period	1.86
Infant period	1.80
Neonatal period	
Under 1 day	1.56
1–6 days	1.44
7–27 days	2.00
1–5 months	2.56
6–11 months	2.55

Source: U.S. Department of Health, Education, and Welfare.[3]

national vital statistics (Table C-4). The relationship also holds true at each age level. Table 4-4 compares the ratios of nonwhite to white mortality for 1968. The contrast is greatest in the postneonatal period when environmental and socioeconomic conditions have an especially large influence on infant mortality.

Between 1945 and 1968, mortality declined among both the white and nonwhite groups. Except for fetal mortality, the decline was at a more rapid rate among white infants (Table 4-5). Note that an increase in mortality among infants less than 1 day old occurred among nonwhites. This may be associated, in part, with increasing proportions of blacks born in hospitals and, as a result, more complete and accurate live birth and death registration.

MATERNAL AGE

The percentage distribution of 1968 live births shows that a larger proportion of infants are born to nonwhite mothers under 20 years of age than to white mothers under 20 (Table 4-6). Even though the mortality rates for whites and nonwhites are strikingly different, the patterns in fetal, neonatal, and postneonatal mortality by maternal age are similar (Figure 4-4 and Table C-2). The rates are high for infants born to mothers under 15 years of age. They drop to their lowest rate generally in the 20- to 34-year-age range and rise again thereafter. The highest rates are fetal death rates among births to mothers 45 years or older for both race groups.

TABLE 4-5 Percentage Change 1945–1948 in Mortality for Whites and Non-Whites by Age of Death: United States

Rate (ratio)	Percent Change 1945–1968	
	White	Nonwhite
Fetal period	−35.5	−39.0
Infant period	−46.1	−39.5
Neonatal period	−36.9	−28.1
Under 1 day	−20.9	+ 7.1
1–6 days	−40.7	−38.9
7–27 days	−68.3	−67.5
1–5 months	−60.0	−49.7
6–11 months	−71.8	−64.1

Source: U.S. Department of Health, Education, and Welfare.[3]

BIRTH ORDER

Fetal, neonatal, and postneonatal mortality are consistently higher among nonwhite infants than among white infants for each birth order (Table C-3). The differences decrease with higher birth orders for fetal and neonatal mortality but not for postneonatal mortality.

There were slight differences in 1968 between the percentage of white and nonwhite births by order of birth (Table 4-7). The most marked difference is in the highest birth order—6 percent of white and 14 percent of nonwhite births are sixth or higher births; that is, among the birth-order group that experiences the highest risk of death in the first year of life.

CAUSE OF DEATH

Nonwhite infants have higher death rates than white infants for virtually all causes of death (Table C-5). The only exceptions are congenital malformations and hemolytic diseases of the newborn. Lower nonwhite mortality from hemolytic disease is due to the fact that the Rh-negative factor is less common among blacks and that mortality from Rh incompatibility is lower.[7] The greatest differences are among infants with gastritis group conditions and "symptoms and ill-defined conditions"; the death rates for these two conditions for nonwhite infants are 6.2 and 5.4 times as high, respectively, as the rates for white infants. For most causes, the differences between the nonwhite and white are greater in the postneonatal than in the neonatal period (Table C-6).

As large as the relative differences appear, they tend to mask the number of deaths from causes that have smaller ratios. Of 257,410 infant deaths, for example, in the 3 years 1965 to 1967, the four largest causes of death were postnatal asphyxia and atelectasis, with 42,168 deaths; neonatal disorders arising from certain diseases in the mother during pregnancy, with 39,889 deaths; immaturity unqualified, with 39,568 deaths; and congenital malformations, with 37,275 deaths. In all, the four causes account for 61.7 percent of infant deaths, and the differences in experience by race are relatively small, with ratios ranging from 0.87 to 2.18. From this it seems clear that the relative differences between neonatal and postneonatal mortality of nonwhite and white infants relate more to environmental and socioeconomic conditions that affect numerically smaller groups of infants. Biologic factors have smaller relative ratios, and their effect on nonwhite and white infants is more nearly equal.

GEOGRAPHIC VARIATION

Fetal and infant mortality rates vary widely by state (Table 4-8 and Table C-7). The relative variation (2.84 and 2.89) was greatest among fetal death ratios and postneonatal mortality rates. The fetal death ratio ranged from 10.4 in Utah to 29.5 in Mississippi; the postneonatal rate ranged from 3.8 in Iowa and Vermont to 11.0 in Missis-

TABLE 4-6 Percentage Distribution of Live Births by Color of Mother and Age: 1968, United States

Age of Mother (years)	Percent of Live Births	
	White	Nonwhite
Under 15	0.1	1.1
15–19	14.6	28.0
20–24	38.2	32.8
25–29	27.1	19.3
30–34	12.2	10.9
35–39	5.9	5.9
40–44	1.7	1.8
45 and over	0.1	0.1
All ages	99.9	99.9

Source: U.S. Department of Health, Education, and Welfare.[5]

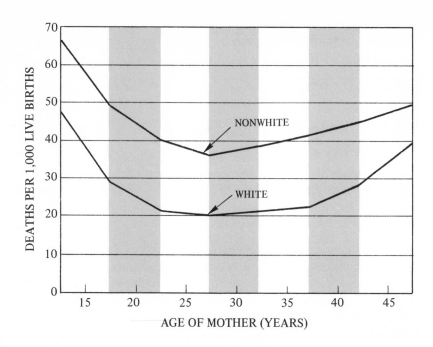

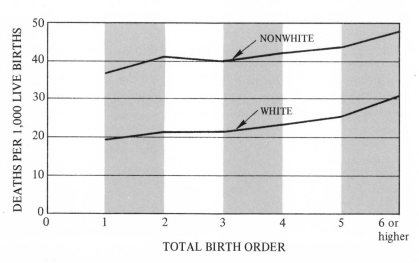

FIGURE 4-4   Infant mortality rates by age of mother and by total birth order, each by color: United States, 1960 live-birth cohort. (See Appendix C, Tables C-2 and C-3.)

TABLE 4-7 Percentage Distribution of Live Births by Color of Mother and Total Birth Order: 1968, United States

Total Birth Order	Percent of Live Births	
	White	Nonwhite
First	37.9	35.3
Second	27.1	22.0
Third	15.8	13.7
Fourth	8.7	9.0
Fifth	4.6	6.1
Sixth and over	5.8	13.9
All orders	99.9	100.0

Source: U.S. Department of Health, Education, and Welfare.[5]

sippi. Even the rate with least variation, the neonatal rate, varied 91 percent between North Dakota (12.8) and Mississippi (24.5).

When the states are divided into quartiles by infant mortality rates, they cluster geographically (Figure 4-5). In general, states in the Great Plains and West have the lowest mortality and states in the Southeast have the highest. While racial composition of state populations is an important factor, among white infants alone there is more than 50 percent variation among states.

The differences between nonwhite and white infant deaths are evident for virtually every state in every component rate, irrespective of the relative proportion of nonwhite infants. Where there are exceptions, most are based on small numbers. For some, such as Minnesota and Oklahoma, a plausible explanation may be that lower neonatal mortality among nonwhite infants is related to deficient registration

TABLE 4-8 Range and Ratio of Highest to Lowest Death Rates by States: 1968, United States

Rate (ratio)	Range of State Rates	Ratio of Highest to Lowest
Fetal period	10.4–29.5	2.84
Infant period	16.9–35.5	2.10
Neonatal period	12.8–24.5	1.91
Postneonatal period	3.8–11.0	2.89

Source: U.S. Department of Health, Education, and Welfare.[5]

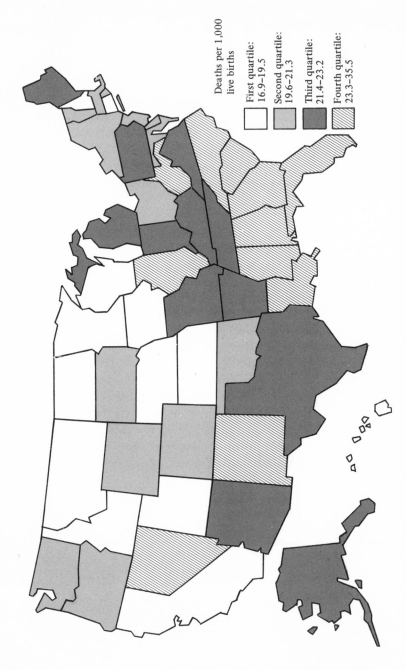

FIGURE 4-5 Infant mortality rates among states in quartiles: United States, 1968. (See Appendix C, Table C-7.)

Deaths per 1,000
live births

First quartile:
16.9–19.5

Second quartile:
19.6–21.3

Third quartile:
21.4–23.2

Fourth quartile:
23.3–35.5

of Indian deaths. In Hawaii, for example, lower rates for nonwhite infants may be because of the large Oriental population, which appears to have lower fetal mortality.

NONWHITE RACES

Individual races in the nonwhite group also show differences in mortality, some of great magnitude. In 1968, infant mortality was highest among blacks, followed by Indians. The rate for whites was double that for Chinese and Japanese infants (Table 4-9).

Nationwide studies of registration completeness—the most recent of which was for January to March 1950—showed that live-birth registration was grossly deficient for American Indians.[8,9] Although registration completeness has improved in recent years, the true relative position of the rates for black and Indian infants is still difficult to determine.

In the neonatal period, the highest mortality (24.3 per 1,000 live births) is for black infants. Neonatal mortality for Indian and white infants is almost equal, but the rate for Indian infants is probably understated by deficient registration. In the postneonatal period, black and Indian infants experienced mortality roughly three times that of white infants.

The rates for Chinese and Japanese infants are unusually low and they may be inaccurate. A recent study in California, for example, demonstrated that they may be attributed to inconsistencies in re-

TABLE 4-9   Infant, Neonatal, and Postneonatal Mortality Rates by Race: 1968, United States

Race	Infant Mortality Rate	Neonatal Mortality Rate	Postneonatal Mortality Rate
White	19.2	14.7	4.5
Black	36.2	24.3	11.9
Indians (including Aleuts, Eskimos)	29.0	13.7	15.4
Chinese	8.9	6.9	2.1
Japanese	10.3	7.9	2.4
Other races	15.4	11.7	3.6
All races	21.8	16.1	5.7

Source: U.S. Department of Health, Education, and Welfare.[3,5]

cording and coding racial and ethnic categories from birth and death records.[10] When data from linked live-birth and infant death certificates were used, and race was determined from the birth record, there were significant increases in the cohort infant mortality rates over those routinely derived for both Oriental groups (Table 4-10). The rates for Indians, Japanese, and the other races category markedly increased; the rate for the Chinese group also increased but it retained a still favorable position relative to the white group. The authors attributed this phenomenon to the tendency to record the death of an infant of mixed parentage as "white," whereas its birth would be recorded according to the race of the nonwhite parent. The study, in addition to shedding better light on nonwhite infant mortality, demonstrates clearly the advantages of cohort data over conventional data.

SOCIOECONOMIC LEVEL

For a number of years, investigators in Great Britain have used the occupation of the father as an index of socioeconomic status in assigning live-birth and infant death records to one of five social classes. Analyses of mortality by social class consistently have shown increasing fetal and infant mortality with decreasing social class. Baird, in Aberdeen, Scotland, introduced the height of the mother as an added

TABLE 4-10 Comparison of Infant Mortality Rates by Race Using Conventional Death Certificates and Linked Live-Birth–Death Records (Cohort) Data: 1965–1967, California

Race	Infant Mortality Rate	
	Conventional	Cohort
White	19.9	19.3
Black	32.1	32.3
Indian	13.9	29.0
Chinese	12.9	16.1
Japanese	13.6	22.0
Other races	9.1	21.3
All races	20.8	20.6

Source: Norris FD, Shipley PW.[10]

indicator of social class, hypothesizing that her height was a good indicator not only of the social class of her husband but a reflection of the social class of her father as well.[11-13] He also implicated the level of her nutrition as a contributing factor to her height, indicating that the foundation of the mother's reproductive history is associated with her early growth and development.

A comprehensive study of 80,000 stillbirths and infant deaths among 1½ million children born in England and Wales during 1949 and 1950 describes some of the interrelationships between biologic and socioeconomic factors.[14-19] Among factors studied were mother's age, parity, social class, previous loss and cause of death, birth spacing, and multiple births. Once again, father's occupation was inversely related to infant mortality. Moreover, the variation in stillbirth, neonatal, and postneonatal mortality could not be explained by the maternal age and parity distributions among the social class groups.

The most comprehensive British study—one combining demographic factors with a host of obstetric and other medical factors for a nationwide group—is that of the National Birthday Trust.[20-24] This study was based on 16,994 single live births during the week beginning March 3, 1958, and 7,117 single stillbirths and neonatal deaths in the months of March, April, and May 1958. Perinatal mortality in the lowest social class was twice that in the highest social class, but the effects of maternal age, parity, and social class acted independently of each other.

In the United States, a large-scale study of more than 436,000 white single live births in New York State (exclusive of New York City) demonstrated that an inverse gradient existed between fetal, neonatal, and postneonatal mortality and the level of the father's occupation.[25] The study of infants born in 1950, 1951, and 1952 found that even when the rates were adjusted for mother's age and birth order, the relationships between mortality and father's occupational level prevailed (Appendix C, Table C-8).

Several studies published in the early 1960's suggest that mortality in general, and infant and neonatal mortality in particular, are no longer sensitive indices of the nation's health status.[26-30] These studies used midcentury Census-tract data from Hartford, Connecticut, Syracuse, New York, and Providence, Rhode Island, and found no significant relationship between infant mortality and social class. The main argument against Census-tract studies, however, is that the socioeconomic status of a tract is determined by an average of characteristics and, therefore, combinations of Census tracts result in socioeco-

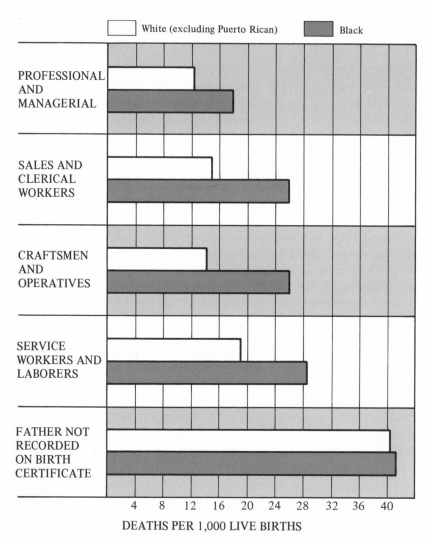

DEATHS PER 1,000 LIVE BIRTHS

Note: Rates are infant deaths under 28 days, 1961–1963, per 1,000 live births, 1962, multiplied by 3.
SOURCE: Shapiro *et al.*[28] Based on Densen, P. M.: unpublished data for 1961–1963 from the New York City Health Department.

FIGURE 4-6 Neonatal mortality rates by occupation of father and race: New York City, 1961–1963.

nomic heterogeneity in each category. The result is that differences in mortality may be attenuated or even disappear.

A study of neonatal mortality by father's occupational class in New York City for 1961, 1962, and 1963 showed gradients in mortality similar to the New York State study a decade earlier.[31] The data in the New York City study were prepared separately for white and black infants, and the occupation groups have been consolidated somewhat (Figure 4-6). For infants with father's occupation specified, black mortality is about one-and-one-half times white mortality. Those infants with no father recorded on the birth certificate are presumed to be illegitimate; for them, mortality for both black and white infants is very high and about equal.

More recent national data support the inverse relationship between risk of death in infancy and parental socioeconomic status.[32] The National Natality and National Infant Mortality surveys of 1964–1966 examined three indices of socioeconomic status: education of father, education of mother, and family income for the year before the birth or infant death. Only legitimate live births were analyzed. For white infants, all three indices were strongly associated with risk of death. The rates showed a regular and substantial decrease from the lowest of five classes to the central class. The rates were quite similar in the three highest socioeconomic classes, regardless of which of the three variables was used to define the classes. The trends for black infants were less regular, especially in the two highest socioeconomic groups, in part because of their smaller numbers. Mortality rates were lower in the central class, however, than in either of the two lowest classes. The decline in mortality with increasing socioeconomic status was seen in all age-at-death categories for both black and white infants. (See Table C-9 for rates by mother's education.)

ILLEGITIMACY

The number of illegitimate births is estimated to be about 340,000 annually in the United States. The rates have increased from 3.8 percent of live births in 1940 to 9.7 percent in 1968. Among white births, about 5 percent are illegitimate, while among nonwhite births, 31 percent are illegitimate.

Data from the 1950–1952 New York study suggest very high mortality among illegitimate births. Table C-8 includes nearly 13,000 white infants whose father's occupation is not classified; almost all of these infants are illegitimate. The fetal and neonatal mortality rates

TABLE 4-11   Fetal and Neonatal Mortality Rates by Legitimacy Status: 1950–
1952, New York State, Exclusive of New York City

Legitimacy Status	Fetal Death Rate	Neonatal Mortality Rate
Legitimate	15.7	16.1
Illegitimate	22.7	22.8
TOTAL	15.9	16.3

Source: Chase HC.[25]

for them are markedly higher than for other infants (Table 4-11). If
similar differences exist for nonwhite infants, the fact that 31 percent
of the nonwhite infants are illegitimate could have a significant bear-
ing on nonwhite death rates.

BIRTH WEIGHT

For most infants, birth weight increases with length of gestation. (Infants, however, may be of low birth weight from impaired intrauterine
growth even though born at full term.) There are decided advantages
in considering birth weight and length of gestation simultaneously, as
has been done in special studies.[33]

Infant mortality is inversely related to birth weight until birth
weight reaches 4,000 grams or more; infants weighing more than
4,000 grams, as infants weighing less than 2,500 grams, have increased
risk of death. Mortality among live-born low-birth-weight infants
(2,500 grams or less) is 17 times higher than mortality rates among
infants weighing more than 2,500 grams (Appendix C, Table C-11).
In the neonatal period, the ratio is 30:1. The magnitude of the relative difference in mortality by birth weight exceeds that of any reported differences by age at death, geographic area, maternal age,
birth order, race, socioeconomic status, or legitimacy. Low-birth-
weight infants constitute about 8 percent of live births. Not only
do they experience higher mortality rates, but the absolute number
of deaths among the low-birth-weight infants during the first year of
life exceeds the number of deaths among the remaining 92 percent
of live-born infants. Stated another way, a high proportion of deaths
during the first year of life occurs among a relatively small group of
infants.

Infant mortality by birth weight is lowest for infants who weigh between 3,501 grams and 4,000 grams. In the heaviest infants—those weighing more than 4,000 grams—mortality is higher but not to the magnitude of mortality among low-birth-weight infants. The higher rates among the heaviest infants is found for both white and nonwhite infants in both neonatal and postneonatal periods.

Immaturity associated with low-birth-weight infants is a biologic handicap that imposes added risk. Not only is the infant subject to greater risk of mortality but numerous studies have shown that survivors have increased risk for central nervous system disorders such as cerebral palsy, epilepsy, and mental retardation. Maturity is, therefore, perhaps considered to be of greatest importance in the prognosis for a newborn infant.

MATERNAL AGE

The low-birth-weight ratio is highest among infants of mothers under age 20 years (Table 4-12). The variation by age is significant because, to some extent, it explains the higher mortality among infants born to young mothers.

RACE

For infants weighing more than 2,500 grams, infant mortality for nonwhite infants is twice the rate for white infants. For both white

TABLE 4-12   Percent of Infants 2,500 Grams or Less by Age of Mother: 1960 and 1968, United States

Age of Mother (years)	Percent 2,500 Grams or Less	
	1960	1968
Under 15	16.0	18.2
15–19	9.9	10.6
20–24	7.4	7.7
25–29	6.9	7.1
30–34	7.5	7.7
35–39	7.9	9.1
40–44	8.3	9.4
45 and over	9.6	8.8
TOTAL	7.7	8.3

Source: U.S. Department of Health, Education, and Welfare.[4,5]

and nonwhite infants, mortality is very high for low-birth-weight infants and their overall experiences are nearly the same. The percent of nonwhite low-birth-weight infants, however, is about twice that of white low-birth-weight infants (Appendix C, Table C-12). Nearly one in every five low-birth-weight infants dies before reaching its first birthday.

For neonatal and postneonatal mortality, however, the comparative rates for white and nonwhite infants of low birth weight are quite different (Appendix C, Table C-11). In the neonatal period, the risk of death for nonwhite infants is about 13 percent lower than for white infants. The reasons for this are not clear. It may be due, in part, to deficient registration of very small nonwhite infants who die soon after birth. Or, it may be due to the fact that the nonwhite infants, although low in weight, are of longer average gestations and, consequently, are better equipped to survive. In the postneonatal period, mortality in nonwhite low-birth-weight infants is over two times the rate in white infants.

In national data, black infants constitute about 90 percent of the nonwhite infants. Data from Hawaii for 1951, provide some insight into the percentage of low-birth-weight infants for specific racial groups[34] (Table 4-13). Although a relatively high proportion of Filipino infants weighed 2,500 grams or less at birth, the neonatal death rate among these infants was lower than that among infants of all other races, except Chinese. The significance of this may be that, regardless of birth weight, many of the Filipino infants were full term and fully developed (Table 4-14).

TABLE 4-13   Percent of Live Births 2,500 Grams or Less by Race: 1951, Hawaii

Race of Infant	Percent of Single Live Births Weighing 2,500 Grams or Less, 1951
Japanese	6.0
Caucasian	6.1
Chinese	7.3
Hawaiian	7.9
Filipino	12.1
All races	7.3

Source: Taff MA, Jr, Wilbar CL.[34]

TABLE 4-14   Neonatal Death Rates among Low-Birth-Weight Infants by Race: 1951, Hawaii

Race of Infant	Neonatal Death Rates among Low-Birth-Weight Infants
Japanese	160.4
Caucasian	152.3
Chinese	119.4
Hawaiian	150.0
Filipino	143.7
All races	152.2

Source: Taff MA, Jr, Wilbar CL.[34]

Infant mortality varied from 17 per 1,000 for Japanese infants to 50 per 1,000 for Hawaiian infants in 1951–1954, but the rates do not rank precisely with the proportions of low-birth-weight infants.[35] Thus, one must conclude that the proportion of low-birth-weight infants is not the only factor affecting the differences among the racial groups, but that other determinants must be operating as well.

SOCIOECONOMIC LEVEL

The twofold difference in the proportion of nonwhite and white low-birth-weight infants is an indicator of the effect of socioeconomic factors as well as biologic conditions. In the 1950–1952 New York State study of white births, the proportion of low-birth-weight infants increased as socioeconomic level declined (Appendix C, Table C-14). Among infants whose fathers were professionals, the proportion who weighed 2,500 grams or less was 6.1 percent, while for infants whose fathers were nonfarm laborers, it was higher—8.1 percent. The highest proportion, 11.5 percent, was among presumed illegitimate infants for whom the information regarding the father was absent. The occurrence of low-birth-weight infants increases with declining socioeconomic level in almost every maternal age group.

Recently, the North Carolina State Department of Health published fetal, neonatal, and perinatal mortality rates by education of the mother.[36] The proportions of low-birth-weight deliveries decreased as the mother's education increased for both white and nonwhite infants (Table C-15). The relative difference between blacks and whites was

least among the lowest education group (1.47 : 1) and progressed
steadily to the highest education group (2.17 : 1).

The 1964–1966 national data show similar patterns.[32] The distribution of births by birth weight and mother's education is shown in
Table C-12. Among whites, the percentage of low-birth-weight infants
declines regularly with increasing socioeconomic status. The trend for
blacks is similar but not as striking. In both races, there is higher percentage of births over 3,500 grams as socioeconomic status increases.

Mortality rates by birth weight and mother's education are given in
Appendix C, Table C-13. Among births weighing 2,500 grams or less,
there was no consistent relationship between mortality and socioeconomic status. The most striking relationship between infant mortality
and socioeconomic class is found in births falling in the most normal
weight range—3,001 to 4,000 grams. For births in these weight groups,
a threefold range of mortality is associated with education for both
racial groups.

BIRTH INTERVAL

Information from a number of studies suggests that certain patterns of
childbearing are associated with higher mortality among infants.[37–40]
When the interval between pregnancies is less than 2 years or more
than 6 years, there are higher risks of fetal and neonatal death and
prematurity in the offspring.

Birth intervals appear to be associated with socioeconomic status.
In the United States, short intervals are more frequent among wives
of laborers, for example, than among wives of professionals.[37]

PREVIOUS LOSS

Some investigators have hypothesized that certain women may be re-
productively more efficient, because an undue number of pregnancy
losses appear to be concentrated in a relatively small group of women,
and the type of reproductive loss tends to be repeated.

A vital-records analysis of death rates among women with second
and higher birth orders is found in Appendix C, Table C-16. The analysis is somewhat limited but highly suggestive that in large population
groups there is support for a hypothesis of repeated loss by type of
loss. The fetal mortality experienced in previous pregnancies of

mothers whose current births terminated in fetal death was higher than the previous postnatal mortality rates. For mothers whose current births terminated in neonatal, postneonatal, and even early childhood deaths (1 to 4 years of age), the prior postnatal mortality rate was higher than the prior fetal mortality. For mothers whose current births resulted in infants who survived to 5 years of age, the prior fetal and postnatal mortality rates were lower than for the groups whose current pregnancies ended in a fetal or neonatal death.

Other studies have demonstrated that women whose last previous pregnancy ended either in a fetal death or low-birth-weight infant had relatively high incidence of fetal deaths, neonatal deaths, low-birth-weight infants, or significant congenital anomalies in the subsequent pregnancy. Also, the type of loss in succeeding pregnancies was repetitive.[41]

SUMMARY

By far, birth weight exerts the greatest impact on infant mortality. Yet, birth weight is, of itself, an outcome measure, associated with various biologic and sociodemographic influences. The percent of low-birth-weight infants, for example, declines both with increasing lengths of gestation and with increasing levels of socioeconomic status although the death rates among such infants vary little from social class to social class.

Neonatal death rates do vary considerably by socioeconomic status among infants weighing more than 2,500 grams at birth. It seems, therefore, that low socioeconomic status is associated with higher infant and neonatal mortality on two counts: Women of low social status have proportionately more low-birth-weight babies, and their optimal-weight babies experience higher mortality than do infants in higher social classes.

Differences in infant death by race are considerable, but they are also obliquely associated with socioeconomic variables. Two-to-one ratios between mortality of nonwhite and white infants are not uncommon, especially in the postneonatal period when environmental and social conditions predominate over biologic factors. In the neonatal period, when biological factors exert a greater influence, the difference among races is not as great. In the white group alone, infant mortality varies inversely with socioeconomic status regardless of whether status is measured by the father's occupation or the mother's education. If presumed-illegitimate infants are excluded, the difference between the two ends of the eight-level occupational scale is about 50 percent.

A coarse assessment of the relative association between mortality at various ages and a number of variables is shown in Appendix C, Table C-17. Although the data are now 20 years old, they are the most recent encompassing this array of variables for simultaneous review. Each rate is related to the experience of all single white infants in a specific age-at-death group; the highest risk groups emerge with the highest ratios. Almost without exception, the highest ratios are for low-birth-weight infants. Following these, but at much lower levels, are the presumed-illegitimate infants, mothers 40 years and older, fathers 45 years and older; and seventh or higher birth order in the fetal, neonatal, and postneonatal periods. In the early childhood period (1 to 4 years of age), infants of large families show the greatest relative risk.

In general, demographic studies of infant mortality, such as those reviewed in this chapter, allow assessments about the population at large, while avoiding some of the biases related to certain special groups. Because they are usually based on large samples, a number of factors can be studied simultaneously that could not be studied in smaller samples. There are, however, certain limitations to demographic studies. The size of the numbers requires a considerable investment to merely collect and process the data and because of the large number of sources involved, the data are often not as complete, consistent, and accurate as is desirable.

REFERENCES

1. United States Department of Health, Education, and Welfare: Advance re-report—final mortality status, 1969. Monthly Vital Statistics Report, 21(4), supplement to July 25, 1972
2. United States Department of Health, Education, and Welfare: Births, marriages, divorces, and deaths for May 1972. Monthly Vital Statistics Report, Provisional Statistics from the National Center for Health Statistics, 21(5), July 27, 1972
3. United States Department of Health, Education, and Welfare: Vital Statistics of the United States, 1968. Vol II—Part A, Washington, D.C., 1969
4. United States Department of Health, Education, and Welfare: Vital Statistics of the United States, 1960. Vol I, Washington, D.C., 1962

5. United States Department of Health, Education, and Welfare: Vital Statistics of the United States, 1968. Vol I, Washington, D.C., 1970
6. United States Department of Health, Education, and Welfare: Vital Statistics of the United States, 1960. Vol II—Part A, Washington, D.C., 1963
7. Wintrobe MM: Clinical Hematology. Philadelphia, Lea & Febiger, 1967
8. Grove RD: Studies in completeness of birth registration. I. Completeness of birth registration in the United States, December 1, 1939, to March 31, 1940. U.S. Bureau of the Census, Vital Statistics—Special Reports, Vol 17, No 18, 1943
9. Shapiro S, Schachter J: Birth registration completeness in the United States and geographic areas, 1950. U.S. Department of Health, Education, and Welfare, Vital Statistics Special Reports, Vol 39, No 2, 1954
10. Norris FD, Shipley PW: A closer look at race differentials in California's infant mortality, 1965–67. HSMHA Health Rep 86:810–814, 1971
11. Baird D: Social Class and Fetal Mortality. Lancet 253(6476):531–535, 1947
12. Baird D: Preventive Medicine in Obstetrics. New Engl J Med 246:561–568, 1952
13. Baird D, Illsley R: Environment and Childbearing. Proc R Soc Med 46:53–59, 1953
14. Morris JN, Heady JA: Social and Biological Factors in Infant Mortality. I. Object and Methods. Lancet 268(6859):343–349, 1955
15. Daly C, Heady JA, Morris JN: Social and Biological Factors in Infant Mortality. III. The Effects of Mother's Age and Parity on Social Class Differences in Infant Mortality. Lancet 268(6861):445–448, 1955
16. Heady JA, Stevens CF, Daly C, Morris JN: Social and Biological Factors in Infant Mortality. IV. The Independent Effects of Social Class, Region, the Mother's Age and Her Parity. Lancet 268(6862):499–502, 1955
17. Morris JN, Heady JA: Social and Biological Factors in Infant Mortality. V. Mortality in Relation to the Father's Occupation, 1911–1950. Lancet 268 (6863):554–560, 1955
18. Heady JA, Morris JN: Social and Biological Factors in Infant Mortality. VI. Mother's Who Have Their Babies in Hospitals and Nursing Homes. Br J Prev Soc Med 10:97–106, 1956
19. Morrison SL, Heady JA, Morris JN: Social and Biological Factors in Infant Mortality. VIII. Mortality in the Postneonatal Period. Arch Dis Child 34:101–114, 1959
20. Butler NR, Bonham DG: Perinatal Mortality. First Report of the 1958 British Perinatal Mortality Survey. Edinburgh and London, E & S Livingstone Ltd, 1963
21. Pringle MLK, Butler NR, Davie R: 11,000 Seven-Year-Olds. First Report of the National Child Development Study (1958 Cohort). London, Longmans, Green & Co Ltd, 1966
22. Butler NR, Alberman ED (ed): Perinatal Problems. Second Report of the 1958 British Perinatal Survey. Edinburgh and London, E & S Livingstone Ltd, 1969
23. Feldstein MS, Butler NR: Analysis of Factors Affecting Perinatal Mortality. Br J Prev Med 19:128–134, 1965

24. Feldstein MS: A Method of Evaluating Perinatal Mortality Risk. Br J Prev Soc Med 19:135–139, 1965

25. Chase HC: The Relationship of Certain Biologic and Socio-Economic Factors to Fetal, Infant, and Early Childhood Mortality. I. Father's Occupation, Parental Age, and Infant's Birth Rank (1961). II. Father's Occupation, Infant's Birthweight, and Mother's Age (1962). III. Previous Loss (1963). New York State Department of Health, Albany, New York

26. Willie CV: A Research Note on the Changing Association Between Infant Mortality and Socioeconomic Status. Soc Force 37:221–227, 1959

27. Stockwell EG: Infant Mortality and Socioeconomic Status: A Changing Relationship. Milbank Mem Fund Q 40:101–111, 1962

28. Willie CV, Rothney WB: Racial, Ethnic, and Income Factors in the Epidemiology of Neonatal Mortality. Am Sociol Rev 27:522–526, 1962

29. Stockwell EG: A Critical Examination of the Relationship Between Socioeconomic Status and Mortality. Am J Public Health 53:956–964, 1963

30. Stockwell EG: Use of Socioeconomic Status as a Demographic Variable. Public Health Rep 81:961–966, 1966

31. Shapiro S, Schlesinger ER, Nesbitt REL, Jr.: Infant Perinatal, Maternal, and Childhood Mortality in the United States. Cambridge, Harvard Press, 1968

32. National Center for Health Statistics: Infant Mortality Rates: Socioeconomic Factors. Department of Health, Education, and Welfare. Washington, D.C., Government Printing Office, 1972 (PHS Publ No 72-1045, Ser 22, No 14)

33. Yerushalmy J, van den Berg BJ, Erhardt CL, Jacobziner H: Birth Weight and Gestation as Indices of "Immaturity." Am J Dis Child 109:43–53, 1965

34. Taff MA, Jr, Wilbar CL, Jr: Immaturity of Single Live Births According to Weight, with Particular Reference to Race. AMA J Dis Child 85:279–284, 1953

35. Connor A, Bennett CG, Louis LSK: Birth Weight Patterns by Race in Hawaii. Hawaii Med J 16:626–632, 1957

36. North Carolina State Board of Health: Perinatal Mortality Statistics, 1968. Raleigh. (no publication date)

37. Schachter J: Child Spacing as Measured from Data Enumerated in the Current Population Survey, United States, April 1950 and April 1954. Vital Statistics Special Reports, U.S. Office of Vital Statistics, Vol 47, No 3, October 9, 1958

38. Woodbury RM: Causal Factors in Infant Mortality. Department of Labor, Children's Bureau. Washington, D.C., Government Printing Office, 1925. (Publ No 142)

39. Douglas JWB: Some Factors Associated with Prematurity: The Results of a National Survey. J Obstet Gynecol Br Emp 57:143–170, 1950

40. Shapiro S, Abramowicz M: Pregnancy Outcome Correlates Identified through Medical Record-Based Information. Am J Publ Health 59:1629–1650, 1969

41. Shapiro S, Ross LJ, Levine HS: Relationship of selected prenatal factors to pregnancy outcome and congenital anomalies. Am J Publ Health 55:268–282, 1965

FIVE

Maternal
and Infant
Health Services

In the analysis of the 1968 New York City infant birth and death records, adequate maternal health services are found to be associated with an increased probability of infant survival. This relationship prevails, regardless of the time of infant death—fetal, neonatal, or postneonatal. Because our index for adequate health services is based on indicators of services and not actual care delivered, we felt it would be important to assess the overall organization and delivery of maternal and infant health services in the United States and particularly those programs aimed at reaching high-risk women and infants.

Such an undertaking, however, would be extremely complex and require new data and original investigations far beyond the scope of this study. On the basis of available information it is difficult, if not impossible, to determine how much of our national medical and health-dollar resources are committed to maternal and infant care. Even at the federal level, which in fiscal year 1971 made up only 25 percent of all health expenditures, the picture is not clear. The federal–state medicaid program, for instance, reports that 11 million children and their mothers are covered for services; no federal data exist, however, that indicate how many of the 6.1 billion fiscal year 1971 medicaid dollars purchased maternal and infant services. The amount, moreover, could be sizable; the State of California, for example, reports that in 1970, its medicaid program covered more than 51,000 births, or 14 percent of the total births in the state.*

Even among federal programs in which the funds are specifically

*F. D. Norris, personal communication, September 1972.

earmarked for maternal and child health services, comparative data
are not readily available. With the exception of the family planning
program, for example, the largest sum of federal maternal and child
health services money is a formula grant program. Grants are made to
the states based on a complicated formula that favors rural areas and
financial need. The grants, authorized by Section 501 of the Social
Security Act, are intended to "extend and improve" traditional maternal and child health services such as maternity care, well-child con-
ferences, immunizations, and crippled children services. The grants
totaled nearly $118 million in fiscal year 1971. Based on fiscal year
1970 trends, state and local governments probably spent an additional
$230 million in delivering these services.

Despite the statistical obstacles, we felt that specific projects designed to reduce infant deaths needed to be acknowledged and available data at least to be summarized. Two federally sponsored programs, the Maternity and Infant Care (MIC) projects and neonatal intensive care units (NICU's), lend themselves to such cursory examinations. Together, they represent only a small fraction of all maternal
and infant care, yet, they are an important part of it. While the combined programs accounted for less than two tenths of 1 percent of all
federal health expenditures in fiscal year 1971, or about $39 million,
they attempted to respond to a congressional mandate to lower infant
mortality by funding specific health projects to meet the needs of
identified, high-risk women and infants.

CONTENT OF CARE

Before examining the effect of MIC and NICU projects, it is useful to
look briefly at the content of maternal and infant health services. The
content, as we have chosen to describe it, is based largely on the recommendations of the medical profession; it is not, therefore, what is
provided to all mothers and infants, but what should be provided.
This distinction is important. For whatever reasons, economic or social, only about one fourth of the mothers in the New York City
study received care that conceivably could meet these standards*
(Table 3-15).

---

*Minimum American College of Obstetricians and Gynecologists standards spec-
ify that care should be initiated in the first trimester and that the pregnant
woman should have at least 13 visits. Only those women meeting our criteria for
adequate care could possibly have met these criteria.

FAMILY PLANNING

The most favorable childbearing age for the mother appears to be between 20 and 30 years of age, with an interval of 3 or more years between pregnancies.[1] Greater risks are associated with high-birth orders and advanced maternal age. The most important single factor, although it affects a relatively small proportion of births, is an unfavorable previous pregnancy.[2] The American College of Obstetricians and Gynecologists (ACOG) recommends that family planning services be made available to all hospital gynecological patients and to women soon after delivery.[3] The House of Delegates of the American Medical Association has approved recommendations developed by ACOG that sexually active teenage girls have access to contraceptive advice and methods and that the "physician so consulted should be free to prescribe or withhold contraceptive advice in accordance with his best judgment in the best interests of his patient."[4]

Legislative restraints on the distribution and use of contraceptives have been eliminated, for all practical purposes, by a 1972 Supreme Court ruling that a state may not prohibit distribution of contraceptives to single persons when they are legally available to married couples.[5]

A recent study of prematurity and unwanted pregnancies, however, indicates that preventing unwanted pregnancies, through family planning or otherwise, has little or no effect on prematurity rates.[6] A study conducted by researchers at the University of North Carolina shows that preventing unwanted pregnancies among blacks changed the prematurity rates marginally—from 10.6 percent to 10.7 percent. Among whites, the difference was similarly insignificant—from 5.0 percent to 4.9 percent.

Abortion represents a last resort in family planning methods, a backup service for contraception failure. Before 1967, all states imposed strict legal limitations on abortions. By July 1971, however, 17 states had liberalized their abortion laws. Four of these, Alaska, Hawaii, New York, and Washington, permit abortions by physicians at the request of the pregnant woman, with varying permissable limits on the length of the pregnancy involved.[7]

In 1970, more than 180,000 legal abortions were reported to the U.S. Department of Health, Education, and Welfare's Center for Disease Control.[8] In the first half of 1971, immediately after New York State freedom-of-choice legislation had become effective, more than 94,000 abortions were reported in New York City alone—more than double the number reported during the previous 6 months.[9]

The effect of liberalized abortion laws on reducing infant death rates, however, is unclear. From two recent studies[10,11] —neither of which incorporated measures of the women's social status—it appears that, with the exception of marital status, women with the most favorable characteristics for producing a viable infant are also most likely to undergo abortion. Table 5-1 briefly summarizes the characteristics of the women from the abortion studies and contrasts these characteristics with corresponding neonatal death rates from our New York City study population and the percent of our study population

TABLE 5-1 Demographic Characteristics of Two Populations of Women Having Abortions Compared to Total Population of Live Births: New York City, 1968

Mother's Characteristics	National Abortion Study[a]		New York City Abortion Study[b]		1968 New York City Infant Study	
					Neonatal Death Rate	Percent Population
	Number	Percent	Number	Percent		
Age						
17 and under	7,172	9.8	5,395	6.2	23.6	4.8
18–19	10,524	14.4	9,161	10.6	20.3	8.7
20–29	40,851	56.0	50,551	58.5	15.5	63.7
30–34	8,049	11.0	12,122	14.1	15.9	14.4
35 and older	6,392	8.8	8,715	10.1	19.0	8.4
Not stated			437	0.5		
Parity						
First	34,354	47.1	35,746	41.4	14.1	36.5
Second	13,783	18.9	16,040	18.6	15.6	26.2
Third	10,980	15.0	13,603	15.7	16.7	15.9
Fourth or more	13,871	19.0	19,712	22.8	22.4	21.4
Not stated			1,280	1.5		
Marital Status						
Wed	21,843	29.9	30,233	35.0	14.6	81.5
Unwed	51,145	70.1	56,148	65.0	25.7	18.5
Single	(40,814)	(55.9)				
Widowed/divorced/ separated	(10,331)	(14.2)				
Ethnicity						
White	50,590	69.3	39,152	45.3	12.2	56.2
Nonwhite	22,398	30.7	47,229	54.7	22.4	43.8
Puerto Rican			(9,287)	(10.8)	(19.1)	(15.8)
TOTAL	72,988	100.0	86,381	100.0	16.7	100.0

[a] Data from Tietze C, Lewis S.[11]
[b] Data from Pakter J.[10]

with the characteristics. Thus, for example, women 17 years old and younger have the highest neonatal death rate, have the smallest number of births, and are the least likely to obtain an abortion. In contrast, the overwhelming percentage of those who do obtain abortions are 20 to 29 years of age and have the most favorable neonatal death rate.

The greatest potential impact of liberalized abortion laws would appear to be in reducing the number of births out-of-wedlock and, thereby, reducing the overall neonatal mortality rate. If, for example, the women in our study of New York City births in 1968 had had abortions at the approximate rates shown for whites and nonwhites in the study of abortions among New York City residents and those rates were adjusted to meet the percentages of married and unmarried, there would have been about 9,000 fewer out-of-wedlock births, 230 fewer deaths among illegitimate youngsters, 12,000 fewer in-wedlock births, and 138 fewer deaths among legitimate youngsters. Overall, the neonatal death rate would have decreased from 16.7 per 1,000 to 16.2 per 1,000—or less than 3 percent.

From 1960 to 1971, the neonatal death rates in New York City fluctuated widely from year to year.[10] The general trend has been downward. In light of this fluctuation, coupled with an overall decline in neonatal deaths nationally,[12] it seems unwise, as yet, to attribute improved infant survival rates to increased abortions among high-risk women.

The American Public Health Association has recommended standards for abortions. The standards cover referral, counseling, public education, surgical care including personnel, facilities, patient safety, and data reporting for planning and evaluation.[13]

GENETIC COUNSELING

Originally, genetic counseling was intended to inform parents of the numerical odds for hereditary or congenital conditions occurring in their future offspring and to help them reach a decision about planning a pregnancy. It is usually offered or sought when a genetic disease or condition has occurred in the family of one or both of the parents or in their previous children. Genetic counseling services vary in complexity. They may be a simple exposition of the one-in-four risks of cystic fibrosis, or they may include biochemical determinations, chromosomal studies, and family pedigree investigations. Recently, counseling has been extended to the identification of serious genetic

defects during fetal life. Hereditary disorders may be detected ante-
natally by study of amniotic fluid cells obtained by amniocentesis.[14]
In proper hands, the procedure is considered safe and reliable. The information provides a factual basis for parents to decide whether to
continue or terminate the pregnancy.

PRECONCEPTION CARE

By the time of the first prenatal examination, "the fetus has already
passed the most critical period of its development. Furthermore, the
effects of various noxious influences on the germ cells before fertili-
zation cannot be nullified by earlier prenatal care."[15] Preconception
care services are aimed at improving the health of women who anticipate pregnancy and avoiding hazards to the fetus. Emphasis is placed
on routine visits to a physician several months before a pregnancy is
planned, "to insure an adequate diet, to detect and treat any systemic
disease, and to correct endocrine imbalance prior to conception," as
well as to counsel about the hazards of drugs and x rays.[16]

ANTEPARTUM CARE

Ideally, antepartum (or prenatal) care is a "planned program of obser-
vation, education, and medical management of pregnant women."[17]
Its original focus was on the early detection and treatment of toxemia
and other life-threatening complications of pregnancy. It now encom-
passes all the elements of health supervision of a presumably healthy
pregnant woman, with definitive diagnosis and prompt treatment of
abnormalities related to or associated with pregnancy.

   Care during pregnancy is one of the "relatively few areas of medical practice in which clearly formulated minimum standards are available concerning time for initiation of medical care, frequency of
patient visits, and content of professional care."[18] The standards are
accepted by medical practitioners and health agencies. Women should
be examined as soon as pregnancy is suspected. Prenatal visits are
normally scheduled every 4 weeks for the first 28 weeks of pregnancy,
every 2 weeks thereafter until the thirty-sixth week, and then weekly
until delivery.[17] The first visit, once pregnancy has been established,
allows for a detailed social, family, and medical and obstetrical history; a complete physical examination with particular attention to
the breasts and pelvic area; and laboratory tests including urine analysis, blood count, serological examination for syphilis, rubella anti-
body test when indicated, blood grouping and Rh determination, and

cytology screening for genital tract cancer. Counseling begins on nutrition, exercise, rest, anxiety, and marital relations.

On subsequent visits, blood pressure, weight, urinalysis, and any unusual symptoms are recorded. On certain visits, abdominal and vagi-
nal examinations and hemoglobin or hematocrit determinations are
performed; counseling continues. Weight gain, with particular attention to sudden increase in the second half of the antepartum period,
is followed. Severe caloric restriction is considered damaging to the
developing fetus and it is recommended that "weight-reduction re-
gimes, if needed, should be instituted only after pregnancy has terminated."[19] Medications, other than vitamin–iron supplements, are
limited to those "absolutely necessary to the effective management of
the problem at hand" and "specifically proved or acknowledged by
all to be harmless during pregnancy."[17]

INTRAPARTUM CARE

Usually in the United States, intrapartum and immediate postpartum
care is provided in a hospital. All but 1.5 percent of the deliveries in
1968 took place in hospitals.[20] Standards for hospital care are recommended by the American College of Obstetricians and Gynecologists.[21] These cover requirements for labor and delivery areas, patient
housing units, and auxiliary facilities.

POSTPARTUM CARE

Four or 5 days of hospitalization following delivery are generally considered desirable. Early ambulation, starting 4 to 6 hours after delivery, is routine immediate postpartum care in the absence of specific
contraindications. Anti-Rh immune globulin is administered within
72 hours of delivery to Rh-negative women who have not been previously sensitized. Family planning counseling begins. A 6- to 8-week
postpartum examination is essential to be sure complete involution
of the pelvic structures has taken place and no abnormalities are
present.

INTERCONCEPTIONAL CARE

Interconceptional care begins after regular postpartum care is completed. It includes periodic breast and pelvic examinations and PAP
smears and continues as long as the possibility of another pregnancy
exists. While highly desirable as a routine service, interconceptional

care (particularly contraceptive services) is of special importance to
women, who for any reason, are considered to be at high risk for
subsequent pregnancies.

NORMAL INFANT CARE

The American Academy of Pediatrics recommends that there be one
person in the delivery room with primary responsibility for care of
the newborn infant.[22] It calls for the availability of trained personnel
and adequate equipment for resuscitation of the newborn and maintenance of the infant's body temperature. Assessment of physical
status by Apgar score should be made at 1 minute and 5 minutes
of age and by a simple examination of the infant before transfer to
the nursery or, as a less desirable alternative, on admission to the nursery. One percent silver nitrate is recommended as a prophylactic
agent against gonorrheal ophthalmia. The infant should be properly
identified while mother and infant are still in the delivery room.

The Academy's recommendations for transitional care, given at
nursery admittance, include specific, timed observations with assessment of growth and development. Bathing is deferred until the infant's temperature and other vital signs stabilize. Regular nursery care
involves consideration of each infant's bassinet and equipment as an
individual isolation unit. Handwashing with a recommended anti-
septic is mandatory on entering the nursery and before and after
handling an infant. Wearing long-sleeved gowns is not necessary in the
nursery unless an infected or potentially infected infant is handled.
Wearing masks is not recommended for routine duties by nurses or
physicians.

Bathing infants with a 3 percent hexachlorophene solution has been
discontinued because danger of brain damage from such solutions
has been demonstrated in experimental animals. In the presence of
a staphylococcal outbreak, it may be used, for a short term, as part
of an infection-control program according to the Food and Drug Administration and the Center for Disease Control.[23]

A screening test for phenylketonuria, involving determination of
the phenylalanine blood level during the newborn's hospital stay, is
required in most states.[24]

HIGH-RISK-INFANT CARE

There is general agreement that a pediatrician, and, preferably, one
skilled in the care of the newborn, should be present at the delivery

of a high-risk infant.[21,22] The nursery and the physician responsible for care of the infant should be notified of the anticipated birth.[22] Particular attention must be paid to maintenance of body temperature in the delivery room and during transport to the nursery. A physician and nurse should see the infant on arrival at the nursery. The temperature of the infant and the immediate environment should be monitored frequently. Oxygen should be given in the minimum concentration only as long as needed, preferably monitored by arterial blood gas measurements, to minimize the danger of retrolental fibroplasia. If transfer of the infant to a regional intensive care unit is indicated, proper preparation of the infant and accompaniment by an experienced attendant are essential.

OLDER INFANT CARE

In its standards for child health care, the American Academy of Pediatrics suggests monthly visits for the first 6 months of life and bimonthly visits thereafter until the infant is 1 year old.[25] The Academy also recommends a "health appraisal" for every infant. Included in the health appraisal are a medical and developmental history; a physical examination to evaluate physical, mental, and emotional development; detection of deviations; and suitable immunizations and laboratory tests. Consultation with the parents includes advice about feeding and nutrition, immunization, accident prevention, specific corrective procedures, and health protection; interpretation of child development; assistance in the prevention and management of behavior problems; referral for indicated consultative services; and promotion of family well-being.

MATERNITY AND INFANT CARE PROJECTS

Section 508 of the Social Security Act provides the legislative authority for MIC projects "to help reduce the incidence of mental retardation and other handicapping conditions . . . and to help reduce infant and maternal mortality . . .".

The program, originally placed in the Children's Bureau of the Social and Rehabilitation Service, U.S. Department of Health, Education, and Welfare, was transferred to the Department's Health Services and Mental Health Administration in 1969 as the Maternal and Child Health Services.

Early policies for funding applicant MIC projects were published by the Children's Bureau in 1964. The legislative mandate to reduce infant and maternal mortality, however, was added in the 1967 amendments to the Social Security Act and revised policies had not been issued by late 1972.

From the outset, the projects were aimed at bringing comprehensive maternal and infant health services to the poor, especially in inner-city and rural areas, where existing services were most inadequate. Emphasis was placed on increasing the number of maternity clinics providing a broad spectrum of diagnostic and specialist consultation services, hospitalization during the prenatal period as well as during labor and delivery for high-risk patients, intensive care for high-risk infants, and various other services such as public health nursing, medical social work, nutrition services, dental care, homemaker services, drugs, and transportation. (The 1967 amendments added family planning services to the list.)

Originally, agencies eligible to receive grants were state health agencies and, with their consent, the health agency of any political subdivision of the state. The 1967 amendments broadened eligible agencies to include, with state agency consent, public and nonprofit private agencies, institutions, and organizations.

SCOPE

There were 56 MIC projects in operation by the end of fiscal year 1971. They report 141,000 new maternity admissions and 42,600 new infant admissions during the preceding 12 months; new family planning admissions totaled 130,000.[26] Federal budget estimates indicate services were provided to 144,000 mothers and 49,000 infants in fiscal year 1972, and services will be provided to 152,000 mothers and 53,000 infants in fiscal year 1973.[27]

Patient eligibility varies from project to project. In a sizable number, for example, hospitalization is available only to women at very high risk, but outpatient prenatal and postpartum care and family planning are available to all women in a designated geographic area. In other projects, services are limited to women at especially high risk, but complete care, including hospitalization, is given to all women admitted to the projects. Present MIC policy states that diagnostic services and prenatal clinic care "should be available for any woman living in the project area."[28] The revised policy statement, which will reflect the 1967 legislative changes, is as yet unapproved. The draft, however, expands the eligibility requirement and forcefully specifies:

"Prenatal, postnatal, family planning . . . and diagnostic services must be available to any woman living in the project area without requirement or determination of financial eligibility."[29]

In general, the projects are credited with accelerating the organization of comprehensive health care for mothers and infants in their target areas and with serving as models for delivering maternal and infant health services in low-socioeconomic areas. They have also been credited with promoting the team-care concept among physicians and other health professionals. Most of the projects have used new types of health personnel, especially health aides.[30]

Many of the projects, however, have a continuing struggle to maintain standards and to meet the needs of all women in their area with limited funds. A national conference on MIC projects early in 1970 identified existing problems and deficiencies in the projects, as well as their strengths and contributions.[30] Key recommendations included:

● State and local governments give MIC projects higher financial priority. The federal matching formula should be amended to allow special aid to poor areas.

● Escalation of training and use of paramedical personnel, particularly the nurse–midwife, obstetrical associate, pediatric nurse practitioner, and pediatric assistant.

● Nonphysician health professionals should provide routine prenatal care for the normal obstetric patient after an initial evaluation by a physician, support the patient during labor, deliver normal patients, provide routine postpartum care, and counsel and evaluate in infant and interconceptional care.

FINANCING

At present, Maternity and Infant Care projects are financed on a 75 percent federal and 25 percent state or local matching formula for special projects. The law requires, however, that effective July 1, 1973, each state will be required to have such special projects (15 do not have MIC projects), and funding for all special projects will be included in the state formula grants for maternal and child health services. A report by the U.S. General Accounting Office predicts the shift in funding will bring about substantial changes in the amount of funds available to many states.[31] Thirty-eight states would receive increases from $10,000 to nearly $2.7 million and 16 states would receive decreases;

New York would receive the largest decrease—more than $8.8 million. It is important to note that while the changes in the law will require each state to have at least one MIC project, Children and Youth project, NICU, and family planning unit, it does not require them to have more than one each.

Maternity and Infant Care project grants during fiscal year 1972 totaled slightly more than $38 million in federal funds. They ranged from a low of $92,000 each for Augusta, Maine, and Sherman, Texas, projects to a high of $3.36 million for the Chicago project. All but four of the projects are funded through state and county health departments, as the original authorizing legislation required. Most are operated through teaching hospitals.

SELECTED MIC PROJECTS

Following are descriptive reports on selected MIC projects. Data were supplied by the individual projects. Each report tends to suggest that infant mortality rates have declined when MIC services have been provided; while it is tempting to attribute the declines solely to the projects, it seems unwise to do so until controlled evaluations are available.

New York City   The Maternity and Infant Care–Family Planning Project in New York City is a large program. It received more than $3.2 million in federal MIC funds for fiscal year 1972. To date, program efforts have focused on maternity care with infant care provided by other agencies.

The project was expanded in 1968 with specific Maternal and Child Health Services family planning grants to a clinic network.[32] Each clinic is affiliated with a hospital that provides medical supervision and staffing by board-certified or board-eligible obstetricians and, in an increasing number of instances, certified nurse–midwives. The prenatal, postpartum, and family planning services include medical, nurse–midwife, nutrition, public health nursing, social work and related services, and extensive use of community aides. Preconceptional and interconceptional care include annual medical examinations, semiannual breast and pelvic checks for users of contraceptive pills, and selected laboratory examinations. Fertility services are also provided. A Clearing House for Abortion Appointments, located in the project central office is supported by funds from a private foundation; it was begun before the July 1, 1970, effective date of state legislation legalizing abortion on request. Free pregnancy testing has been offered to all women, regardless of income, since spring 1970.

Nine New York City health districts in the boroughs of Manhattan, Brooklyn, and the Bronx are served by the program. In all, the three boroughs record more than 100,000 births each year. The average 1963 infant mortality rate in the nine districts served by the program was 30.3 per 1,000 live births.* In 1967, when the program was barely under way in most of the districts, the average rate had fallen to 28.4 per 1,000—a decrease of 6.3 percent in 4 years. In 1970, the average rate was 25.4 per 1,000, a decline of 10.6 percent in the 3 years the program was operative.

The infant mortality rate in 14 health districts not served by the program was 21.3 per 1,000 in 1967, and it fell 4.2 percent to 20.4 in 1970, while citywide, the rate declined 9.6 percent from 23.9 in 1967 to 21.6 in 1970.

The most striking decline is reported for the Mott Haven health district, the area that received the heaviest concentration of MIC services. In this district, the infant mortality rate fell from 33.6 per 1,000 live births in 1967 to 18.8 in 1970, a reduction of 44 percent (Figure 5-1).

Some information is also available on neonatal mortality among MIC-project infants and among the total population in the MIC districts. In 1967, the last year for which complete information on neonatal mortality rates is available, the rate for the districts was 23.2 deaths per 1,000 live births. Neonatal mortality among MIC infants whose mothers resided in the districts was 18.2 per 1,000 births, or 21.5 percent lower.

Providence   The Rhode Island Department of Health MIC Project is attached to St. Joseph's Hospital, Providence. The project is small, covering about 300 deliveries annually.[33] It provides services to women residing in six of 16 inner-city Census tracts and statewide to pregnant adolescents and unmarried women.

Federal MIC funds for fiscal year 1972 amounted to $176,000. The project provides the usual range of services; family planning is provided for 1 year after delivery. Infants receive care until their first birthday.

The project has provided services to about half of the pregnant women in the six Census tracts since 1966. Between 1966 and 1968, the infant mortality rate in this area ranged between 47.4 and 53.4

*N. Nicholas, personal communication, March 1972.

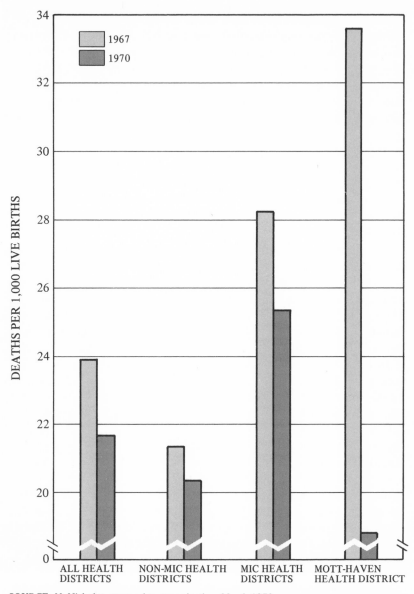

SOURCE: N. Nicholas, personal communication, March 1972.

FIGURE 5-1   Infant mortality rates in health districts with and without Maternity and Infant Care projects: New York City, 1967 and 1970.

per 1,000 live births.* The rate declined to 35.4 in 1969 and 25.2 in 1970, or 29 percent. The infant mortality rate in the 10 inner city Census tracts not served by the project was 28.7 in 1969; it declined to 21.4 in 1970, or 25 percent.

Chicago   During fiscal year 1972, the Chicago project received the largest federal grant of any MIC project—$3.36 million. All women who come to a board of health prenatal clinic are registered in the MIC project. All registered women "receive the same services, which include a 50 gram glucose meal with one hour post prandial blood sugar test, testing for sickle cell disease, social-service guidance, and nutritional guidance as well as routine prenatal care."† Patients receive care from the project until about their seventh month, at which time they are referred to a participating hospital where the remainder of their care is provided by hospital staff. Four groups of high-risk patients, about 2,000 women per year in all, receive special arrangements for their delivery at hospitals affiliated with the project.[34]

One of the high-risk groups consists of women 15 years of age or younger at time of conception. During the period from January 1, 1965, through June 30, 1967, the neonatal mortality rate among their infants was 19.0 per 1,000 live births; among offspring of all other patients of this age, it was 36.8.

Intrapartum and neonatal care appear to have been important factors in the difference in rates. A neonatal mortality rate of 26.4 per 1,000 live births was attributed to birth injury and asphyxia in the non-MIC group and compared to a rate of 10.6 per 1,000 in the project group. Among blacks in both groups, an even greater difference is shown: 30.8 per 1,000 among nonproject infants and 9.5 per 1,000 among MIC infants.

Albuquerque   The New Mexico MIC project, begun in March 1969, is located in the Bernalillo County Medical Center, Albuquerque. Prenatal care is provided in the center and five satellite clinics. The clinics are staffed by obstetricians and obstetrical residents from the center.[35] A special prenatal clinic is conducted for patients with obstetrical problems. Nurse–midwives are employed, but mainly for patient education. While family planning services are provided during the maternity cycle, women are referred to a voluntary agency for family plan-

*D. B. Casey, personal communication, March 1972.
†J. Zackler, personal communication, April 1972.

ning after their postpartum visit. In 1970, a neonatologist and other
qualified personnel were employed to care for high-risk infants.
Follow-up care of high-risk infants and a limited number of other infants is provided through a special clinic. During fiscal year 1972, the
project received $49,500 in federal MIC funds.

In the 3 years of the project, with about 1,200 deliveries a year
during 1970 and 1971, the neonatal mortality rate dropped from
21.4 deaths per 1,000 live births among the project population in
1969 to 12.2 in 1971—an annual decline of more than 21 percent per
year.

In the absence of a controlled study, the decline in neonatal mortality among the MIC project infants between 1970 and 1971 appears
to result from improved neonatal and perinatal services and facilities
instituted during 1970. The proportion of low-birth-weight infants
declined only slightly during the period.

Los Angeles   The Los Angeles MIC project has provided comprehensive prenatal and postpartum care since 1967. Federal funds amounted
to nearly $1.4 million for fiscal year 1972. The project is centered in
the Los Angeles County–University of Southern California Medical
Center and four community-based clinics.[36] The project serves two
major areas of Los Angeles. The average perinatal mortality rate for
the two MIC districts for 1966 and 1967 was 34.5 fetal and neonatal
deaths per 1,000 live births and fetal deaths. The corresponding rate
in two large districts not served by the project was 33.3 per 1,000.
The average perinatal mortality rate declined 13.0 percent to 30.3 per
1,000 in the MIC districts in 1969–1970; the rate in non-MIC districts
declined 8.1 percent to 30.6 per 1,000.

IMPACT

Reports from the selected MIC projects generally show declining neonatal, infant, or perinatal mortality rates among project populations.
In most instances, however, data on comparison or control groups are
inadequate, absent, or tenuous; lack of such control data, coupled
with the small size of some of the MIC populations make it hazardous
to reach definitive conclusions about the impact of the projects on
infant death.

The only major overall evaluation of the MIC program to date was
begun in 1966. The study sought to determine whether MIC care improved the outcome of pregnancy and to identify the components of
prenatal care that are most beneficial to women and their infants.[37]

The study employed a risk-adjustment technique to compare outcomes in the MIC population with other clinic populations, taking into account maternal age, parity, height, and weight.[38] While the results of the undertaking are not yet available—and the data generated from it is deemed "limited and not very useful"[31] —a preliminary study of prematurity rates (birth weights under 2,500 grams) has been reported.[37] The determination of risk included the outcome of the last pregnancy in addition to age, parity, height, and weight of the mother. The study compared prematurity rates among single offspring of different risk groups of black women in 13 MIC projects with prematurity rates among offspring of similar risk groups in the study population of the National Institute of Neurological Disease and Blindness's Collaborative Perinatal Research Project. No discernible differences were found in the outcomes in the two groups.

The results of the preliminary study are difficult to assess, in part because of the nature of the National Institute's study population and the scope of services received by them. This group of women received care during their entire maternity cycle, and presumably at other times as well, from university teaching centers. Infant mortality, in contrast to prematurity, can be affected by care during and after the neonatal period. In general, it is doubtful that this group met the general requirements for a control group.

NEONATAL INTENSIVE CARE UNITS

A number of published and unpublished reports point to the effectiveness of neonatal intensive care units (NICU's) in reducing infant mortality among high-risk newborn infants—especially when intensive neonatal care is preceded by intensive prenatal care.

Recent evidence strongly suggests that lowered neonatal mortality after intensive care is accompanied by more favorable long-term outcomes among surviving infants, even among those of very low birth weight. Infants with a birth weight of 1,500 grams who received neonatal intensive care at the University College Hospital in London have been examined at intervals of 6 months in the outpatient department of the hospital.[39] The children were clinically assessed and developmentally screened on each visit; they were psychometrically tested at 4 and 5 years of age. Among a total of 68 children, whose ages ranged from 9 months to 4 years at the last examination (including four on whom reports were received from abroad), 59 (or 87 percent) were considered normal in physical and mental development,

four (or 6 percent) of doubtful mental but normal physical development, and five (or 7 percent) of abnormal physical or mental development. As the London report points out, the finding that only 13 percent of the infants were of doubtful or definitely abnormal mental or
physical development sharply contrasts with findings that one third to
more than one half of similar children who received traditional newborn care are moderately to severely handicapped.[40]

The conclusions from the British study are reinforced by the findings in a Finnish investigation of even smaller infants, those less than
1,250 grams at birth,[41] and by findings in a U.S. investigation of
babies weighting 1,500 grams or less at Monmouth Medical Center,
New Jersey.

As with the MIC program, legislative authority for a federal NICU
program is found in Section 508 of the Social Security Act. The federal program is administered by the Maternal and Child Health Services under its special project grants. It is, however, considerably less
ambitious than the $38 million MIC program.

SCOPE

It is unclear how many NICU's are operating in the United States at
present. Neither the American Hospital Association, the American
College of Obstetricians and Gynecologists, or the American Academy
of Pediatrics maintains a registry. Only eight units receive direct federal project money.

While the NICU's may provide services only to infants of mothers
delivering in the hospital where the unit is located, in most instances
the units function as regional centers or referral centers for other local
hospitals.

Because they require highly complicated, expensive equipment and
specially trained nurses and other personnel, Swyer has recommended,
based on Canadian experience, that NICU's be large enough for efficient operation and be limited in number.[43] In light of the appeal of
special services to hospital administrators and trustees, physicians, and
the general public, critical studies are needed to acertain an adequate
population base and unit size for optimal operation.

FINANCING

Federal financing of NICU's falls under the special project grant
money for maternal and infant health services as is the case with MIC

money. The present matching formula—75 percent federal, 25 percent state or local—is also subject to the pending changes cited for the MIC projects.

In general, NICU's are expensive to operate. According to the Maternal and Child Health Services, annual operating costs in fiscal year 1972 were $753,000. They increased from $450,000 each for fiscal year 1971 and 1970. There is, it should be pointed out, no readily available information on per-bed or per-patient expenses.

SELECTED NICU PROJECTS

Following are descriptive reports on selected NICU projects. Data were supplied largely by the individual projects.

University of Texas In 1970, the Robert B. Green Hospital at the University of Texas Medical School, San Antonio, reorganized its traditional newborn service into intensive, intermediate, low-birth-weight, and minimal care units.* In 1969, the hospital's neonatal mortality rate had been 25.0 deaths per 1,000 live births; by 1971, it fell to 13.1 per 1,000. Among infants weighing 1,500 to 2,000 grams at birth, the rate dropped from 180 per 1,000 live births in 1969 to 78 in 1971.

The rate decline was achieved in the absence of any successful efforts to reach mothers for prenatal care; about half the mothers had not received prenatal care and another 15 percent had received minimal care only.

Mount Zion A similar before-and-after mortality rate decline was recorded at Mount Zion Hospital, San Francisco.† A perinatal intensive care unit was opened shortly after the appointment of a full-time neonatologist to the staff in late 1966. The overall Mount Zion neonatal mortality rate dropped from 33.5 deaths per 1,000 live births in 1966 to a low of 8.8 per 1,000 in 1970. Among infants weighing 2,500 ' grams or less, the rate fell from 218 deaths per 1,000 in 1966 to 66 per 1,000 in 1970, and among those weighing 1,500 grams or less, it fell from 792 per 1,000 in 1966 to 375 per 1,000 in 1970.

Vanderbilt A neonatal intensive care nursery was opened at Vanderbilt University Hospital in the early 1960's. The neonatal mortality

---

*H. W. Diserens, personal communication, May 1972.
†M. Markarian, personal communication, April 1972.

rate of 23.3 per 1,000 live births during the period 1950–1960 fell to 18.6 per 1,000 in 1963–1968.[44] During the same period, the rate among infants weighing 2,500 grams or less at birth fell from 214 to 121 per 1,000. Among those who weighed between 1,000 and 2,500 grams, mortality decreased from 118 to 65 per 1,000, essentially the same rate of decline (43 percent) as in the entire low-birth-weight group.

Wisconsin   In Wisconsin, a statewide NICU network was begun in 1967.[45] Initially, it focused on neonatal deaths that were judged preventable by upgrading knowledge and techniques in community hospitals or preventable by regional intensive care centers. Preventable neonatal deaths were suspected to constitute between eight and ten deaths per 1,000 live births—about half of these, it was judged, could be saved by improving care in community hospitals, and half could be saved by regional intensive care centers.

Institutes, or workshops, on recognition and management of perinatal problems were offered throughout the state starting in 1967. A physician–nurse team visited hospitals on request to review policies, procedures, equipment, facilities, and records involved in maternal and newborn care. Four regional intensive care units were opened in 1968 and 1969, and another was opened in 1971; two more are planned to complete the statewide network.

The statewide neonatal mortality rate declined from 16.9 to 14.9 between 1960 and 1968. In 1969, the rate dropped to 11.9 and remained at about the same level in 1970. Almost all of the recent decrease has been among infants dying the first day after birth, with a slight decline among the 1- to 7-day olds. There was no decline, however, in the mortality rate among infants 8 to 27 days old.

Arizona   The impact of regionalized neonatal intensive care on infant mortality in a large state with a relatively sparse population is illustrated by the Arizona program where neonatal intensive care centers were established in 1967.[46] Newborns who need special care are transported to the centers by ambulance, helicopter, and conventional aircraft. Services following hospital discharge are provided by state public health nurses.

During the first 3 years of the program, the fatality among transported infants with respiratory-distress syndrome was 32 percent; among those who remained in the hospitals where they were born, it was 59 percent. The most striking change, however, was among infants weighing 1,001 to 2,500 grams at birth who were born in hospitals with intensive care centers. The neonatal mortality rate among these children fell from about 100 to 59 deaths per 1,000 live births.

Quebec   Usher reports a 1967–1968 survey in Quebec Province, Canada, in which deaths among infants weighing more than 1,000 grams were compared among three types of hospitals: hospitals with neonatal intensive care units, hospitals routinely using referral neonatal intensive care units, and other hospitals.[47] All hospitals were in the Montreal and Quebec city metropolitan areas; all recorded more than 1,000 births per year. The perinatal mortality rates were 15.0, 17.2, and 19.9 per 1,000 live births, respectively. Most of the differences were attributed to outcome among low-birth-weight infants.

The differences undoubtedly would have been greater if smaller maternity units—those with less than 1,000 births annually—had been included. Perinatal mortality rates appear to be inversely related to the number of maternity beds available, the percentage of maternity beds occupied, and the newborn census.[48]

IMPACT

In assessing the impact of NICU's, it is important to keep two things in mind: First, only about 8 to 10 percent of the infants born in any 1 year would normally need such services, and, second, the infants who do need the services (generally those weighing 2,500 grams or less) account for about two thirds of our annual infant mortality rate.

From the before-and-after data reported here by the five U.S. NICU's, it appears that the units can be expected to reduce mortality among low-birth-weight infants from 40 to 70 percent. While the units did not report results for comparable weight groups of infants in all cases and the study groups are limited to before-and-after populations, all showed a consistent and striking decline in deaths.

It should be pointed out, however, as it was in the discussion of the MIC projects prematurity rates, that infant mortality can also be affected by care after the neonatal period. No information was provided on the long-term survival of the NICU infants.

REFERENCES

1. Day RL: Factors influencing offspring: Number of children, interval between pregnancies, and age of parents. Am J Dis Child 113:179–185, 1967

2. Schlesinger ER, Allaway NC: Use of child loss data in evolving priorities in maternal health services. Am J Public Health 47:570–577, 1957

3. The American College of Obstetricians and Gynecologists: Standards for Obstetric–Gynecologic Hospital Services. The American College of Obstetricians and Gynecologists, Chicago, 1969

4. American Medical Association: Teenage Pregnancy. Statement adopted by House of Delegates of the American Medical Association, Atlantic City, June 1971. AMA, Chicago

5. Eisenstadt v. Baird, 405 U.S. 438 (1972)

6. Morris NM, Udry JR, Chase CL: Reduction of prematurity rates by the prevention of unwanted pregnancies. Presentation to the Maternal and Child Health Section at the 100th Annual Meeting of the American Public Health Association, Atlantic City, November 16, 1972

7. Checklist for Abortion Laws in the United States. Association for the Study of Abortion, New York, 1971

8. Center for Disease Control: Family Planning Evaluation: Abortion Surveillance Report-Legal Abortions, United States Annual Summary, 1970. U.S. Department of Health, Education, and Welfare, Atlanta, 1971

9. Harris D, O'Hare D, Pakter J, et al: Legal abortion 1970–1971: The New York City experience. Presented at the ninety-ninth annual meeting of the American Public Health Association, Minneapolis, October 10–15, 1971

10. Pakter J: An 18 month experience in New York City with the liberalized abortion law. NY Med, September 1972

11. Tietze C, Lewit S: Joint program for the study of abortion (JPSA): early medical complications of legal abortion. Stud Fam Plann 3(6):97–124, June 1972

12. U.S. Department of Health, Education, and Welfare, HSMHA, NCHS, Monthly vital statistics reports. 19(9), November 30, 1970, 20(9), November 29, 1971, and 21(9), November 27, 1972

13. American Public Health Association: Recommended standards for abortion services. Am J Public Health 61:396–398, 1971

14. Gerbie AB, Nadler HL, Gerbie MV: Amniocentesis in genetic counseling: Safety and reliability in early pregnancy. Am J Obstet Gynecol 109:765–768, 1971

15. Friesen RF: Pre-pregnancy care—Logical extension of prenatal care. Can Med Assoc J 103:495–597, 1970

16. Siddall AC: The gynecologist's role in comprehensive medical care. Am J Public Health 59:657–662, 1969

17. The American College of Obstetricians and Gynecologists: Manual of Standards in Obstetric–Gynecologic Practice. Second edition. Chicago, 1965

18. Donabedian A, Rosenfeld LS: Some factors influencing prenatal care. New Engl J Med 265:1–6, 1961

19. Committee on Maternal Nutrition: Maternal Nutrition and the Course of Pregnancy: Summary Report. Food and Nutrition Board, National Research Council, National Academy of Sciences, Washington, DC, 1970

20. National Center for Health Statistics: Vital Statistics of the United States, 1968: Vol I—Natality. Department of Health, Education, and Welfare. Washington, DC, Government Printing Office, 1971. PHS

21. American College of Obstetricians and Gynecologists: Standards for Obstetric–Gynecologic Hospital Services. The American College of Obstetricians and Gynecologists, Chicago, 1969

22. American Academy of Pediatrics: Standards and Recommendations for Hospital Care of Newborn Infants. Fifth edition. American Academy of Pediatrics, Evanston, Illinois, 1971

23. FDA: CDC issue statement recommending reevaluation of nursery techniques when staphylococcal infections occur. Am Acad Pediatr Newsl 23:1–2, 1972

24. Maternal and Child Health Service: Recommended Guidelines for PKU Programs for the Newborn. Department of Health, Education, and Welfare, Health Services and Mental Health Administration, Washington, DC, Government Printing Office, 1971 (PHS Publ No 2160)

25. Council on Pediatric Practice: Standards of Child Health Care. American Academy of Pediatrics, Evanston, Illinois, 1967

26. Maternal and Child Health Service: Promoting the Health of Mothers and Children fy 1971. Health Services and Mental Health Administration, Department of Health, Education, and Welfare, Washington, DC, Government Printing Office, 1971 (Publ No. 72-5002)

27. Office of Management and Budget: The Budget of the United States Government, Appendix, Fiscal 1973. Washington, DC, Government Printing Office, 1972

28. United States Department of Health, Education, and Welfare: Grants for Maternity and Infant Care Projects. Social and Rehabilitation Service, Children's Bureau. Policies and Procedures. 1964. Washington, DC, 1964

29. United States Department of Health, Education, and Welfare: Grants for Maternity and Infant Care Projects. Health Services and Mental Health Administration, Maternal and Child Health Services. Policies and Procedures. Washington, DC, 1970

30. Position Papers and Recommendations and Participant Lists of the National Conference of Maternity and Infant Care Projects, Washington, DC, January 5–7, 1970. Maternal and Child Health Service, Rockville, Maryland, 1970

31. United States General Accounting Office: Report of the Committee on Ways and Means, House of Representatives. Maternal and Child Health Programs, Authorized by Title V, Social Security Act. Washington, DC, Department of Health, Education, and Welfare, 1972 [GAO Publ. No B-164031(3)]

32. Maternity Care and Family Planning: Progress Report 1970. New York City Maternity and Infant Care–Family Planning Projects, New York, 1971

33. Maternity and Infant Care Project of the Rhode Island Department of Health for St. Joseph's Hospital, July 1, 1970, to June 30, 1971, Providence, Rhode Island, 1971

34. Zackler J, Andelman SL, Bauer F: The young adolescent as an obstetric risk. Am J Obstet Gynecol 103:305–312, 1969

35. Annual Progress Report, New Mexico Maternity and Infant Care Project, Calendar Year 1971. University of New Mexico School of Medicine, Albuquerque, 1972

36. County of Los Angeles Health Department Maternity and Infant Care Project, Program Year 1970–1971. Los Angeles, 1971
37. Hebel R, et al: Prenatal care and prematurity. Presented at the annual meeting of the American Medical Association, Atlantic City, June 21, 1971
38. Hebel R, Entwisle MD, Tayback M: A risk-adjustment technique for comparing prematurity rates among clinic populations. HSMHA Health Rep 86:946–952, 1971
39. Rawlings G, et al: Changing prognosis for infants of very low birth weight. Lancet 1:516–519, 1971
40. Lubchenco LO, Delivoria-Papadopoulos M, Searls D: Long-term follow-up studies of prematurely born infants. II. Influence of birth weight and gestational age on sequelae. J Pediatr 80:509–512, 1972
41. Vapaavuori EK, Räihä NCR: Intensive care of small premature infants: I. Clinical findings and results of treatment. Acta Paediatr Scand 59:353–362, 1970
42. Madden PC: An investigation of the effects of neonatal intensive care upon the intellectual development and social functioning of very low birthweight infants. Abstract of a doctoral dissertation submitted to the faculty of the Graduate School of Education of Rutgers University–State University of New Jersey, New Brunswick, June 1972
43. Swyer PR: The regional organization of special care for the neonate. Pediatr Clin N Am 17:761–776, 1970
44. Stahlman M: What evidence exists that intensive care has changed the incidence of intact survival. Problems of Neonatal Intensive Care Units. Report of the fifty-ninth Ross Conference on Pediatric Research. Columbus, Ohio, Ross Laboratories, 1969
45. Graven SN, Howe G, Callon H: Perinatal health care studies and program results in Wisconsin, 1964–1970. Presented at the spring session of the American Academy of Pediatrics, San Diego, April 24–27, 1972
46. Meyer HBP, Daily WJR: A report to the Maricopa County Pediatric Society on the current status of the Arizona State Newborn Intensive Care and Transport Program, Phoenix, Arizona, February 1972
47. Usher RH: Clinical implications of perinatal mortality statistics. Clin Obstet Gynecol 14:885–925, 1971
48. Tokuhata GK, et al: Hospital and related characteristics associated with perinatal mortality: An empirical analysis for Pennsylvania births. Division of Research and Biostatistics, Pennsylvania Department of Health, Harrisburg, May 1971

Supplementary Tables for Chapter 1

TABLE A-1 Ninety-five Percent Confidence Limits for Infant Mortality Rates[a]: New York City Live-Birth Cohort, 1968

Risk Category and Three-Factor Index	Confi- dence Limit	Total	White Native Born	White Foreign Born	Puerto Rican	Black Native Born	All Others
			Deaths per 1,000 Live Births				
	L[b]	20.6	14.2	13.5	23.2	33.5	21.1
Total risk groups		_21.9_	_15.2_	_15.3_	_25.4_	_35.7_	_24.5_
	U[c]	23.3	16.2	17.4	27.8	38.0	28.4
	L	12.1	11.2	10.1	11.1	14.2	11.1
Adequate		_13.3_	_12.6_	_12.9_	_18.8[d]_	_21.0_	_18.0_
	U	14.6	14.1	16.4	29.7	30.0	27.5
	L	17.4	12.2	12.5	18.7	23.0	16.7
Intermediate		_18.5_	_13.7_	_15.0_	_21.2_	_25.4_	_20.9_
	U	19.7	15.4	18.0	24.0	28.0	26.1
	L	33.4	22.8	16.0	28.4	44.6	26.6
Inadequate		_35.6_	_25.8_	_20.4_	_32.2_	_48.1_	_33.9_
	U	37.9	29.3	25.9	36.5	51.9	43.1
	L	11.2	8.5	7.5	14.3	17.4	12.7
No risk		_12.1_	_9.5_	_9.4_	_17.5_	_20.4_	_17.1_
	U	13.0	10.6	11.8	21.4	23.9	22.6
	L	7.5	7.3	4.7	4.5	6.3	2.7
Adequate		_8.7_	_8.6_	_7.4_	_12.2[d]_	_13.1[d]_	_8.2[d]_
	U	10.1	10.2	11.0	26.6	24.1	19.1

TABLE A-1 *(Continued)*

Risk Category and Three-Factor Index	Confidence Limit	Total	White Native Born	White Foreign Born	Puerto Rican	Black Native Born	All Others
		Deaths per 1,000 Live Births					
	L	10.0	7.1	5.9	12.6	12.0	12.2
Intermediate		_11.2_	_8.5_	_8.7_	_16.4_	_15.3_	_18.0_
	U	12.6	10.2	12.4	21.3	19.4	25.7
	L	18.5	12.6	10.3	15.0	24.4	13.1
Inadequate		_21.0_	_16.1_	_16.4_	_21.0_	_30.2_	_22.1_[d]
	U	23.8	20.4	24.8	28.6	37.4	34.9
	L	23.3	14.1	10.2	20.2	31.2	20.6
Sociodemographic only		_24.9_	_16.9_	_13.2_	_23.3_	_34.3_	_27.7_
	U	26.6	20.3	17.2	26.8	37.7	36.6
	L	8.6	5.4	4.4	1.7	12.4	10.3
Adequate		_12.3_	_9.7_	_9.2_	_14.1_[d]	_30.8_[d]	_31.8_[d]
	U	17.1	16.0	16.9	50.9	63.4	74.1
	L	16.1	9.4	7.9	15.1	20.0	7.0
Intermediate		_18.1_	_13.2_	_11.7_	_18.9_	_23.7_	_12.9_
	U	20.3	18.0	16.7	23.6	28.1	21.7
	L	31.8	19.5	12.5	23.4	38.4	31.9
Inadequate		_34.7_	_25.3_	_19.3_	_28.6_	_43.1_	_45.7_[d]
	U	37.9	32.9	28.6	34.9	48.3	63.5
	L	25.3	21.5	20.6	21.9	34.7	13.7
Medical–obstetric only		_27.7_	_24.4_	_26.3_	_28.5_	_41.7_	_21.1_
	U	30.3	27.7	33.4	37.1	50.0	31.2
	L	19.3	19.3	13.7	5.2	6.8	9.9
Adequate		_22.6_	_23.2_	_21.2_	_19.0_[d]	_18.5_[d]	_24.7_[d]
	U	26.5	27.8	31.4	48.6	40.3	50.9
	L	21.0	16.7	23.8	14.1	22.7	8.6
Intermediate		_24.2_	_20.9_	_33.3_	_20.9_	_30.6_	_17.2_[d]
	U	27.9	26.1	45.3	29.9	40.4	30.8
	L	39.6	30.1	8.1	32.5	53.2	10.7
Inadequate		_46.4_	_40.6_	_18.9_	_48.2_[d]	_67.8_	_26.6_[d]
	U	54.3	53.6	37.2	68.9	86.1	54.8
	L	39.1	31.5	20.8	32.8	48.7	30.1
Sociodemographic and medical–obstetric		_42.0_	_36.9_	_26.5_	_38.1_	_54.2_	_40.6_
	U	45.0	43.2	33.7	44.2	60.3	53.6

TABLE A-1 (*Continued*)

Risk Category and Three-Factor Index	Confi-dence Limit	Total	White Native Born	White Foreign Born	Puerto Rican	Black Native Born	All Others
				Deaths per 1,000 Live Births			
	L	23.5	17.1	19.7	19.5	22.1	9.5
Adequate		__29.9__	__24.6__	__32.3__[d]	__53.1__[d]	__51.3__[d]	__35.1__[d]
	U	38.0	34.2	49.7	115.8	101.1	89.9
	L	31.6	30.4	14.4	25.5	33.1	29.2
Intermediate		__35.2__	__38.7__	__21.4__	__32.0__	__39.7__	__43.2__[d]
	U	39.1	49.1	30.6	40.0	47.6	61.8
	L	49.9	37.7	19.7	37.0	59.1	20.9
Inadequate		__55.1__	__50.8__	__32.2__[d]	__45.7__	__68.1__	__37.4__[d]
	U	60.8	67.1	49.6	56.7	78.4	61.7

[a] Rate in underscored bold type indicates actual calculated rate.
[b] Lower confidence limit.
[c] Upper confidence limit.
[d] Based on 100–999 live births.

TABLE A-2 Ninety-five Percent Confidence Limits for Neonatal Mortality Rates[a]: New York City Live-Birth Cohort, 1968

Risk Category and Three-Factor Index	Confi-dence Limit	Total	White Native Born	White Foreign Born	Puerto Rican	Black Native Born	All Others
				Deaths per 1,000 Live Births			
	L[b]	15.7	11.3	10.8	17.3	23.7	16.3
Total risk groups		__16.7__	__12.2__	__12.4__	__19.1__	__25.4__	__19.3__
	U[c]	17.8	13.2	14.3	21.1	27.2	22.9
	L	10.1	9.2	9.2	10.4	7.8	9.8
Adequate		__11.1__	__10.4__	__11.7__	__17.8__[d]	__12.9__	__16.3__
	U	12.3	11.8	14.9	28.5	20.1	25.4
	L	13.0	9.5	9.6	14.0	15.6	12.9
Intermediate		__13.9__	__10.8__	__11.7__	__16.1__	__17.7__	__16.8__
	U	14.8	12.2	14.3	18.5	20.1	21.8
	L	24.8	17.7	11.3	20.5	31.9	18.8
Inadequate		__26.4__	__20.4__	__15.2__	__23.6__	__34.9__	__25.3__
	U	28.1	23.5	20.1	27.2	38.1	33.4

TABLE A-2 (*Continued*)

Risk Category and Three-Factor Index	Confidence Limit	Total	White Native Born	White Foreign Born	Puerto Rican	Black Native Born	All Others
		Deaths per 1,000 Live Births					
	L	8.3	6.4	6.5	10.1	11.4	9.7
No risk		_9.1_	_7.2_	_8.3_	_12.7_	_13.9_	_13.6_
	U	9.9	8.2	10.5	15.9	17.0	18.5
	L	5.7	5.2	4.5	4.5	2.9	2.7
Adequate		_6.7_	_6.4_	_7.1_	12.2^d	7.8^d	8.2^d
	U	7.9	7.8	10.7	26.6	17.0	19.1
	L	7.2	5.1	5.0	8.9	7.0	10.2
Intermediate		_8.3_	_6.3_	_7.4_	_12.2_	_9.6_	_15.6_
	U	9.6	7.8	10.7	16.3	12.9	22.9
	L	13.4	10.0	7.9	9.0	17.0	6.7
Inadequate		_15.5_	_13.0_	_13.4_	_13.6_	_22.1_	13.5^d
	U	18.0	16.9	21.2	19.7	28.7	24.2
	L	16.0	10.4	6.8	13.8	20.4	16.0
Sociodemographic only		_17.4_	_12.9_	_9.3_	_16.4_	_22.9_	_22.0_
	U	18.9	16.0	12.5	19.4	25.7	29.5
	L	7.3	5.4	3.8	1.7	2.7	10.3
Adequate		_10.8_	_9.7_	_8.3_	14.1^d	13.2^d	31.8^d
	U	15.4	16.0	15.8	50.9	38.5	74.1
	L	10.6	6.8	4.5	10.5	11.9	5.0
Intermediate		_12.2_	_10.0_	_7.4_	_13.6_	_14.9_	_10.1_
	U	14.0	14.3	11.5	17.7	18.6	18.1
	L	21.8	13.3	8.2	15.4	25.9	23.8
Inadequate		_24.3_	_18.2_	_13.9_	_19.6_	_29.8_	35.2^d
	U	27.0	24.4	22.0	24.9	34.3	50.3
	L	21.2	18.3	16.8	17.4	27.3	13.0
Medical–obstetric only		_23.3_	_21.1_	_21.8_	_23.4_	_33.4_	_20.3_
	U	25.6	24.3	28.3	30.9	40.7	30.2
	L	16.9	16.9	11.7	5.2	3.3	7.8
Adequate		_20.0_	_20.7_	_18.6_	19.0^d	12.3^d	21.2^d
	U	23.7	25.3	28.1	48.6	31.5	46.2
	L	18.0	14.4	18.9	12.0	18.7	8.6
Intermediate		_20.9_	_18.4_	_27.1_	_18.2_	_25.7_	17.2^d
	U	24.2	23.4	37.7	26.6	34.4	30.8

TABLE A-2 *(Continued)*

Risk Category and Three-Factor Index	Confidence Limit	Total	White Native Born	White Foreign Born	Puerto Rican	Black Native Born	All Others
				Deaths per 1,000 Live Births			
Inadequate	L	30.2	22.4	5.2	23.1	39.3	10.7
		36.2	**31.4**	**14.2**^{d}	**36.1**^{d}	**52.9**	**26.6**^{d}
	U	43.4	42.7	31.0	53.8	69.8	54.8
Sociodemographic and medical–obstetric	L	30.1	26.0	15.7	25.7	35.9	19.8
		32.7	**30.8**	**21.2**	**30.4**	**40.7**	**28.4**
	U	35.4	36.5	28.0	36.0	46.2	39.5
Adequate	L	19.6	14.3	17.2	14.3	14.1	5.4
		25.5	**21.2**	**29.0**^{d}	**44.2**^{d}	**38.5**^{d}	**26.3**^{d}
	U	33.2	30.3	45.8	103.0	83.9	76.8
Intermediate	L	23.6	23.3	11.0	19.1	24.1	18.1
		26.8	**30.3**	**17.1**	**24.8**	**29.8**	**29.2**^{d}
	U	30.4	39.4	25.5	32.2	37.0	44.7
Inadequate	L	38.4	33.0	12.3	29.3	43.7	13.7
		43.1	**45.3**	**22.5**^{d}	**37.3**	**51.2**	**27.4**^{d}
	U	48.3	60.7	37.8	47.4	60.0	49.0

^{a}Rate in underscored bold type indicates actual calculated rate.
^{b} Lower confidence limit.
^{c} Upper confidence limit
^{d} Based on 100–999 live births.

TABLE A-3 Ninety-five Percent Confidence Limits for Postneonatal Mortality Rates^a: New York City Live-Birth Cohort, 1968

Risk Category and Three-Factor Index	Confidence Limit	Total	White Native Born	White Foreign Born	Puerto Rican	Black Native Born	All Others
				Deaths per 1,000 Live Births			
Total risk groups	L^b	4.9	2.6	2.2	5.3	9.1	3.6
		5.3	**3.0**	**3.0**	**6.3**	**10.2**	**5.1**
	U^c	5.7	3.5	4.0	7.5	11.4	7.1
Adequate	L	1.8	1.6	0.4	0.0	4.2	0.2
		2.2	**2.2**	**1.1**	**1.0**^{d}	**8.1**	**1.7**
	U	2.8	2.9	2.3	5.6	14.2	6.1

TABLE A-3 *(Continued)*

Risk Category and Three-Factor Index	Confidence Limit	Total	White Native Born	White Foreign Born	Puerto Rican	Black Native Born	All Others
				Deaths per 1,000 Live Births			
	L	4.1	2.3	2.2	3.9	6.4	2.4
Intermediate		4.6	2.9	3.3	5.1	7.7	4.1
	U	5.2	3.7	4.7	6.6	9.2	6.6
	L	8.3	3.9	3.1	6.8	11.4	5.3
Inadequate		9.2	5.3	5.2	8.7	13.2	8.6
	U	10.2	7.0	8.1	11.0	15.3	13.2
	L	2.6	1.8	0.6	3.3	4.8	1.8
No risk		3.0	2.3	1.2	4.9	6.5	3.6
	U	3.5	2.9	2.2	7.0	8.6	6.4
	L	1.4	1.5	0.0	0.0	1.4	0.0
Adequate		1.9	2.2	0.3	0.0^d	5.2	0.0^d
	U	2.6	3.1	1.7	17.8	13.3	14.3
	L	2.3	1.5	0.4	2.4	3.8	0.7
Intermediate		2.9	2.2	1.3	4.2	5.7	2.4
	U	3.6	3.1	3.0	6.7	8.3	6.1
	L	4.2	1.8	0.8	4.1	5.2	3.4
Inadequate		5.5	3.2	3.0	7.3	8.1	8.6^d
	U	7.2	5.3	7.7	12.0	12.0	17.7
	L	6.6	2.6	2.3	5.3	9.6	2.9
Sociodemographic only		7.5	3.9	3.8	6.9	11.4	5.7
	U	8.5	5.6	5.9	9.0	13.5	10.0
	L	0.5	0.0	0.0	0.0	4.8	0.0
Adequate		1.6	0.0	0.9	0.0^d	17.6^d	0.0^d
	U	3.7	5.5	5.0	61.6	45.1	55.8
	L	4.7	1.5	2.1	3.4	6.5	0.6
Intermediate		5.8	3.2	4.3	5.3	8.8	2.8
	U	7.1	5.9	7.7	7.9	11.6	8.2
	L	8.9	4.3	2.2	6.2	10.7	4.9
Inadequate		10.4	7.1	5.4	8.9	13.2	10.6^d
	U	12.2	11.1	11.1	12.4	16.4	20.1
	L	3.6	2.4	2.4	2.6	5.5	0.0
Medical–obstetric only		4.4	3.4	4.5	5.1	8.3	0.8
	U	5.5	4.7	7.7	8.9	12.1	4.5

TABLE A-3 *(Continued)*

Risk Category and Three-Factor Index	Confidence Limit	Total	White Native Born	White Foreign Born	Puerto Rican	Black Native Born	All Others
			Deaths per 1,000 Live Births				
	L	1.6	1.4	0.5	0.0	0.8	0.1
Adequate		2.7	2.6	2.5	0.0[d]	6.2[d]	3.5[d]
	U	4.2	4.4	7.3	41.5	22.4	19.5
	L	2.3	1.3	2.7	0.7	2.2	0.0
Intermediate		3.4	2.6	6.2	2.7	4.9	0.0[d]
	U	4.9	4.7	12.2	6.9	9.3	13.7
	L	7.1	4.8	0.6	5.2	8.5	0.0
Inadequate		10.2	9.2	4.7[d]	12.0[d]	14.9	0.0[d]
	U	14.2	16.1	17.0	23.6	24.1	33.3
	L	8.0	4.1	2.9	5.4	10.9	6.8
Sociodemographic and medical–obstetric		9.3	6.1	5.3	7.7	13.5	12.2
	U	10.8	8.8	8.9	10.7	16.7	20.1
	L	2.2	1.1	0.4	0.2	1.5	0.2
Adequate		4.4	3.3	3.2[d]	8.8[d]	12.8[d]	8.8[d]
	U	7.9	7.7	11.6	49.0	46.2	49.0
	L	6.7	4.9	1.6	4.4	6.7	6.7
Intermediate		8.4	8.4	4.3	7.2	9.9	13.9[d]
	U	10.5	13.4	9.4	11.1	14.2	25.6
	L	9.8	2.0	3.6	4.8	12.6	2.7
Inadequate		12.1	5.5	9.7[d]	8.3	17.0	10.0[d]
	U	15.0	12.0	21.1	13.3	22.4	25.5

[a]Rate in underscored bold type indicates actual calculated rate.
[b] Lower confidence limit.
[c] Upper confidence limit.
[d] Based on 100–999 live births.

TABLE A-4 Mean Birth Weight (Grams) by Risk Category, Three-Factor Health Services Index, and Ethnic Group: New York City Live-Birth Cohort, 1968

Risk Category and Three-Factor Index	Total	White Native Born	White Foreign Born	Puerto Rican	Black Native Born	All Others
			Mean Birth Weight (grams)			
Total	3,161	3,213	3,290	3,136	3,008	3,136
Adequate	3,236	3,230	3,314	3,200	3,122	3,142
Intermediate	3,185	3,227	3,297	3,173	3,069	3,160
Inadequate	3,051	3,133	3,232	3,074	2,932	3,092
No risk	3,209	3,232	3,290	3,158	3,086	3,155
Adequate	3,245	3,241	3,305	3,218	3,164	3,173
Intermediate	3,216	3,238	3,303	3,182	3,125	3,145
Inadequate	3,122	3,174	3,215	3,098	3,008	3,161
Sociodemographic only	3,109	3,173	3,311	3,120	2,994	3,099
Adequate	3,245	3,219	3,363	3,185	3,044	3,036
Intermediate	3,156	3,222	3,315	3,162	3,049	3,147
Inadequate	3,034	3,091	3,262	3,071	2,948	3,051
Medical–obstetric only	3,171	3,195	3,263	3,167	3,020	3,152
Adequate	3,203	3,196	3,276	3,184	3,138	3,127
Intermediate	3,194	3,216	3,248	3,214	3,089	3,189
Inadequate	3,052	3,120	3,275	3,060	2,866	3,090
Socioeconomic and medical–obstetric	3,088	3,170	3,280	3,119	2,931	3,137
Adequate	3,239	3,232	3,346	3,171	2,996	3,158
Intermediate	3,135	3,173	3,296	3,158	3,012	3,187
Inadequate	2,977	3,077	3,180	3,063	2,852	3,041

TABLE A-5 T-Test Values for Significance of Differences in Mean Birth Weight by Ethnic Group, Mother's Risk Category, and Three-Factor Health Services Index: New York City Live-Birth Cohort, 1968

Risk Category/ Three-Factor Index/Ethnic Group	White Native Born	White Foreign Born	Puerto Rican	Black Native Born	All Others
			T-Test Values		
No Risk/Adequate					
White					
Native born					
Foreign born	6.75**				
Puerto Rican	−1.02	−3.66**			
Black native born	−4.19**	−6.99**	−1.79		
All others	−3.35**	−6.16**	−1.57	0.33	
TOTAL	1.11	−6.84**	1.21	4.52**	3.60**
No risk/Intermediate					
White					
Native born					
Foreign born	7.13**				
Puerto Rican	−6.29**	−10.59**			
Black native born	−13.33**	−15.80**	−5.11**		
All others	−7.18**	−10.52**	−2.50*	1.31	
TOTAL	−5.40**	−10.59**	4.19**	12.61**	5.67**
No risk/Inadequate					
White					
Native born					
Foreign born	2.43*				
Puerto Rican	−5.20**	−5.99**			
Black native born	−12.64**	−10.93**	−5.47**		
All others	−0.62	−2.22*	2.76**	6.72**	
TOTAL	−6.26**	−6.03**	1.94	11.14**	−1.96
No risk/Total					
White					
Native born					
Foreign born	9.54**				
Puerto Rican	−10.77**	−15.49**			
Black native born	−23.49**	−24.87**	−8.09**		
All others	−8.11**	−12.54**	−0.31	5.98**	
TOTAL	−8.51**	−14.34**	7.89**	21.79**	5.81**
Sociodemographic risk only/Adequate					
White					
Native born					
Foreign born	6.50**				
Puerto Rican	−0.69	−3.51**			
Black native born	−4.39**	−7.78**	−2.25*		
All others	−3.85**	−6.70**	−2.04*	−0.12	
TOTAL	1.81	−6.74**	1.25	5.26**	4.55**

TABLE A-5 *(Continued)*

Risk Category/ Three-Factor Index/Ethnic Group	White Native Born	White Foreign Born	Puerto Rican	Black Native Born	All Others
			T-Test Values		
Sociodemographic risk only/Intermediate					
White					
Native born					
Foreign born	6.55**				
Puerto Rican	−4.74**	−11.71**			
Black native born	−14.04**	−20.70**	−10.32**		
All others	−3.92**	−9.01**	−0.84	5.30**	
TOTAL	−6.68**	−14.60**	−0.70	14.90**	0.57
Sociodemographic risk only/Inadequate					
White					
Native born					
Foreign born	8.64**				
Puerto Rican	−1.37	−10.51**			
Black native born	−10.08**	−16.54**	−10.17**		
All others	−1.67	−7.91**	−0.92	4.41**	
TOTAL	−4.81**	−13.30**	−3.85**	11.76**	−0.80
Sociodemographic risk only/Total					
White					
Native born					
Foreign born	13.51**				
Puerto Rican	−5.96**	−19.61**			
Black native born	−20.70**	−32.44*	−15.46**		
All others	−5.15**	−14.66**	−1.49	7.36**	
TOTAL	−9.26**	−24.18**	−1.60	22.61**	0.81
Medical–obstetric risk only/Adequate					
White					
Native born					
Foreign born	4.09**				
Puerto Rican	−0.26	−1.96			
Black native born	−1.66	−3.51**	−0.87		
All others	−1.85	−3.54**	−1.02	−0.22	
TOTAL	0.87	−4.09**	0.44	1.91	2.09*

TABLE A-5 (*Continued*)

Risk Category/ Three-Factor Index/Ethnic Group	White Native Born	White Foreign Born	Puerto Rican	Black Native Born	All Others
			T-Test Values		
Medical–obstetric risk only/Intermediate White					
Native born					
Foreign born	1.68				
Puerto Rican	−0.15	−1.55			
Black native born	−7.38**	−6.91**	−5.76**		
All others	−1.07	−2.08*	−0.91	3.48**	
TOTAL	−2.42*	−3.23**	−1.25	7.40**	0.19
Medical–obstetric risk only/Inadequate White					
Native born					
Foreign born	4.33**				
Puerto Rican	−1.91	−5.36**			
Black native born	−8.77**	−9.93**	−5.41**		
All others	−0.68	−3.79**	0.62	4.41**	
TOTAL	−3.55**	−6.62**	−0.31	8.75**	−0.90
Medical–obstetric risk only/Total White					
Native born					
Foreign born	5.39**				
Puerto Rican	−1.97*	−5.66**			
Black native born	−13.86**	−14.46**	−8.27**		
All others	−2.28*	−5.29**	−0.71	5.83**	
TOTAL	−3.89**	−7.89**	0.31	13.73**	1.05
Sociodemographic and medical–obstetric risks/Adequate White					
Native born					
Foreign born	3.68**				
Puerto Rican	−0.96	−2.71**			
Black native born	−4.22**	−5.98**	−1.98*		
All others	−1.15	−2.87**	−0.14	1.79	
TOTAL	0.43	−4.00**	1.10	4.59**	1.30

TABLE A-5 *(Continued)*

Risk Category/ Three-Factor Index/Ethnic Group	White Native Born	White Foreign Born	Puerto Rican	Black Native Born	All Others
			T-Test Values		
Sociodemographic and medical–obstetric risks/Intermediate					
White					
Native born					
Foreign born	5.46**				
Puerto Rican	−0.81	−6.79**			
Black native born	−8.53**	−13.50**	−8.77**		
All others	0.50	−3.81**	1.13	6.43**	
TOTAL	−2.64**	−9.26**	−1.89	10.83**	−2.16*
Sociodemographic and medical–obstetric risks/Inadequate					
White					
Native born					
Foreign born	2.97**				
Puerto Rican	−0.55	−3.82**			
Black native born	−8.68**	−10.10**	−10.43**		
All others	−0.87	−3.16**	−0.59	4.76**	
TOTAL	−4.53**	−6.96**	−5.35**	10.17**	−1.77
Sociodemographic and medical–obstetric risks/Total					
White					
Native born					
Foreign born	6.86**				
Puerto Rican	−3.79**	−10.45**			
Black native born	−17.85**	−21.74**	−14.62**		
All others	−1.54	−6.44**	0.88	9.32**	
TOTAL	−8.03**	−14.32**	−3.14**	19.04**	−2.48*
Total/Adequate					
White					
Native born					
Foreign born	11.00**				
Puerto Rican	−1.69	−5.96**			
Black native born	−7.48**	−11.87**	−3.26**		
All others	−5.47**	−9.76**	−2.39*	0.88	
TOTAL	1.85	−11.20**	2.05*	8.06**	5.92**

TABLE A-5   *(Continued)*

Risk Category/ Three-Factor Index/Ethnic Group	White Native Born	White Foreign Born	Puerto Rican	Black Native Born	All Others
			T-Test Values		
Total/Intermediate					
White					
Native born					
Foreign born	10.61**				
Puerto Rican	−9.04**	−16.54**			
Black native born	−27.72**	−30.42**	−15.35**		
All others	−7.40**	−13.50**	−1.40	8.94**	
TOTAL	−11.85**	−19.22**	2.32*	26.00**	2.90**
Total/Inadequate					
White					
Native born					
Foreign born	8.67**				
Puerto Rican	−6.64**	−13.50**			
Black native born	−24.01**	−24.90**	−16.44**		
All others	−2.94**	−8.76**	1.24	10.79**	
TOTAL	−12.72**	−17.31**	−3.46**	22.84**	−3.11**
Total/Total					
White					
Native born					
Foreign born	16.81**				
Puerto Rican	−17.87**	−27.77**			
Black native born	−51.39**	−50.99**	−24.19**		
All others	−11.46**	−20.22**	0.06	16.19**	
TOTAL	−22.24**	−30.60**	6.43**	47.02**	3.67**

**Significant at 1 percent level.
*Significant at 5 percent level.

TABLE A-6 Mean Birth Weight (Grams) by Education of Mother and Ethnic Group: New York City Live-Birth Cohort, 1968

Education of Mother	Total	White			Black			All Others
		Native Born	Foreign Born	Puerto Rican	Native Born	Foreign Born	Puerto Rican	
				Mean Birth Weight (grams)				
None, elementary	3,164	3,136	3,330	3,134	2,975	3,168	3,084	3,149
High school, 1–3 years	3,083	3,146	3,270	3,122	2,975	3,121	3,016	3,094
High school, 4 years	3,185	3,229	3,298	3,175	3,034	3,146	3,128	3,142
College, 1–3 years	3,197	3,225	3,235	3,170	3,070	3,178	3,152	3,178
College, 4 years or more	3,215	3,222	3,230	3,231	3,158	3,168	3,355[a]	3,130
Not stated	3,138	3,207	3,277	3,080	2,954	3,182	3,061	3,133
TOTAL	3,161	3,213	3,290	3,136	3,008	3,153	3,071	3,186

[a] Mean based on less than 20 live births.

TABLE A-7 T-Test Values for Significance of Differences in Mean Birth Weight by Ethnic Group within Mother's Education Groups: New York City Live-Birth Cohort, 1968

T-Test Values

Mother's Education and Ethnic Group	White			Black			Chinese	Japanese	All Others
	Native Born	Foreign Born	Puerto Rican	Native Born	Foreign Born	Puerto Rican			
NONE, ELEMENTARY									
White									
Native born									
Foreign born	11.18**								
Puerto Rican	-0.13	-19.13**							
Black									
Native born	-7.46**	-24.80**	-11.98**						
Foreign born	1.21	-7.76**	1.63	7.50**					
Puerto Rican	-1.38	-7.71**	-1.54	2.80**	-2.15*				
Chinese	0.38	5.01**	0.49	4.08**	-0.39	1.36			
Japanese	0.92	0.02	0.99	1.51	0.80	1.13	0.92		
All others	0.96	-0.57	1.04	2.00*	0.74	1.30	0.89	-0.35	
TOTAL	1.69	-19.42**	4.47**	16.42**	-0.21	2.40*	0.31	-0.81	-0.77

TABLE A-7 (Continued)

T-Test Values

Mother's Education and Ethnic Group	White			Black			Chinese	Japanese	All Others
	Native Born	Foreign Born	Puerto Rican	Native Born	Foreign Born	Puerto Rican			
HIGH SCHOOL (1–3 years)									
White									
Native born									
Foreign born	9.40**								
Puerto Rican	−2.66***	−11.17**							
Black									
Native born	−19.74**	−21.59**	−16.70**						
Foreign born	−1.11	−6.07**	−0.04	6.07**					
Puerto Rican	−4.49**	−8.32**	−3.66***	1.30	−2.78**				
Chinese	1.07	−1.69	1.60	4.48**	1.46	3.37**			
Japanese	−1.93	−2.86**	−1.75	−0.61	−1.62	−0.86	−2.70**		
All others	−0.51	−1.82	−0.26	1.17	−0.23	0.76	−1.21	1.19	
TOTAL	−9.51**	−15.38**	−5.73***	19.67***	−1.69	2.29*	−2.37*	1.40	−0.14
HIGH SCHOOL (4 years)									
White									
Native born									
Foreign born	9.50**								
Puerto Rican	−6.41**	−11.99**							
Black									
Native born	−33.03**	−30.26**	−13.54**						
Foreign born	−6.39**	−10.49**	−1.80	7.38***					
Puerto Rican	−3.10**	−5.14**	−1.35	2.58***	−0.45				
Chinese	−3.89**	−6.32**	−1.83	2.85***	−0.73	−0.17			
Japanese	−1.91	−3.16**	−0.89	1.48	−0.34	−0.06	0.05		

All others	−0.48	−1.75	0.55	2.78**	0.94	1.21	1.64	1.04	
TOTAL	−13.63**	−16.64**	1.34	30.40**	2.97**	1.67	2.19*	1.06	−0.33

COLLEGE (1–3 years)

White									
Native born									
Foreign born	0.65								
Puerto Rican	−1.89	−2.03*							
Black									
Native born	−10.59**	−7.72**	−2.76**						
Foreign born	−1.83	−1.91	0.21	3.31**					
Puerto Rican	−0.64	−0.71	−0.16	0.59	−0.20				
Chinese	−0.54	−0.70	0.46	1.95	0.28	0.36			
Japanese	−1.46	−1.54	−0.83	0.27	−0.80	−0.42	−1.06		
All others	−0.26	−0.38	0.44	1.52	0.31	0.28	0.09	0.75	
TOTAL	−4.21**	−2.55*	0.90	9.68**	0.72	0.38	0.01	1.08	−0.12

COLLEGE (4 years or more)

White									
Native born									
Foreign born	0.56								
Puerto Rican	0.17	0.02							
Black									
Native born	−2.96**	−2.73**	−1.17						
Foreign born	−1.58	−1.62	−0.99	0.20					
Puerto Rican	0.45	0.40	0.44	0.57	0.57				
Chinese	−2.49*	−2.51*	−1.77	−0.41	−0.58	−0.89			
Japanese	−2.25*	−2.23*	−1.88	−0.93	−1.04	−0.88	−0.86		
All others	−3.91**	−3.79**	−2.54*	−1.56	−1.60	−0.99	−1.28	−0.04	
TOTAL	−1.44	−1.19	−0.32	2.96**	−1.37	−0.47	2.26*	2.10*	3.68**

**Significant at 1 percent level.
*Significant at 5 percent level.

163

TABLE A-8 Ninety-five Percent Confidence Limits for Infant Mortality Rates by Mother's Education, Three-Factor Health Services Index, and Ethnic Group[a]: New York City Live-Birth Cohort, 1968

Risk Category and Three-Factor Index	Confidence Limit	Total	White Native Born	White Foreign Born	Puerto Rican	Black Native Born	All Others
	L[b]	20.6	14.2	13.5	23.2	33.5	21.1
Total infant deaths		21.9	15.2	15.3	25.4	35.7	24.5
	U[c]	23.3	16.2	17.4	27.8	38.0	28.4
	L	12.1	11.2	10.1	11.1	14.2	11.1
Adequate care		13.3	12.6	12.9	18.8[d]	21.0	18.0
	U	14.6	14.1	16.4	29.7	30.0	27.5
	L	17.4	12.2	12.5	18.7	23.0	16.7
Intermediate care		18.5	13.7	15.0	21.2	25.4	20.9
	U	19.7	15.4	18.0	24.0	28.0	26.1
	L	33.4	22.8	16.0	28.4	44.6	26.6
Inadequate care		35.6	25.8	20.4	32.2	48.1	33.9
	U	37.9	29.3	25.9	36.5	51.9	43.1
	L	26.9	17.4	7.4	35.0	35.4	16.4
Education not stated		31.0	23.5	13.0	45.5	46.0	30.0[d]
	U	35.7	31.0	21.1	59.2	59.8	50.4
	L	11.7	12.0	5.8	0.0	0.7	0.0
Adequate care		18.1	20.2[d]	15.9[d]	e	e	e
	U	26.8	31.9	34.7	257.5	163.8	208.5
	L	20.7	10.4	7.0	26.7	22.7	6.8
Intermediate care		25.9	17.5	15.2[d]	40.1[d]	36.2[d]	20.9[d]
	U	32.4	27.7	28.9	58.1	54.7	48.7
	L	37.2	26.1	0.1	36.7	38.7	22.3
Inadequate care		45.5	42.1[d]	3.8[d]	54.4[d]	54.2[d]	48.6[d]
	U	55.5	64.4	21.2	77.8	73.7	92.3
	L	25.3	23.9	12.5	22.6	42.2	21.1
None, elementary		27.7	32.8	15.9	26.0	50.7	29.5
	U	30.3	44.0	20.2	29.9	60.8	40.1
	L	10.8	1.2	5.7	12.3	12.9	7.1
Adequate care		16.9	10.3[d]	11.5[d]	37.9[d]	e	e
	U	25.2	37.2	20.6	88.3	182.5	100.7
	L	19.4	21.3	10.4	17.0	29.2	12.3
Intermediate care		22.4	33.6[d]	14.5	21.0	39.4	20.7[d]
	U	25.8	50.4	19.7	26.0	52.0	32.7
	L	32.9	24.7	14.7	26.2	48.3	27.4
Inadequate care		37.3	40.4[d]	22.3	32.0	60.5	43.7[d]
	U	42.3	62.2	32.6	39.0	75.6	66.0

TABLE A-8 *(Continued)*

Risk Category and Three-Factor Index	Confi-dence Limit	Total	White Native Born	White Foreign Born	Puerto Rican	Black Native Born	All Others
	L	26.7	18.8	11.6	22.0	34.1	21.1
High school, 1–3 years		**28.5**	**21.8**	**16.3**	**25.4**	**37.4**	**29.6**
	U	30.4	25.3	22.2	29.2	41.1	40.3
	L	15.1	12.1	4.4	10.3	13.4	22.0
Adequate care		**20.4**	**17.9**	**12.1**^{d}	**28.2**^{d}	**36.6**^{d}	**60.0**^{d}
	U	26.9	25.6	26.4	61.5	79.8	130.8
	L	18.8	14.5	8.1	16.5	20.4	16.1
Intermediate care		**21.1**	**18.5**	**13.7**	**20.4**	**24.5**	**26.3**^{d}
	U	23.7	23.5	21.6	25.3	29.4	40.5
	L	35.9	22.9	14.2	26.7	43.8	15.6
Inadequate care		**39.2**	**29.2**	**24.9**^{d}	**32.6**	**49.1**	**28.5**^{d}
	U	42.8	37.1	40.3	39.8	55.0	47.9
	L	18.2	13.4	12.4	15.5	28.9	17.0
High school, 4 years		**19.4**	**14.7**	**15.2**	**19.4**	**31.9**	**22.1**
	U	20.6	16.1	18.5	24.3	35.2	28.7
	L	12.1	11.6	9.9	3.4	13.2	3.3
Adequate care		**13.7**	**13.4**	**13.9**	**10.6**^{d}	**22.2**^{d}	**10.3**^{d}
	U	15.5	15.5	18.9	24.7	35.1	24.0
	L	15.2	11.0	10.4	13.7	20.0	13.4
Intermediate care		**16.7**	**12.9**	**14.2**	**18.4**	**23.4**	**19.9**
	U	18.3	15.1	19.0	24.3	27.4	28.5
	L	29.8	19.9	13.6	16.5	38.0	21.9
Inadequate care		**32.9**	**24.3**	**21.2**	**24.5**	**43.8**	**33.2**^{d}
	U	36.3	29.6	31.6	35.0	50.4	48.5
	L	11.5	8.9	11.1	6.1	19.5	11.7
Some college or higher		**12.9**	**10.3**	**15.2**	**15.1**^{d}	**25.3**	**17.7**
	U	14.5	11.9	20.4	31.1	32.9	25.8
	L	8.3	7.8	6.5	2.2	1.5	6.2
Adequate care		**10.1**	**9.7**	**11.3**	**18.5**^{d}	**7.2**^{d}	**15.4**^{d}
	U	12.3	12.0	18.3	66.8	21.0	31.7
	L	10.7	7.3	12.3	4.6	13.5	9.5
Intermediate care		**12.9**	**9.5**	**19.0**	**16.8**^{d}	**20.7**	**17.8**^{d}
	U	15.5	12.4	28.1	43.0	30.4	30.4
	L	17.3	10.8	6.6	0.2	28.6	8.3
Inadequate care		**22.0**	**16.0**	**16.4**^{d}	**8.4**^{d}	**42.3**^{d}	**20.6**^{d}
	U	27.9	22.9	33.8	46.8	60.5	42.4

^{a} Rate in underscored bold type indicates actual calculated rate.

^{b} Lower confidence limit.

^{c} Upper confidence limit.

^{d} Based on 100–999 live births.

^{e} Less than 100 live births; rate not computed.

Supplementary Tables for Chapter 2 and New York City Birth and Death Record Forms

TABLE B-1 Number of Live Births by Sociodemographic Risks: New York City Live-Birth Cohort, 1968

Sociodemographic Risk[a]	Total Number of Infants at Risk[b]
TOTAL	56,719
Age of mother/ total birth order	28,056
All under 15	437
15–19/2 or more	5,158
20–24/4 or more	4,566
25–29/5 or more	5,085
30–34/first child or 6 or more	5,993
35–39/first child or 5 or more	4,227
All 40 or more	2,590
Education of mother (completed years) 8 or less	18,734
Illegitimate births	26,293

[a] All sociodemographic risks are identifiable at the first prenatal visit.
[b] Number at risk is less than sum for separate risks because of multiple risks in some cases.

TABLE B-2 Number of Live Births by Medical–Obstetric Risks: New York City Live-Birth Cohort, 1968

Medical–Obstetric Risk[a]	Number of Infants	Medical–Obstetric Risk Identifiable		
		At 1st Pre-natal Visit	During Pregnancy	At Labor
TOTAL	41,053	34,490	5,918	7,760
Previous pregnancy history				
Death among previous live births	5,447	5,447		[b]
Previous fetal death				
gestation less than 20 weeks	16,492	16,492		[b]
gestation 20 weeks or more	4,240	4,240		[b]
Previous delivery within year	3,665	3,665		[b]
Conditions present during pregnancy				
Pre-eclampsia	2,979		2,979	[b]
Eclampsia	56		56	[b]
Hypertensive disease	932	932	932	[b]
Uterine bleeding, not in labor				
1st trimester	473		473	[b]
2nd trimester	210		210	[b]
3rd trimester	598		598	[b]
trimester not stated	116		116	[b]
Pyelonephritis	417	417	417	[b]
Heart disease	480	480		[b]
Diabetes	1,079	1,079		[b]
Syphilis	313	313		[b]
Tuberculosis	110	110		[b]
German measles				
1st trimester	23		23	[b]
Narcotic addiction	251	251		[b]
Benign or malignant neoplasm	375	375		[b]
Laboratory findings				
Positive serology	726	726		[b]
Positive cytology	249	249		[b]
Indications for operative delivery				
Maternal and fetal complications				
Rupture of uterus	12			12
Violent accident or trauma	3			3
Placenta previa, premature separation, abruptio placentae	667			667
Fetal distress	1,450			1,450
Bleeding	33		33	33
Previous Cesarean section	3,359	3,359		[b]

TABLE B-2 (*Continued*)

Medical–Obstetric Risk[a]	Number of Infants	Medical–Obstetric Risk Identifiable		
		At 1st Prenatal Visit	During Pregnancy	At Labor
Cardiac disease, diabetes, tuberculosis	205	205		b
Toxemia, nephritis, pyelitis	200		200	b
Prolonged labor	1,474			1,474
Congenital malformations of the mother making normal delivery impossible	16	16		b
Habitual abortion, Rh incompatibility	62	62		b
Maternal exhaustion	12			12
Elderly primipara	120	120		b
Cesarean section with premature rupture of membranes	264			264
Abnormal presentation				
Transverse arrest	1,016			1,016
Persistent occiput posterior position	749			749
Breech presentation	1,640			1,640
Other abnormal presentation	405			405
Dystocia				
Cephalo-pelvic disproportion	2,292	2,292		b
Cervical dystocia	21			21
Nonengagement of head	7			7
Impacted shoulders	2			2
Contraction ring	2			2
Dystocia associated with pelvic tumor, fibroids, ovarian cancer	55	55	55	b
Dystocia due to short cord	3		3	

[a] Number at risk is less than the sum for separate risks because of multiple risks in some cases.
[b] Category not applicable.

TABLE B-3 Alternative Combinations of Total Birth Order and Age of Mother for Categorizing Sociodemographic Risk

Alternative	Total Birth Order		Age of Mother (years)
I	5th and higher	or	All under 15
		or	All 40 and over
II	1	and	Under 15 or 30 and over
	2,3	and	Under 20 or 35 and over
	4	and	Under 25 or 35 and over
	5, 6th and higher	and	All ages
III	1	and	Under 15 or 30 and over
	2,3	and	Under 20 or 40 and over
	4	and	Under 25 or 40 and over
	5	and	Under 30 or 35 and over
	6th and higher	and	All ages
IV	1	and	Under 15 or 30 and over
	2–4	and	Under 20 or 40 and over
	5	and	Under 25 or 40 and over
	6th and higher	and	All ages

CERTIFICATE OF BIRTH

Birth No._____

DATE FILED

1. FULL NAME OF CHILD (Type or Print) | First Name | Middle Name | Last Name

2. SEX

3a. NUMBER OF CHILDREN born of this pregnancy
3b. If more than one, number of this child in order of birth

4a. DATE OF CHILD'S BIRTH (Month) (Day) (Year)
4b. Hour ____ AM / PM

5. PLACE OF BIRTH
a. New York City
b. Borough
c. Name of Hospital or Institution. If not in hospital, street address.

6a. MOTHER'S FULL MAIDEN NAME
6b. MOTHER'S AGE at time of this birth
6c. MOTHER'S BIRTHPLACE, City and State. If not U. S. A., Country.

7. MOTHER'S USUAL RESIDENCE
a. State
b. County
c. City, town or location.
d. Inside city limits (Specify Yes or No)
e. Street and house number

8a. FATHER'S FULL NAME
8b. FATHER'S AGE at time of this birth
8c. FATHER'S BIRTHPLACE, City and State. If not U.S.A., Country

I hereby certify that this child was born alive at the hour and on the date stated above, and that all the facts stated in this certificate and report of birth are true to the best of my knowledge, information and belief.

(Signed)_____

Name of Signer_____ C.R.N. / R.N. / D.O. / M.D.

(Type or Print)

Address_____

Date of Report_____19___

Given name added from a supplemental report _____
(Date of)

_____
Borough Registrar.

BUREAU OF RECORDS AND STATISTICS — DEPARTMENT OF HEALTH — THE CITY OF NEW YORK

Print here the mailing address of mother→
Copy of this certificate will be mailed to her when it is filed with the Department of Health.

Name._____
Address._____ Apt._____
City._____ State._____ Zip Code._____

Each question MUST be answered.

CONFIDENTIAL MEDICAL REPORT

Only for scientific purposes approved by the Board of Health; not open to inspection or subject to subpoena

Name of Child._____ Birth No._____

2H (Rev. 69)

2H (Rev. 69)
450M - 722032 (69)

THIS CERTIFICATE NOT VALID UNLESS FILED IN THE HEALTH DEPARTMENT.
DO NOT WRITE IN THIS SPACE, MARGIN RESERVED FOR CODING AND BINDING.

Cert. No.

Died : Date

Place

170

9. PREVIOUS BIRTHS

		1.	10a. Date of Last Previous Live Birth	10b. Date of Last Previous Fetal Death

9a. If none check here ☐

9b. Are now living?

9c. Were born alive now dead?

Were born dead (fetal death)
- **9d.** Less than 20 weeks gestation
- **9e.** 20 weeks plus gestation

10a. Date of Last Previous Live Birth — Month Day Year

10b. Date of Last Previous Fetal Death — Month Day Year

11a. Mother's Race (White, Negro, etc.)

12a. Mother's Education (Highest grade completed)
- Elementary (0, 1, 2, 3...... or 8)
- High School (1, 2, 3, or 4)
- College (1, 2, 3, 4, or 5+)

13. Date last normal menses began — Month Day Year

14. Date of first prenatal visit. If none, so state — Month Day Year

11b. Father's Race (White, Negro, etc.)

12b. Father's Education (Highest grade completed)
- Elementary (0, 1, 2, 3...... or 8)
- High School (1, 2, 3, or 4)
- College (1, 2, 3, 4, or 5+)

15. Mother's Blood Group and RH

16. Total number of prenatal visits

17. Conditions present during THIS pregnancy (check one or more items):

- 01 ☐ Pre-eclampsia
- 02 ☐ Eclampsia
- 03 ☐ Hypertensive disease
- 04 ☐ Uterine bleeding not associated with labor. Check trimester
  - 05 ☐ 1st   06 ☐ 2nd   07 ☐ 3rd
- 08 ☐ Pyelo-nephritis
- 09 ☐ Heart disease
- 10 ☐ Diabetes
- 11 ☐ Syphilis
- 12 ☐ Tuberculosis
- 13 ☐ German measles. Check trimester
  - 14 ☐ 1st   15 ☐ 2nd   16 ☐ 3rd
- 17 ☐ Other viral disease. Specify
- 18 ☐ Check trimester   19 ☐ 1st   20 ☐ 2nd   3rd
- 21 ☐ Narcotic Addiction
- 22 ☐ Benign or malignant neoplasm or related conditions. Specify
- 23 ☐ Other condition. Specify
- 24 ☐ Injury or operation. Specify
- 99 ☐ None known

18. During THIS pregnancy were the following tests done:

a. Serologic test for Syphilis: ☐ No ☐ Yes   Date........   Result........

b. Cytologic test for CA of Cervix: ☐ No ☐ Yes   Date........   Result........ (Check One) ☐ Unsatisfactory ☐ Positive ☐ Negative ☐ Suspicious ☐ Other, Specify

19. Method of induction. If not induced, state "none"........ Indication........

20. Method of stimulation (augmentation). If not stimulated, state "none"........ Indication........

21. Specify manual, instrumental, or operative procedures used. If none, so state........

22. Indications for procedures........

23. Indicate by X whether mother was .... private physician's patient ☐ .... general service patient ☐

24. Did delivery occur on ambulance service? ☐ Yes ☐ No

25. Weight at birth .... lbs. .... ounces or .... grams
  1. ....   2. ....

26. What was position at delivery? ....

27. Duration of labor: 1st stage .... hours; 2nd stage .... hours .... minutes   **28.** Apgar Score: 1 minute .... ; 5 minute ....

29. Congenital abnormality? (circle one): Questionable Yes No

30. Birth injury? (circle one) Questionable Yes No

31. Describe abnormality and/or injuries........

If Cesarean section primary or repeat? ....

Side labels (left column)

- Plurality
- Institution
- Nativ. M F R
- Ed. M   Ed. F
- Bld. Type Rh
- Conditions
- Sero.   Cyto.
- Labor — Ind.   Stim.
- Delivery
- A   P
- Labor — 1   2
- Apgar — 1   5
- Cong. Malf.
- O W

171

CERTIFICATE OF FETAL DEATH

Did heart beat after birth? .... *Was there movement of voluntary muscles?* ....
Such cases must be reported by filing a certificate of birth and a certificate of death.

Certificate No. ....

DATE FILED

1. SEX OF FETUS
☐ Male
☐ Female
☐ Undetermined

2a. NUMBER OF CHILDREN born of this pregnancy

2b. If more than one, number of this child in order of birth

3a. DATE OF DELIVERY OR OPERATION FOR DELIVERY (Month) (Day) (Year)

3b. Hour ☐ AM ☐ PM

4. PLACE OF DELIVERY
a. New York City
b. Borough

c. Name of Hospital or Institution. If not in hospital, street address.

5a. MOTHER'S FULL MAIDEN NAME

5b. MOTHER'S AGE at time of this delivery

5c. MOTHER'S BIRTHPLACE, City and State. If not U. S. A., Country.

6. MOTHER'S USUAL RESIDENCE
a. State
b. County
c. City, town or location
d. Inside city limits (Specify Yes or No)
e. Street and house number

7a. FATHER'S FULL NAME

7b. FATHER'S AGE at time of this delivery

7c. FATHER'S BIRTHPLACE, City and State. If not U. S. A., Country.

8. I hereby certify that I attended professionally (at) (after) this delivery which occurred at the hour and on the date stated above, that all the facts stated in this certificate are true to the best of my knowledge, information and belief.

Signature .... ☐ D.O. ☐ M.D.

Name of Physician .... (Type or Print)

Address ....

Date .... 19 ....

FUNERAL DIRECTOR'S CERTIFICATE

I hereby certify that I have been employed as Funeral Director herein by .... of ....

This statement is made to obtain a permit for the burial or cremation of the fetus described in this certificate.

Signature of Funeral Director

State License No.

Address

PLACE OF BURIAL OR CREMATION

DATE of Burial or Cremation

BUREAU OF RECORDS AND STATISTICS   DEPARTMENT OF HEALTH   THE CITY OF NEW YORK

CONFIDENTIAL MEDICAL REPORT

Each question MUST be answered.

Only for scientific purposes approved by the Board of Health; not open to inspection or subject to subpoena

Surname of Mother .... Certificate No. ....

8H (Rev. 69)

8H (Rev. 69)
135M - 722052 (69)

DO NOT WRITE IN THIS SPACE, MARGIN RESERVED FOR CODING AND BINDING

172

1.

2. OXX XXX

9. PREVIOUS BIRTHS

	Were born alive	Were born dead (fetal death)
	9.a. Are now living?	Less than 20 weeks gestation	20 weeks plus gestation

If none check here

9.a. Were born alive
9.b. Are now living?
9.c. Less than 20 weeks gestation
9.d. 20 weeks plus gestation
9.e.

11a. Mother's Race (White, Negro, etc.)

12a. Mother's Education (Highest grade completed)
Elementary (0, 1, 2, 3, ... or 8)
High School (1, 2, 3, or 4)
College (1, 2, 3, 4, or 5+)

11b. Father's Race (White, Negro, etc.)

12b. Father's Education (Highest grade completed)
Elementary (0, 1, 2, 3, ... or 8)
High School (1, 2, 3, or 4)
College (1, 2, 3, 4, or 5+)

10a. Date of Last Previous Live Birth — Month Day Year

10b. Date of Last Previous Fetal Death — Month Day Year

13. Date last normal menses began — Month Day Year

14. Date of first prenatal visit — If none, so state — Month Day Year

15. Mother's Blood Group and RH

16. Total number of prenatal visits

17. Conditions present during THIS pregnancy (check one or more items)

01 ☐ Pre-eclampsia
02 ☐ Eclampsia
03 ☐ Hypertensive disease
04 ☐ Uterine bleeding not associated with labor. Check trimester
   1st ☐ 05   2nd ☐ 06   3rd ☐ 07

08 ☐ Pyelo-nephritis
09 ☐ Heart disease
10 ☐ Diabetes
11 ☐ Syphilis
12 ☐ Tuberculosis

13 ☐ German measles
   Check trimester
   1st ☐ 14   2nd ☐ 15   3rd ☐ 16
17 ☐ Other viral disease. Specify
18 ☐ Syphilis
   Check trimester
   1st ☐ 19   2nd ☐ 20   3rd ☐ ...
21 ☐ Narcotic Addiction

22 ☐ Benign or malignant neoplasm or related conditions. Specify
23 ☐ Other condition. Specify
24 ☐ Injury or operation. Specify
99 ☐ None known

18. During THIS pregnancy were the following tests done:
a. Serologic test for Syphilis: ☐ No ☐ Yes Date........ Result........
b. Cytologic test for CA of Cervix: ☐ No ☐ Yes Date........ Result: ☐ Unsatisfactory ☐ Positive ☐ Negative ☐ Suspicious
   (Check One) ☐ Other, Specify........

19. Method of induction
   If not induced, state "none"........ Indication........

20. Method of stimulation (augmentation)
   If not stimulated, state "none"........ Indication........

21. Specify manual, instrumental, or operative procedures used. If none, so state.

22. Indications for procedures.

23. Indicate by X whether mother was
   private physician's patient ☐
   general service patient ☐

24. Did delivery occur on ambulance service? ☐ Yes ☐ No
   Specify fetal or maternal

25. Fetal death was caused by
   Part I. a. Immediate cause.
   b. Due to.
   c. Due to.
   If Cesarean section primary or repeat?........
   If so, give date........

Part II. Other significant conditions of fetus or mother

26. Did fetal death occur before labor?........ during labor?........ If during labor, give stage.
   before operation?........ during operation?........
   27. Was autopsy performed?........

ITEMS 28 and following ones to be answered only when 16 or more weeks gestation have been completed

28. Weight at birth........ lbs........ ounces or........ grams
   1. 2.

29. What was position at delivery?........

30. Duration of Labor: 1st stage........ hours; 2nd stage........ hours........ minutes

31. Congenital abnormality? (circle one) Yes No Questionable

32. Birth injury? (circle one) Yes No Questionable

33. Describe abnormality and/or injuries.

Plurality

Institution

Nativ. MF B

Ed. M   Ed. F

Bld. Type Rh

Conditions

Sero.   Cyto.

Labor Ind. Stim.

Delivery

A   P

Labor 1   2

Cons.   Malf.

Lab   Died Oper.

Autopsy

Cause FD

O W

DO NOT WRITE IN THIS SPACE, MARGIN RESERVED FOR CODING AND BINDING

CERTIFICATE OF DEATH

Certificate No. ....

17H (Rev. 69)
437.5M - 722032 (69)

DATE FILED ....

1. NAME OF DECEASED ....
(Type or Print)
First Name .... Middle-Name .... Last Name

MEDICAL CERTIFICATE OF DEATH (To be filled in by the Physician)

2. PLACE OF DEATH
a. New York City
b. Borough
c. Name of Hospital or Institution. If not in hospital, street address

3a. DATE AND HOUR OF DEATH
(Month) (Day) (Year)
3b. Hour .... AM / PM
4. SEX
5. APPROXIMATE AGE
M on ....

6. I HEREBY CERTIFY THAT (I attended the deceased)* (a staff physician of this institution attended the deceased)* (Dr. ....
attended the deceased)* from .... 19........, to ...., 19........ and last saw h........ alive at .... M on ....

19........ I further certify† that traumatic injury or poisoning DID NOT play any part in causing death, and that death did not occur in any unusual
manner and was due entirely to NATURAL CAUSES. *Cross out words that do not apply. † See first instruction on reverse of certificate.

Witness my hand this........ day of........ 19........ Signature ....
Name of Physician .... Address ....
Type or Print

D.O.
M.D.

PERSONAL PARTICULARS (To be filled in by Funeral Director)

7. USUAL RESIDENCE
a. State
b. County
c. City or Town
d. Inside city limits (Specify Yes or No)
e. Street and house number
f. Length of residence or stay in City of New York immediately prior to death

8. SINGLE, MARRIED, WIDOWED or DIVORCED (Write in word)

9. NAME OF SURVIVING SPOUSE (If wife, give maiden name)

10. DATE OF BIRTH OF DECEDENT
(Month) (Day) (Year)

11. AGE at last birthday
Yrs.
If UNDER 1 year: mos. / days
If LESS than 1 day: hrs. or / min.

12a. USUAL OCCUPATION (Kind of work done during most of working life, even if retired.)
b. KIND OF BUSINESS or INDUSTRY

13. SOCIAL SECURITY NO.

14. BIRTHPLACE (State or Foreign Country)

15. OF WHAT COUNTRY WAS DECEASED A CITIZEN AT TIME OF DEATH

16. ANY OTHER NAME(S) BY WHICH DECEDENT WAS KNOWN

17. NAME OF FATHER OF DECEDENT

18. MAIDEN NAME OF MOTHER OF DECEDENT

19a. NAME OF INFORMANT
b. RELATIONSHIP TO DECEASED
c. ADDRESS

Institution
Boro-Resid.
Area-Dist.
R C
Native. Dec.
Cause 1
Operation
Att.-Autop.
Cem.
Type Accid.
Occurrence

THIS CERTIFICATE NOT VALID UNLESS FILED IN THE HEALTH DEPARTMENT.
DO NOT WRITE IN THIS SPACE, MARGIN RESERVED FOR CODING AND BINDING.

174

17H (Rev. 69)

20a. NAME OF CEMETERY OR CREMATORY | LOCATION (City, Town or Country and State) | c. DATE of Burial or Cremation

21a. FUNERAL DIRECTOR | b. ADDRESS

BUREAU OF RECORDS AND STATISTICS — DEPARTMENT OF HEALTH — THE CITY OF NEW YORK

Certificate No.

PHYSICIAN'S CONFIDENTIAL MEDICAL REPORT

I am submitting herewith a confidential report of the cause of death of:

FULL NAME OF DECEASED (Type or Print) | 22. COLOR OR RACE OF DECEDENT

23. DEATH WAS CAUSED BY:

(Describe Below)

| | INTERVAL BETWEEN ONSET AND DEATH |

N.B. Enter only one cause each for (a), (b), and (c).

1
a. IMMEDIATE CAUSE. This does not mean the mode of dying such as heart failure, asthenia, etc. It means the disease or complication which caused death.

PART 1

a. Immediate Cause

b. Due to or as a consequence of

c. Due to or as a consequence of

b. and c. ANTECEDENT. CAUSES. Morbid conditions, if any, giving rise to the above cause (a) stating the underlying cause last.

2
Conditions contributing to the death, but not related to the terminal condition mentioned in Part 1. (a)

PART 2

Other Significant Conditions

24. IF DEATH OF FEMALE

Any history of pregnancy in last 6 months? | If so, was she delivered?

If Yes, date of delivery | Liveborn or stillborn?

25. OPERATION

Date of (If none, so state) | Major findings of operation

26. AUTOPSY—Date of (If none, so state)

Signature _____ D.O. M.D.

Address _____

BUREAU OF RECORDS AND STATISTICS—DEPARTMENT OF HEALTH—THE CITY OF NEW YORK

175

....M.D.

† CAUTION TO PHYSICIANS: BEFORE SIGNING READ THIS ENTIRE STATEMENT CAREFULLY

Section 878-1.0 of the Administrative code for the City of New York provides that the death of any person from criminal violence or by a casualty or by a suicide, or suddenly while in apparent health, or when unattended by a physician, or in any suspicious or unusual manner, shall be reported forthwith to the office of the Chief Medical Examiner. Only the Medical Examiner may issue a death certificate in such cases.

FAILURE TO REPORT TO THE MEDICAL EXAMINER IS A MISDEMEANOR

† Section 205.03 (a) (2) of the New York City Health Code provides that if a death from natural causes occurs elsewhere than in a hospital, the death must be reported by the licensed physician in attendance or by his duly authorized medical associate, provided that whoever reports the death, certifies (by signing the certification provided on the left hand margin of this side of the certificate) that he has visited the scene of death, viewed the body, and has found no evidence of suspicions or unusual circumstances.

TO FUNERAL DIRECTORS

This certificate must be accompanied by the Confidential Medical Report. No permit for the disposal of the body can be granted until the Confidential Medical Report is filed. Divulging the information contained in the Confidential Medical Report, or delivery of that Report to any one other than a licensed funeral director, or an official of the Bureau of Records and Statistics of the Department of Health designated to receive such reports, will result in the prosecution under the provisions of the Health Code.

Removal of bodies prohibited without permit. Except when such removal is ordered in connection with an investigation conducted by a Medical Examiner, a District Attorney or the Police Department, Section 205.23 of the Health Code prohibits the removal of the body of a human being, who died in the City of New York, unless a permit therefor has been obtained from the Department of Health.

Permission to remove dead bodies granted by telephone. In keeping with Section 205.23, the Department of Health will grant to registered funeral directors by telephone, permission for the removal of a body from the place of death to another location within the city for preparation for burial, provided the application is made by a registered funeral director who has the certificate of death in his possession at the time of telephoning.

FUNERAL DIRECTOR'S CERTIFICATE

It is hereby certified that the undersigned has been employed to dispose of the remains of ....

by .... of ....

who is the .... and the nearest surviving relative or next of kin of the deceased. This statement is
    (Relationship)

made to obtain a permit for disposition of the remains of the deceased.

Name of establishment... State Business Registration No...................

By.. State License No...................
    (Signature of registered funeral director)

    To be Filled in by the Funeral Director When Obtaining Removal Permit by Telephone

Telephone Removal No................... granted by...(Burial Clerk)

Date................... Hour................... (A.M.) (P.M.) ....
    (Funeral Director)

Deaths that are even remotely associated with an earlier accident, must be referred to the Medical Examiner.

DO NOT WRITE IN THIS SPACE, RESERVED FOR HEALTH DEPARTMENT RECORDS.

176

Supplementary Tables for Chapter 4

TABLE C-1   Fetal Deaths and Death Ratios by Color and Infant Deaths and Infant Death Rates by Color and Age: United States, 1968

Age at Death	Total	White	All Others	Total	White	All Others
		Number		Deaths per 1,000 Live Births		
Infant deaths						
Under 1 year	76,263	55,902	20,361	21.8	19.2	34.5
Under 28 days	56,456	42,904	13,552	16.1	14.7	23.0
Under 1 day	33,304	25,305	7,999	9.5	8.7	13.6
Under 1 hour	6,519	4,986	1,533	1.9	1.7	2.6
1–23 hours	26,785	20,319	6,466	7.6	7.0	11.0
1 day	8,153	6,369	1,784	2.3	2.2	3.0
2 days	4,790	3,766	1,024	1.4	1.3	1.7
3 days	2,147	1,664	483	0.6	0.6	0.8
4 days	1,251	905	346	0.4	0.3	0.6
5 days	953	721	232	0.3	0.2	0.4
6 days	677	496	181	0.2	0.2	0.3
7–13 days	2,457	1,818	639	0.7	0.6	1.1
14–20 days	1,453	1,009	444	0.4	0.3	0.8
21–27 days	1,271	851	420	0.4	0.3	0.8
28–59 days	4,721	3,168	1,553	1.3	1.1	2.6
2 months	3,795	2,498	1,297	1.1	0.9	2.2
3 months	2,958	1,934	1,024	0.8	0.7	1.7
4 months	2,057	1,338	719	0.6	0.5	1.2
5 months	1,471	922	549	0.4	0.3	0.9
6 months	1,201	771	430	0.3	0.3	0.7
7 months	939	614	325	0.3	0.2	0.5
8 months	733	484	249	0.2	0.2	0.4
9 months	755	491	264	0.2	0.2	0.4
10 months	588	383	205	0.2	0.1	0.3
11 months	589	395	194	0.2	0.1	0.3
Live births	3,501,564	2,912,224	589,340			
Fetal deaths[a]	55,293	40,206	15,087	15.8	13.8	25.6

[a] Fetal deaths include only those for which the period of gestation was given as 20 complete weeks or more or was not stated.
Source: U.S. Department of Health, Education, and Welfare, Vital Statistics of the United States, 1968. Vol II–Part A, Washington, D.C., 1972.

Appendix C

TABLE C-2 Perinatal and Fetal Death Ratios and Infant Mortality Rates by Age at Death, Color, and Age of Mother: United States, 1960 Birth Cohort

Age of Mother (years)/Color	Rate (ratio) per 1,000 Live Births				
	Mortality Ratio		Mortality Rate		
	Perinatal	Fetal	Neonatal	Postneonatal	Infant
TOTAL	34.5	16.1	18.4	6.7	25.1
Under 15	73.6	32.4	41.2	17.6	58.7
15–19	36.7	14.0	22.7	10.2	32.8
20–24	29.3	12.1	17.3	6.9	24.2
25–29	31.0	14.4	16.6	5.8	22.4
30–34	37.7	19.4	18.3	5.3	23.7
35–39	47.0	27.3	19.7	5.8	25.5
40–44	62.7	39.6	23.1	7.5	30.6
45 and over	93.0	61.8	31.3	9.8	41.1
White	31.0	14.1	16.9	5.3	22.2
Under 15	62.6	30.5	32.1	15.5	47.5
15–19	32.2	11.9	20.4	7.7	28.1
20–24	26.6	10.7	15.9	5.5	21.4
25–29	28.1	12.8	15.3	4.6	20.0
30–34	33.9	17.0	17.0	4.2	21.2
35–39	42.3	23.9	18.4	4.5	22.9
40–44	57.3	35.2	22.0	6.1	28.1
45 and over	87.4	55.6	31.8	7.1	38.9
Nonwhite	53.5	26.8	26.7	14.7	41.4
Under 15	80.1	33.6	46.5	18.8	65.3
15–19	52.4	21.5	30.9	18.6	49.5
20–24	45.5	20.2	25.3	14.8	40.2
25–29	48.7	24.5	24.2	13.1	37.3
30–34	60.2	33.9	26.4	12.0	38.4
35–39	74.6	47.3	27.3	13.9	41.2
40–44	93.9	64.5	29.4	15.4	44.7
45 and over	117.5	88.7	28.9	21.6	50.5

Source: U.S. Department of Health, Education, and Welfare, National Center for Health Statistics (unpublished data).

TABLE C-3 Perinatal and Fetal Death Ratios and Infant Mortality Rates by Age at Death, Color, and Total Birth Order: United States, 1960 Birth Cohort

| Total Birth Order/Color | Rate (ratio) per 1,000 Live Births | | | | |
| | Mortality Ratio | | Mortality Rate | | |
	Perinatal	Fetal	Neonatal	Postneonatal	Infant
TOTAL	34.5	16.1	18.4	6.7	25.1
First	32.4	16.0	16.4	4.9	21.3
Second	28.6	11.2	17.4	6.1	23.5
Third	30.3	13.2	17.1	6.5	23.6
Fourth	34.5	16.1	18.4	6.9	25.3
Fifth	40.4	19.7	20.7	8.2	28.8
Sixth and higher	53.8	28.5	25.3	11.1	36.4
White	31.0	14.1	16.9	5.3	22.2
First	29.2	14.2	15.0	4.1	19.1
Second	26.2	10.2	16.1	5.0	21.1
Third	28.1	12.2	15.9	5.4	21.2
Fourth	32.0	14.8	17.2	5.5	22.7
Fifth	37.5	18.1	19.3	6.3	25.7
Sixth and higher	48.3	24.5	23.7	8.1	31.8
Nonwhite	53.5	26.8	26.7	14.7	41.4
First	53.8	28.1	25.7	10.9	36.6
Second	46.3	19.1	27.2	14.3	41.5
Third	46.5	20.6	25.8	14.7	40.5
Fourth	48.7	23.3	25.4	15.1	40.5
Fifth	52.7	26.3	26.3	16.1	42.4
Sixth and higher	65.8	37.1	28.6	17.6	46.3

Source: U.S. Department of Health, Education, and Welfare. National Center for Health Statistics (unpublished data).

Appendix C

TABLE C-4 Fetal Death Ratios and Infant Mortality Rates by Age at Death and Color: United States, 1935–1968

	Rate (ratio) per 1,000 Live Births							
Year and Color	Fetal	Under 1 Year	Under 28 Days[a]	Under 1 Day	1–6 Days	7–27 Days[b]	1–5 Months	6–11 Months
Total White and Nonwhite								
1968	15.8	21.8	16.1	9.5	5.1	1.5	4.3	1.4
1967	15.6	22.4	16.5	9.6	5.3	1.5	4.5	1.4
1966	15.7	23.7	17.2	9.9	5.5	1.6	4.9	1.3
1965	16.2	24.7	17.7	10.2	5.7	1.7	5.3	1.7
1964	16.4	24.8	17.9	10.2	5.8	1.8	5.1	1.7
1963	15.8	25.2	18.2	10.4	6.0	1.8	5.2	1.7
1962	15.9	25.3	18.3	10.4	6.1	1.9	5.2	1.8
1961	16.1	25.3	18.4	10.3	6.2	1.9	5.2	1.8
1960	16.1	26.0	18.7	10.3	6.4	2.0	5.4	1.9
1959	16.2	26.4	19.0	10.3	6.6	2.1	5.4	1.9
1958	16.5	27.1	19.5	10.2	6.9	2.3	5.6	2.0
1957	16.3	26.3	19.1	9.9	6.8	2.4	5.3	2.0
1956	16.5	26.0	18.9	9.9	6.7	2.2	5.1	2.0
1955	17.1	26.4	19.1	10.0	7.0	2.2	5.2	2.1
1954	17.5	26.6	19.1	9.6	7.1	2.3	5.3	2.2
1953	17.8	27.8	19.6	9.7	7.5	2.4	5.8	2.4
1952	18.3	28.4	19.8	9.7	7.5	2.6	6.0	2.6
1951	18.8	28.4	20.0	9.8	7.7	2.6	5.9	2.5
1950	19.2	29.2	20.5	10.2	7.7	2.7	6.0	2.7
1949	19.8	31.3	21.4	10.5	7.8	3.1	7.0	2.9
1948	20.6	32.0	22.2	10.7	8.2	3.3	6.9	3.0
1947	21.1	32.2	22.8	10.7	8.5	3.5	6.7	2.7
1946	22.8	33.8	24.0	11.4	8.6	4.0	6.8	2.9
1945	23.9	38.3	24.3	11.2	8.5	4.6	9.6	4.4
1944	24.5	39.8	24.7	11.5	8.5	4.7	10.1	4.9
1943	24.5	40.4	24.7	11.6	8.4	4.8	10.5	5.2
1942	25.6	40.4	25.7	12.3	8.5	4.8	9.9	4.8
1941	d	45.3	27.7	13.2	9.0	5.4	11.8	5.9
1940	d	47.0	28.8	13.9	9.4	5.5	12.2	6.0
1939	d	48.0	29.3	14.1	9.6	5.5	12.2	6.6
1938	d	51.0	29.6	14.1	9.6	5.9	13.8	7.7
1937	d	54.4	31.3	14.7	10.0	6.5	15.0	8.2
1936	d	57.1	32.6	15.1	10.7	6.8	15.8	8.7
1935	d	55.7	32.4	15.0	10.5	6.9	15.0	8.3

TABLE C-4 (*Continued*)

Year and Color	Rate (ratio) per 1,000 Live Births							
	Fetal	Under 1 Year	Under 28 Days[a]	Under 1 Day	1–6 Days	7–27 Days[b]	1–5 Months	6–11 Months
White								
1968	13.8	19.2	14.7	8.7	4.8	1.3	3.4	1.1
1967	13.5	19.7	15.0	8.7	4.9	1.3	3.5	1.1
1966	13.6	20.6	15.6	9.0	5.2	1.3	3.7	1.2
1965	13.9	21.5	16.1	9.3	5.2	1.4	4.0	1.3
1964	14.1	21.6	16.2	9.3	5.4	1.4	3.9	1.4
1963[c]	13.7	22.2	16.7	9.5	5.6	1.5	4.0	1.4
1962[c]	13.9	22.3	16.9	9.6	5.7	1.5	4.0	1.4
1961	14.1	22.4	16.9	9.5	5.8	1.6	4.1	1.4
1960	14.1	22.9	17.2	9.6	6.0	1.7	4.2	1.5
1959	14.2	23.2	17.5	9.5	6.2	1.7	4.2	1.5
1958	14.5	23.8	17.8	9.5	6.4	1.9	4.4	1.6
1957	14.5	23.3	17.5	9.3	6.3	2.0	4.2	1.6
1956	14.6	23.2	17.5	9.3	6.3	1.9	4.1	1.6
1955	15.2	23.6	17.7	9.3	6.6	1.8	4.2	1.7
1954	15.5	23.9	17.8	9.0	6.8	2.0	4.3	1.8
1953	15.9	25.0	18.3	9.1	7.1	2.1	4.7	2.0
1952	16.1	25.5	18.5	9.2	7.1	2.2	4.8	2.1
1951	16.7	25.8	18.9	9.3	7.3	2.3	4.8	2.1
1950	17.1	26.8	19.4	9.7	7.4	2.3	5.1	2.3
1949	17.5	28.9	20.3	10.1	7.5	2.7	6.0	2.5
1948	18.3	29.9	21.2	10.3	7.9	2.9	6.1	2.7
1947	18.7	30.1	21.7	10.4	8.2	3.2	5.9	2.4
1946	20.4	31.8	23.1	11.2	8.4	3.6	6.1	2.6
1945	21.4	35.6	23.3	11.0	8.1	4.1	8.5	3.9
1944	[d]	36.9	23.6	11.2	8.1	4.3	9.0	4.3
1943	[d]	37.5	23.7	11.4	7.9	4.4	9.3	4.5
1942	[d]	37.3	24.5	12.1	8.1	4.4	8.7	4.1
1941	[d]	41.2	26.1	12.9	8.4	4.8	10.2	4.9
1940	[d]	43.2	27.2	13.6	8.8	4.8	10.8	5.2
1939	[d]	44.3	27.8	13.8	9.1	4.9	10.7	5.7
1938	[d]	47.1	28.3	13.9	9.0	5.3	12.2	6.6
1937	[d]	50.3	29.7	14.5	9.4	5.9	13.4	7.2
1936	[d]	52.9	31.0	14.9	10.0	6.1	14.1	7.7
1935	[d]	51.9	31.0	14.8	9.9	6.3	13.5	7.4
Nonwhite								
1968	25.6	34.5	23.0	13.6	6.9	2.6	8.7	2.8
1967	25.8	35.9	23.8	14.2	6.9	2.6	9.2	2.8
1966	26.1	38.8	24.8	14.4	7.3	3.1	10.5	3.3
1965	27.2	40.3	25.4	14.4	7.7	3.3	11.3	3.5

TABLE C-4 (*Continued*)

Year and Color	Fetal	Rate (ratio) per 1,000 Live Births						
		Under 1 Year	Under 28 Days[a]	Under 1 Day	1–6 Days	7–27 Days[b]	1–5 Months	6–11 Months
1964	28.2	41.1	26.5	15.0	7.9	3.5	11.0	3.5
1963[c]	26.7	41.5	26.1	14.6	8.1	3.3	11.5	3.8
1962[c]	26.7	41.4	26.1	14.3	8.1	3.6	11.5	3.8
1961	27.0	40.7	26.2	14.2	8.3	3.8	11.0	3.5
1960	26.8	43.2	26.9	14.4	8.5	4.0	12.1	4.3
1959	27.3	44.0	27.7	14.5	8.8	4.2	12.1	4.1
1958	27.5	45.7	29.0	14.3	10.0	4.7	12.4	4.3
1957	26.8	43.7	27.8	13.9	9.3	4.6	11.6	4.3
1956	27.2	42.1	27.0	13.7	8.9	4.4	10.9	4.1
1955	28.4	42.8	27.2	13.9	9.1	4.2	11.3	4.3
1954	28.9	42.9	27.0	13.3	9.4	4.4	11.3	4.6
1953	29.6	44.7	27.4	12.9	9.8	4.7	12.3	5.0
1952	32.2	47.0	28.0	12.8	10.2	5.0	13.3	5.7
1951	32.1	44.8	27.3	12.7	10.0	4.6	12.2	5.3
1950	32.5	44.5	27.5	13.0	9.8	4.8	11.7	5.2
1949	34.6	47.3	28.6	12.8	10.1	5.7	13.5	5.3
1948	36.5	46.5	29.1	12.9	10.4	5.7	12.3	5.0
1947	39.6	48.5	31.0	13.5	11.2	6.2	12.4	5.1
1946	40.9	49.5	31.5	13.4	11.0	7.2	12.5	5.4
1945	42.0	57.0	32.0	12.7	11.3	8.0	17.3	7.8
1944	d	60.3	32.5	13.2	11.3	8.0	18.4	9.4
1943	d	62.5	32.9	13.2	11.7	8.0	19.2	10.3
1942	d	64.6	34.6	14.4	12.0	8.3	19.7	10.2
1941	d	74.8	39.0	15.7	13.5	9.8	23.0	12.8
1940	d	73.8	39.7	16.0	13.7	10.0	22.5	11.5
1939	d	74.2	39.6	16.2	13.5	9.8	22.2	12.5
1938	d	79.1	39.1	15.8	13.4	9.9	24.9	15.1
1937	d	83.2	42.1	16.1	14.7	11.3	26.0	15.1
1936	d	87.6	43.9	16.4	15.6	11.9	27.9	15.9
1935	d	83.2	42.7	16.2	14.8	11.6	25.8	14.7

[a] From 1935 to 1948, this category refers to deaths under 1 month of age.
[b] From 1935 to 1948, this category refers to deaths at 7–29 days of age.
[c] Figures by color exclude data for residents of New Jersey.
[d] Data not available.

NOTE: Data included Alaska beginning with 1959 and Hawaii beginning with 1960. Events that occurred in New Jersey are excluded from data by color in 1962 and 1963, because color was not reported on the vital records for those years.

Source: Annual volumes *Vital Statistics of the United States*, National Center for Health Statistics, Public Health Service, Washington, D.C., U.S. Government Printing Office.

TABLE C-5 Average Annual Infant Mortality Rates for Selected Causes of Death by Age at Death and Color: United States, 1965-1967

Cause of Death (7th Revision—International Classification of Diseases)		Mortality Rate per 100,000 Live Births								
		Infant			Neonatal			Postneonatal		
		Total	White	Nonwhite	Total	White	Nonwhite	Total	White	Nonwhite
Infective and parasitic diseases	(001-138)	30.1	24.4	58.1	3.5	2.8	7.0	26.6	21.6	51.1
Influenza and pneumonia, including pneumonia of newborn	(480-493,763)	258.8	188.0	605.5	68.8	54.2	140.4	190.0	133.8	465.0
All other diseases of respiratory system	(470-475,500-527)	61.3	48.1	126.1	5.4	4.7	8.7	55.9	43.3	117.4
Gastritis and duodenitis, etc.[a]	(543,571,572,764)	45.3	24.0	149.4	7.8	3.7	28.0	37.5	20.4	121.4
All other diseases of digestive system	(530-542,544-570,573-587)	30.1	28.1	40.2	19.8	19.3	22.5	10.3	8.8	17.7
Congenital malformations	(750-759)	342.4	350.3	303.3	227.5	237.7	177.8	114.8	112.6	125.5
Birth injuries	(760,761)	196.3	188.2	235.6	196.0	188.0	235.2	0.3	0.2	0.4[c]
Intracranial and spinal injury at birth	(760)	63.1	55.7	99.4	63.1	55.7	99.4	d	d	d
Other birth injury	(761)	133.2	132.5	136.3	132.9	132.3	135.8	0.3	0.2	0.4[c]
Postnatal asphyxia and atelectasis	(762)	387.3	348.0	579.5	380.5	342.8	564.8	6.8	5.2	14.7
Hemolytic disease of newborn	(770)	36.3	40.6	15.4	36.0	40.3	14.9	0.3	0.2[c]	0.5[c]
Immaturity unqualified	(776)	363.4	302.6	660.9	361.5	301.7	654.1	1.9	0.9	6.9
Neonatal disorders arising from certain diseases of mother during pregnancy, etc.[b]	(765-769,771-774)	366.4	330.5	541.8	348.1	320.0	485.8	18.3	10.5	56.0
Symptoms and ill-defined conditions	(780-793,795)	70.1	40.0	217.4	19.5	8.9	71.2	50.6	31.1	146.3
Accidents	(E800-E962)	84.2	68.8	159.5	10.6	8.1	22.4	73.6	60.6	137.1
Residual	(140-468,590-749,E963-E965)	92.3	81.4	145.4	27.8	26.0	36.8	64.4	55.4	108.6
Certain diseases of early infancy	(760-776)	1,426.0	1,267.6	2,200.8	1,398.4	1,250.4	2,121.6	27.6	17.2	78.7
All causes		2,364.3	2,062.9	3,838.2	1,712.8	1,558.1	2,469.6	651.4	504.8	1,386.6

[a] Includes gastritis and duodenitis; gastroenteritis and colitis, except ulcerative, 4 weeks of age and over; chronic enteritis and ulcerative colitis; diarrhea of newborn.
[b] Includes neonatal disorders arising from certain diseases of mother during pregnancy; ill-defined diseases peculiar to early infancy; immaturity with mention of other subsidiary condition; and other diseases peculiar to early infancy not already shown.
[c] Rate based on a frequency of less than 20 deaths.
[d] Category not applicable.

Source: Based on data in *Vital Statistics of the United States* for the years 1965-1967, Vol. I and Vol. II–Part A.

TABLE C-6 Ratio between Infant Mortality Rates for Nonwhite and White Infants by Age and Cause of Death: United States, 1965–1967

Cause of Death (7th Revision–International Classification of Diseases)		Ratio of Death Rates per 1,000 Live Births Nonwhite/White		
		Infant	Neo-natal	Post-neo-natal
Infective and parasitic diseases	(001-138)	2.38	2.50	2.37
Influenza and pneumonia, including pneumonia of newborn	(480-493,763)	3.22	2.59	3.48
All other diseases of respiratory system	(470-475,500-527)	2.62	1.85	2.71
Gastritis and duodenitis, etc.[a]	(543,571,572,764)	6.23	7.57	5.95
All other diseases of digestive system	(530-542,544-570,573-587)	1.43	1.17	2.01
Congenital malformations	(750-759)	0.87	0.75	1.11
Birth injuries	(760,761)	1.25	1.25	c
Intracranial and spinal injury at birth	(760)	1.78	1.78	d
Other birth injury	(761)	1.03	1.03	c
Postnatal asphyxia and atelectasis	(762)	1.67	1.65	2.83
Hemolytic disease of newborn	(770)	0.38	0.37	c
Immaturity unqualified	(776)	2.18	2.17	7.67
Neonatal disorders arising from certain diseases of mother during pregnancy, etc.[b]	(765-769,771-774)	1.64	1.52	5.33
Symptoms and ill-defined conditions	(780-793,795)	5.44	8.00	4.70
Accidents	(E800-E962)	2.32	2.77	2.26
Residual	(140-468,590-749,E963-E965)	1.79	1.42	1.96
Certain diseases of early infancy	(760-776)	1.74	1.70	4.58
All causes		1.86	1.59	2.71

[a] Includes gastritis and duodenitis; gastroenteritis and colitis, except ulcerative, 4 weeks of age and over; chronic enteritis and ulcerative colitis; diarrhea of newborn.
[b] Includes neonatal disorders arising from certain diseases of mother during pregnancy; ill-defined diseases peculiar to early infancy; immaturity with mention of other subsidiary condition; and other diseases peculiar to infancy not already shown.
[c] Ratio was not computed because rates are based on small numbers.
[d] Category not applicable.

Source: Based on data in *Vital Statistics of the United States* for the years 1965–1967, Vol. I and Vol. II–Part A.

TABLE C-7 Fetal Death Ratios and Infant Mortality Rates by Age and Color: United States and Each State, 1968

State/Color	Rate (ratio) per 1,000 Live Births			
	Fetal	Infant	Neonatal	Postneonatal
Alabama	20.1	26.6	18.7	7.9
White	14.0	20.9	16.4	4.5
Nonwhite	31.9	37.7	23.3	14.4
Alaska	12.1	21.8	15.6	6.2
White	11.6	16.6	13.7	2.9
Nonwhite	13.5	34.7	20.0	14.7
Arizona	11.5	23.0	14.9	8.1
White	10.5	19.7	14.8	4.9
Nonwhite	16.3	38.8	15.9	22.9
Arkansas	16.1	23.2	15.8	7.4
White	12.3	18.6	13.8	4.8
Nonwhite	26.8	36.0	21.3	14.7
California	11.8	19.0	14.0	5.0
White	11.3	18.4	13.7	4.7
Nonwhite	15.3	22.6	16.3	6.3
Colorado	28.7	20.6	15.7	4.9
White	28.1	20.3	15.5	4.8
Nonwhite	40.1	27.3	18.2	9.1
Connecticut	11.4	19.0	14.4	4.6
White	10.1	17.8	13.5	4.3
Nonwhite	22.7	30.1	22.3	7.8
Delaware	15.9	20.2	14.0	6.2
White	12.7	16.0	12.4	3.6
Nonwhite	29.1	37.3	20.4	16.9
District of Columbia	17.6	25.9	18.8	7.1
White	11.2	16.6	11.2	5.4
Nonwhite	18.9	27.7	20.3	7.4
Florida	14.7	24.1	17.4	6.7
White	11.1	19.8	15.1	4.7
Nonwhite	25.1	36.5	23.9	12.6
Georgia	18.0	25.4	16.8	8.6
White	14.5	19.4	14.6	4.8
Nonwhite	25.2	37.6	21.5	16.1
Hawaii	25.3	18.2	13.6	4.6
White	32.7	15.6	13.0	2.6
Nonwhite	22.0	19.2	13.9	5.3

TABLE C-7 *(Continued)*

State/Color	Rate (ratio) per 1,000 Live Births			
	Fetal	Infant	Neonatal	Postneonatal
Idaho	11.2	18.4	13.1	5.3
White	11.2	18.2	13.0	5.2
Nonwhite	9.6[a]	28.8[a]	16.0[a]	12.8[a]
Illinois	13.7	23.4	17.5	5.9
White	11.7	20.0	15.4	4.6
Nonwhite	21.8	37.6	26.0	11.6
Indiana	13.1	21.9	16.4	5.5
White	12.0	20.5	15.6	4.9
Nonwhite	24.3	36.7	24.7	12.0
Iowa	11.6	19.1	15.3	3.8
White	11.5	18.8	15.1	3.7
Nonwhite	15.7[a]	32.2	25.8	6.4
Kansas	11.5	19.4	15.3	4.1
White	10.4	18.5	14.8	3.7
Nonwhite	24.9	30.7	21.6	9.1
Kentucky	14.3	21.9	16.2	5.7
White	13.4	21.0	15.7	5.3
Nonwhite	23.5	31.5	21.5	10.0
Louisiana	14.7	25.3	18.2	7.1
White	9.6	18.2	14.6	3.6
Nonwhite	22.8	36.8	24.0	12.8
Maine	14.7	21.5	15.9	5.6
White	14.5	21.5	15.8	5.7
Nonwhite	30.4[a]	26.1[a]	17.4[a]	8.7[a]
Maryland	13.6	21.3	16.1	5.2
White	12.1	17.9	14.2	3.7
Nonwhite	18.8	33.3	22.6	10.7
Massachusetts	12.2	19.9	15.7	4.2
White	11.9	19.2	15.1	4.1
Nonwhite	16.3	34.2	25.8	8.4
Michigan	13.0	21.6	16.4	5.2
White	11.3	19.3	14.8	4.5
Nonwhite	22.6	34.8	25.8	9.0
Minnesota	11.8	18.4	13.8	4.6
White	11.6	18.1	13.8	4.3
Nonwhite	20.2	26.8	12.5	14.3

TABLE C-7 (*Continued*)

State/Color	Rate (ratio) per 1,000 Live Births			
	Fetal	Infant	Neonatal	Postneonatal
Mississippi	29.5	35.5	24.5	11.0
White	22.3	22.9	18.6	4.3
Nonwhite	36.8	48.1	30.3	17.8
Missouri	15.1	21.4	16.0	5.4
White	13.3	19.3	14.7	4.6
Nonwhite	25.1	33.4	23.3	10.1
Montana	12.3	19.5	14.6	4.9
White	11.5	18.3	14.4	3.9
Nonwhite	22.1	33.2	17.1[a]	16.1
Nebraska	10.6	18.0	14.1	3.9
White	10.0	17.1	13.7	3.4
Nonwhite	19.1	33.0	21.3	11.7
Nevada	14.1	26.5	19.7	6.8
White	13.4	25.5	19.6	5.9
Nonwhite	18.5	33.5	20.3	13.2
New Hampshire	12.0	18.8	14.4	4.4
White	12.1	18.9	14.5	4.4
Nonwhite	[b]	10.4[a]	[b]	[b]
New Jersey	14.1	21.2	16.5	4.7
White	12.5	17.9	14.1	3.8
Nonwhite	21.9	36.5	27.9	8.6
New Mexico	13.0	23.9	16.8	7.1
White	13.0	22.3	16.6	5.7
Nonwhite	13.1	33.5	17.8	15.7
New York	28.5	20.9	15.8	5.1
White	25.2	18.3	14.0	4.3
Nonwhite	44.2	33.5	23.9	9.6
North Carolina	17.0	26.3	18.4	7.9
White	13.0	20.9	16.4	4.5
Nonwhite	26.2	38.7	23.1	15.6
North Dakota	13.0	16.9	12.8	4.1
White	12.8	16.9	13.2	3.7
Nonwhite	16.9[a]	16.9[a]	6.8[a]	10.1
Ohio	13.1	20.3	15.5	4.8
White	12.0	18.7	14.4	4.3
Nonwhite	21.3	32.5	23.5	9.0

TABLE C-7 (*Continued*)

State/Color	Rate (ratio) per 1,000 Live Births			
	Fetal	Infant	Neonatal	Postneonatal
Oklahoma	12.4	20.0	14.8	5.2
White	10.7	19.5	14.9	4.6
Nonwhite	21.7	22.6	14.3	8.3
Oregon	13.8	19.7	14.3	5.4
White	13.4	19.3	14.0	5.3
Nonwhite	23.5	29.0	19.6	9.4
Pennsylvania	16.4	21.7	17.1	4.6
White	14.7	19.6	15.5	4.1
Nonwhite	29.1	37.2	28.3	8.9
Rhode Island	12.0	21.3	16.4	4.9
White	11.8	20.6	15.9	4.7
Nonwhite	14.4[a]	33.6	25.2	8.4
South Carolina	16.8	27.0	16.7	10.3
White	12.4	20.5	15.2	5.3
Nonwhite	23.9	37.4	19.0	18.4
South Dakota	13.6	20.5	15.7	4.8
White	12.4	19.0	15.0	4.0
Nonwhite	22.3	32.4	20.8	11.6
Tennessee	17.0	23.2	16.8	6.4
White	14.7	19.8	15.0	4.8
Nonwhite	25.7	35.8	23.2	12.6
Texas	14.2	22.2	16.3	5.9
White	12.7	19.8	14.9	4.9
Nonwhite	22.7	35.6	24.0	11.6
Utah	10.4	17.6	13.3	4.3
White	10.2	16.6	13.0	3.6
Nonwhite	16.5	52.4	25.4[a]	27.0
Vermont	22.0	19.7	15.9	3.8
White	22.0	19.8	16.0	3.8
Nonwhite	22.7[a]	[b]	[b]	[b]
Virginia	24.1	22.7	17.0	5.7
White	21.4	18.7	14.8	3.9
Nonwhite	32.9	36.2	24.1	12.1
Washington	10.9	19.7	14.2	5.5
White	10.6	19.0	14.0	5.0
Nonwhite	15.6	28.6	16.9	11.7

TABLE C-7 *(Continued)*

State/Color	Rate (ratio) per 1,000 Live Births			
	Fetal	Infant	Neonatal	Postneonatal
West Virginia	15.8	23.4	16.9	6.5
White	15.5	22.4	16.3	6.1
Nonwhite	23.3	42.3	28.9	13.4
Wisconsin	11.5	19.5	14.9	4.6
White	11.0	18.8	14.6	4.2
Nonwhite	20.8	31.2	20.8	10.4
Wyoming	15.1	21.3	17.3	4.0
White	14.4	19.5	16.1	3.4
Nonwhite	27.8^a	55.6^a	41.7^a	13.9^a
United States	15.8	21.8	16.1	5.7
White	13.8	19.2	14.7	4.5
Nonwhite	25.6	34.5	23.0	11.5

[a] Based on less than 20 deaths.
[b] Data not available.
Source: Based on data in *Vital Statistics of the United States,* 1968, Vol. I and Vol. II— Part A.

TABLE C-8   Fetal, Neonatal, Postneonatal, and Early Childhood Mortality Rates by Father's Occupation: New York State, Exclusive of New York City, 1950–1952 Birth Cohort[a]

Father's Occupation at Time of Infant's Birth	Number of Single White Live Births	Percentage Distribution of Live Births	Fetal[b]	Neonatal[c]	Post-neonatal[d]	Early Childhood[e]
Nonagricultural						
Professionals	61,600	14.1	12.8	14.1	3.7	2.4
Managerial	40,966	9.4	13.3	15.2	3.5	2.9
Sales workers	25,095	5.8	14.3	15.0	4.6	2.9
Clerical workers	26,581	6.1	14.9	14.3	3.9	2.8
Craftsmen	105,803	24.3	15.5	16.0	5.0	3.6
Operatives	87,331	20.0	17.8	17.4	6.0	3.5
Service workers	14,882	3.4	17.8	18.3	5.6	4.5
Nonfarm laborers	37,099	8.5	18.0	18.8	9.6	4.9
Agricultural						
Farmers	20,770	4.8	17.7	15.9	6.4	5.5
Farm laborers	3,149	0.7	18.1	20.4	8.3	3.7
Not classified	12,859	2.9	22.7	22.8	6.8	3.4
TOTAL	436,045	100.0	15.9	16.3	5.3	3.5

Mortality Rates column group spans: Fetal[b], Neonatal[c], Post-neonatal[d], Early Childhood[e]

[a] based on single white births.
[b] 20 weeks or more gestation per 1,000 live births and fetal deaths.
[c] Under 28 days per 1,000 live births.
[d] 28 days–11 months per 1,000 survivors to 28 days.
[e] 1–4 years per 1,000 survivors to 1 year.

Source: Chase HC: The relationship of certain biologic and socio-economic factors to fetal, infant, and early childhood mortality. I. Father's occupation, parental age, and infant's birth rank: New York State Department of Health, 1961; and U.S. Department of Health, Education, and Welfare, Children's Bureau, 1964 reprint.

TABLE C-9 Estimated Infant Deaths per 1,000 Legitimate Live Births by Education of Mother and Infant's Race and Age at Death: United States, 1964–1966

	Education of Mother (years)					
Race/Age at Death	All Levels	8 or less	9–11	12	13–15	16 or more
All races						
Less than 1 year	23.0	35.2	27.7	19.5	15.9	20.0
Less than 1 day	9.8	12.4	11.2	8.9	7.0	10.3
1–6 days	5.6	7.0	6.3	5.1	4.8	5.1
7–27 days	1.7	3.6	2.2	1.2	0.5	1.1
1–5 months	4.3	8.1	6.0	2.9	2.7	2.6
6–11 months	1.7	4.1	2.1	1.3	0.9	0.9
White						
Less than 1 year	20.8	32.0	24.6	18.0	15.0	19.6
Less than 1 day	9.1	11.4	10.6	8.5	6.2	10.3
1–6 days	5.3	6.7	5.9	4.8	5.0	4.7
7–27 days	1.4	3.2	1.8	1.1	0.5	1.1
1–5 months	3.5	7.1	4.5	2.6	2.5	2.5
6–11 months	1.5	3.6	1.8	1.1	0.8	1.0
Black						
Less than 1 year	39.5	45.9	41.7		34.0	
Less than 1 day	14.7	16.9	13.1		14.9	
1–6 days	8.3	8.6	8.1		8.3	
7–27 days	3.7	4.9	4.4		2.4	
1–5 months	9.9	11.7	13.3		5.9	
6–11 months	2.9	3.8	2.8		2.5	

Source: National Center for Health Statistics: Infant Mortality Rates: Socioeconomic Factors. Department of Health, Education, and Welfare. Washington, D.C., Government Printing Office, 1972 (PHS Publ. No. 72-1045, Ser 22, No 14).

TABLE C-10 Percentage Distribution of Live Births by Birth Weight and Color: United States, 1960 Live-Birth Cohort

Birth Weight (grams)	Percent of Live Births		
	Total	White	Nonwhite
2,500 or less	7.8	6.8	12.9
2,501 or more	92.2	93.2	87.1
1,000 or less	0.6	0.5	1.0
1,001–1,500	0.7	0.6	1.2
1,501–2,000	1.5	1.3	2.5
2,001–2,500	5.1	4.5	8.3
2,501–3,000	18.5	17.2	25.3
3,001–3,500	38.0	38.1	37.1
3,501–4,000	26.8	28.2	18.9
4,001–4,500	7.5	8.0	4.6
4,501 or more	1.5	1.6	1.2
TOTAL	100.0	100.0	100.0

Source: Chase HC: Infant mortality and weight at birth: 1960 United States birth cohort. Am J Public Health 59:1618–1628, 1969.

TABLE C-11 Infant, Neonatal, and Postneonatal Mortality Rates by Birth Weight and Color: United States, 1960 Live-Birth Cohort

Birth Weight (grams)	Mortality Rate per 1,000 Live Births						Mortality Rate per 1,000 Survivors		
	Under 1 Year			Under 28 Days			28 days–11 months		
	Total	White	Non-white	Total	White	Non-white	Total	White	Non-white
2,500 or less	190.3	191.9	185.7	171.6	177.4	154.8	22.6	17.7	36.6
2,501 or more	11.2	9.7	20.0	5.5	5.1	7.7	5.8	4.6	12.4
1,000 or less	919.3	929.3	893.6	912.8	924.1	883.7	74.0	67.8	84.4
1,001–1,500	548.5	575.6	478.1	521.5	555.1	434.2	56.5	46.2	77.6
1,501–2,000	206.6	219.0	171.8	180.6	198.4	130.3	31.7	25.6	47.7
2,001–2,500	58.4	58.2	59.4	41.4	45.0	30.7	17.7	13.8	29.5
2,501–3,000	19.0	17.3	25.3	9.9	10.1	9.4	9.2	7.3	16.0
3,001–3,500	10.1	8.9	17.4	4.7	4.4	6.4	5.5	4.5	11.1
3,501–4,000	8.0	6.9	17.0	3.6	3.3	6.6	4.3	3.6	10.5
4,001–4,500	8.3	7.0	21.0	4.2	3.6	10.1	4.1	3.4	11.0
4,501 or more	13.3	11.2	28.1	8.7	7.7	16.3	4.6	3.5	11.9
TOTAL	25.1	22.2	41.4	18.4	16.9	26.7	6.9	5.4	15.1

Source: Chase HC: Infant mortality and weight at birth, 1960 United States birth cohort. Am J Public Health 59:1618–1628, 1969.

TABLE C-12 Estimated Average Annual Number of Legitimate Live Births and Percent Distribution by Race and Birth Weight According to Education of Mother: United States, 1964–1965

Race/Birth Weight in Grams	Education of Mother (years)					
	All Levels	8 or Less	9–11	12	13–15	16 or More
	Number of Live Births in Thousands					
All races						
All birth weights	3,572	445	888	1,560	429	249
2,500 or less	281	47	84	110	26	14
2,501–3,000	645	87	174	270	77	37
3,001–3,500	1,397	168	344	615	165	105
3,501–4,000	933	102	213	432	120	66
4,001 and over	317	41	73	132	41	29
White						
All birth weights	3,094	342	724	1,403	393	232
2,500 or less	217	32	63	88	23	11
2,501–3,000	528	58	134	232	70	33
3,001–3,500	1,205	132	278	549	148	99
3,501–4,000	855	88	184	408	113	61
4,001 and over	289	32	65	126	39	28
Black						
All birth weights	421	93	151	138	26	12
2,500 or less	59	14	21	20	*	*
2,501–3,000	108	27	38	36	5	*
3,001–3,500	161	32	59	54	11	*
3,501–4,000	69	13	25	22	5	*
4,001 and over	24	7	8	7	*	*
	Percent Distribution by Birth Weight					
All races						
All birth weights	100.0	100.0	100.0	100.0	100.0	100.0
2,500 or less	7.9	10.6	9.4	7.1	6.0	5.5
2,501–3,000	18.1	19.4	19.6	17.3	17.9	14.7
3,001–3,500	39.1	37.8	38.7	39.4	38.5	42.0
3,501–4,000	26.1	23.0	23.9	27.7	28.0	26.4
4,001 and over	8.9	9.2	8.3	8.5	9.6	11.4

TABLE C-12 *(Continued)*

Race/Birth Weight in Grams	Education of Mother (years)					
	All Levels	8 or Less	9–11	12	13–15	16 or More
Percent Distribution by Birth Weight						
White						
All birth weights	100.0	100.0	100.0	100.0	100.0	100.0
2,500 or less	7.0	9.3	8.7	6.3	5.9	4.9
2,501–3,000	17.1	17.0	18.5	16.6	17.8	14.4
3,001–3,500	38.9	38.5	38.4	39.1	37.7	42.5
3,501–4,000	27.6	25.8	25.5	29.1	28.8	26.2
4,001 and over	9.3	9.4	9.0	9.0	9.8	12.0
Black						
All birth weights	100.0	100.0	100.0	100.0	100.0	100.0
2,500 or less	14.0	14.7	13.7	14.2	*	*
2,501–3,000	25.7	28.8	25.1	26.0	20.8	*
3,001–3,500	38.2	34.8	39.2	39.4	41.5	*
3,501–4,000	16.4	14.0	16.7	15.7	19.9	*
4,001 and over	5.8	7.7	5.4	4.8	*	*

* Estimates of the number of births are not shown for cells with less than 5,000 annual births.

Source: National Center for Health Statistics: Infant Mortality Rates: Socioeconomic Factors. Department of Health, Education, and Welfare. Washington, D.C., Government Printing Office, 1972 (PHS Publ No 72-1045, Ser 22, No 14).

TABLE C-13   Estimated Infant Deaths per 1,000 Legitimate Live Births by Education of Mother and Race and Birth Weight of Infant: United States, 1964–1965

Race/Birth Weight in Grams	All Levels	8 or Less	9–11	12	13–15	16 or More
	Education of Mother (years)					
			Deaths per 1,000 Live Births			
All races						
All birth weights	23.5	36.6	30.0	18.6	16.5	19.7
2,500 or less	185.5	205.9	197.5	167.5	171.8	*
2,501–3,000	19.4	23.4	24.8	14.1	19.7	22.9
3,001–3,500	7.3	13.7	9.5	5.8	3.0	5.9
3,501–4,000	6.6	15.4	8.4	5.1	3.3	3.4
4,001 or more	9.2	16.3	9.1	7.6	5.5	11.8
White						
All birth weights	21.0	32.8	26.0	17.5	15.7	19.0
2,500 or less	184.0	198.3	183.7	177.3	*	*
2,501–3,000	18.2	28.9	21.3	13.0	19.1	21.7
3,001–3,500	6.8	11.5	9.1	5.8	3.0	5.1
3,501–4,000	5.9	14.0	7.6	4.5	2.9	3.7
4,001 or more	7.7	13.9	7.7	6.2	4.4	12.0
Black						
All birth weights	40.7	48.9	47.7	29.4	32.7	*
2,500 or less	188.7	*	*	*	*	*
2,501–3,000	24.6	10.7	35.8	20.3	*	*
3,001–3,500	11.3	20.8	11.7	5.1	*	*
3,501–4,000	14.0	*	15.7	*	*	*
4,001 or more	*	*	*	*	*	*

*Estimates of infant mortality rates are not given for cells in which the average annual number of births was less than 25,000.

Source: National Center for Health Statistics. Infant Mortality Rates: Socioeconomic Factors. Department of Health, Education, and Welfare. Washington, D.C., Government Printing Office, 1972 (PHS Publ No 72-1045, Ser 22, No 14).

TABLE C-14 Percent Low-Birth-Weight Infants (2,500 Grams or Less) by
Father's Occupation and Mother's Age: New York State, Exclusive of New York
City, 1950–1952 Live-Birth Cohort[a]

Father's Occupation at Time of Infant's Birth	Total	Mother's Age (years) at Time of Infant's Birth					
		Under 20	20–24	25–29	30–34	35–39	40 and Over
		Percent 2,500 Grams or Less					
Nonagricultural							
Professional	6.1	7.4	5.7	5.7	6.3	7.8	9.4
Managerial	6.5	8.1	5.9	5.9	6.6	8.1	8.3
Sales workers	6.9	8.3	6.5	6.5	6.7	8.9	9.1
Clerical workers	6.7	6.9	6.4	6.4	6.5	8.1	9.6
Craftsmen	7.1	8.1	6.9	6.7	7.1	8.1	9.9
Operatives	7.5	8.9	7.2	7.0	7.6	8.7	10.0
Service workers	7.6	10.9	7.3	6.7	7.4	8.8	10.4
Nonfarm laborers	8.1	9.2	7.8	7.1	8.7	9.3	10.7
Agricultural							
Farmers	6.0	7.5	5.8	5.7	5.5	6.5	8.2
Farm laborers	6.8	8.6	6.0	7.1	8.1	4.0	8.5[b]
Not classified	11.5	11.9	10.8	10.1	12.3	13.7	13.5
TOTAL	7.1	8.9	6.9	6.5	7.1	8.3	9.6

[a] Based on single white births.
[b] Based on less than 100 births.

Source: Chase HC: The relationship of certain biologic and socio-economic factors to fetal,
infant, and early childhood mortality. II. Father's occupation, infant's birth weight, and
mother's age. New York State Department of Health, 1962.

TABLE C-15 Percentage Distribution of Total Deliveries, Percent Low Birth Weight (2,500 Grams or Less), and Fetal and Neonatal Mortality by Education of Mother and Color: North Carolina, 1968 Birth Cohort

Education of Mother	Distribution of Deliveries			Percent Low Birth Weight			Fetal Mortality[a]			Neonatal Mortality[b]		
	Total	White	Non-white	Total	White	Non-white	Total	White	Non-white	Total	White	Non-white
	Percent			Percent			Rate			Rate		
None or elementary	11.1	8.9	16.3	14.4	12.0	17.6	23.1	18.1	29.5	22.5	20.0	25.7
High school, 1–3 years	34.0	30.0	43.3	12.0	9.8	15.6	15.7	11.3	22.7	19.8	17.6	23.4
High school, 4 years	36.7	39.6	30.0	9.3	7.5	14.8	14.7	12.5	21.5	17.4	16.0	21.7
College, 1–3 years	9.5	11.5	4.6	7.6	6.6	13.3	10.4	7.5	27.5	11.8	11.5	13.4
College, 4 or more years	6.3	7.8	2.8	6.9	6.0	13.0	7.9	6.6	16.6	13.4	10.8	31.1
Not stated	2.4	2.1	3.0	14.9	12.4	19.3	89.8	73.5	117.0	31.6	27.5	38.8
State total	100.0	100.0	100.0	10.6	8.5	15.6	16.9	12.9	26.3	18.3	16.1	23.4

[a] Fetal deaths 20 weeks or more gestation per 1,000 live births and fetal deaths.
[b] Infant deaths under 28 days of age per 1,000 live births.
Source: North Carolina State Board of Health: *Perinatal Mortality Statistics, 1968.* Public Health Statistics Section of the North Carolina State Board of Health, Raleigh, N.C.

TABLE C-16 Death Rates among Previous Births by Outcome of the 1950–1952 Birth: New York State, Exclusive of New York City, 1950–1952 Birth Cohort[a]

Outcome of 1950–1952 Birth Cohort	Previous Loss Rate[b]	Previous Fetal Death Rate[c]	Previous Postnatal Death Rate[d]
Survived to 5 years of age	62.4	22.3	41.1
Died before 5 years of age			
Fetal death	165.4	96.1	76.7
Neonatal death	153.8	56.4	103.3
Postneonatal death	83.9	19.8	65.4
Early childhood death	91.7	22.5	70.8
All births to multiparae	66.3	24.4	43.0

[a] Based on previous reproductive experience of multiparae of single white total births.
[b] Previous fetal and postnatal deaths per 1,000 previous births (fetal deaths and live births).
[c] Previous fetal deaths per 1,000 previous births.
[d] Previous postnatal deaths per 1,000 previous live births.

Source: Chase HC: The relationship of certain biologic and socio-economic factors to fetal, infant, and early childhood mortality. III. Previous loss. New York State Department of Health, 1963.

TABLE C-17 Mortality Rates and Relative Mortality Ratios by Selected Characteristics: New York State, Exclusive of New York City, 1950–1952 Birth Cohort[a]

Characteristic	Fetal[b]		Neonatal[c]		Post-neonatal[d]		Early Childhood[e]	
	Rate	Ratio	Rate	Ratio	Rate	Ratio	Rate	Ratio
Total single white	15.9	100	16.3	100	5.3	100	3.5	100
Nonagricultural								
Professional	12.8	81	14.1	87	3.7	70	2.4	69
Managerial	13.3	84	15.2	93	3.5	66	2.9	83
Sales workers	14.3	90	15.0	92	4.6	87	2.9	83
Clerical workers	14.9	94	14.3	88	3.9	74	2.8	80
Craftsmen	15.5	97	16.0	98	5.0	94	3.6	103
Operatives	17.8	112	17.4	107	6.0	113	3.5	100
Service workers	17.8	112	18.3	112	5.6	106	4.5	129
Nonfarm laborers	18.0	113	18.8	115	9.6	181	4.9	140
Agricultural	17.8	112	16.5	101	6.7	126	5.2	149
Not classified	26.9	169	28.5	175	7.6	143	4.5	129
Mother's age (years)								
Under 20	14.5	91	19.9	122	7.0	132	4.2	120
20–24	11.9	75	15.0	92	5.7	108	3.5	100

TABLE C-17 *(Continued)*

Characteristic	Fetal[b] Rate	Ratio	Neonatal[c] Rate	Ratio	Post-neonatal[d] Rate	Ratio	Early Childhood[e] Rate	Ratio
25–29	13.7	86	15.1	93	4.9	92	3.3	94
30–34	17.5	110	16.6	102	4.6	87	3.3	94
35–39	26.5	167	19.1	117	5.3	100	3.8	109
40 and over	44.4	279	23.6	145	8.2	155	5.3	151
Father's age (years)								
Under 20	13.6	86	20.6	126	5.8	109	3.0	86
20–24	11.9	75	16.1	99	6.3	119	3.5	100
25–29	13.0	82	14.8	91	4.7	89	3.2	91
30–34	14.2	89	15.6	96	4.9	92	3.2	91
35–39	19.3	121	16.6	102	4.9	92	3.9	111
40–44	26.9	169	19.8	121	6.4	121	4.0	114
45 and over	35.9	226	22.8	140	8.7	164	4.5	129
Not stated	28.3	178	26.9	165	7.3	138	4.9	140
Infant's birth rank								
First	16.6	104	15.8	97	3.8	72	2.7	77
Second	11.3	71	15.0	92	4.8	91	3.2	91
Third	15.4	97	16.2	99	5.9	111	3.6	103
Fourth	18.4	116	17.8	109	6.8	128	4.7	134
Fifth	22.8	143	20.9	128	8.2	155	4.8	137
Sixth	28.4	179	19.9	122	11.7	221	6.0	171
Seventh and higher	36.1	227	25.9	159	12.0	226	7.4	211
Weight at birth (grams)								
1,500 or less	374.8	2,357	731.3	4,487	50.4	951	5.1[f]	146[f]
1,501–2,000	135.1	850	209.7	1,287	26.1	492	6.8	194
2,001–2,500	48.9	308	45.0	276	12.6	238	5.9	169
2,501–3,000	10.5	66	10.3	63	6.7	126	3.9	111
3,001–3,500	6.7	42	5.3	33	4.7	89	3.2	91
3,501–4,000	4.7	30	4.2	26	3.7	70	3.2	91
4,001 or more	10.5	66	5.2	32	3.6	68	3.3	94
Presumed legitimacy								
Legitimate	15.9	100	16.1	99	5.3	100	3.5	100
Illegitimate	22.7	143	22.8	140	6.8	128	3.4	97

[a] Based on single white births.
[b] Fetal deaths with 20 completed weeks or more gestation per 1,000 live births and fetal deaths (20 completed weeks or more).
[c] Deaths under 28 days of age per 1,000 live births.
[d] Deaths 28 days–11 months of age per 1,000 survivors to 28 days of age.
[e] Deaths 1–4 years of age per 1,000 survivors to 1 year of age.
[f] Based on less than 100 births.

Source: Chase HC: The relationship of certain biologic and socio-economic factors to fetal, infant, and early childhood mortality. I. Father's occupation, parental age, and infant's birth rank. New York State Department of Health, 1961; and U.S. Department of Health, Education, and Welfare, Children's Bureau, 1964 reprint. Supplemented by unpublished data.

APPENDIX D

Further Research: Objectives and Study Designs

The research objectives, which we considered of utmost priority for maternal and infant health services, are:

- Determination of the influence of patient self-selection factors on the outcome of pregnancy. Identifying the factors that cause one woman to opt for early prenatal care—while another woman, otherwise her apparent peer, does not—will provide useful information for assigning resource-allocation priorities to social and health programs.
- Definition of delivered health services. For a better understanding of the relationship of maternal health care to the various needs or risks of pregnant women, it is crucial to define the content of adequate, intermediate, and inadequate care as used in our New York City study.
- Identify the costs of delivering maternal and infant health services. Measures need to be developed that will identify the present cost of maternal and infant health services, relate those costs to specific elements in the content of care, and allow for the assessment of specific elements of content in relation to the outcome of pregnancy.
- Refinement of maternal risk measures. In our New York City study, we identified 54 percent of the women as at risk, and, of the 54 percent, 95 percent could have been identified at a first prenatal visit. Overall, however, we were able to identify only 71 percent of the women who actually lost their infant. Refinement of the maternal-risk measures should both narrow the number of women assigned risks and increase the identification of women, who, by the present measures, had no risk but nevertheless suffered an infant death.

- Confirmation of New York City study results. Studies similar to the New York City study should be undertaken to validate the associations between maternal risk and health services and infant death. The studies should be conducted using vital records from both urban and rural populations.

There are many study designs that could address these five objectives. We addressed only the gross aspects of six designs and weighed ethical, logistic, and cost implications of each. Both intervention and nonintervention studies were considered by a special group of consultants. The following are their conclusions.

INTERVENTION STUDIES

CONTROLLED CLINICAL TRIAL WITH RANDOM ALLOCATION OF CARE–PRENATAL CARE COMPARED TO NO PRENATAL CARE

In this design, a random sample of women in early pregnancy are randomly allocated to either a *no-care group* or a *care group.* This basic study design must be rejected. It is clearly unethical to withhold usual medical care from a group of pregnant women.

CONTROLLED CLINICAL TRIAL WITH RANDOM ALLOCATION OF CARE–USUAL PRENATAL MEDICAL CARE COMPARED TO SPECIAL PRENATAL HEALTH SERVICES

The basic study design is identical to that described above, except that usual care is not withheld from either group. However, there are legal and ethical questions involved with the random allocation of special health services. For example, some mothers at high risk would be denied the special services because of random allocation. In order to address these concerns, the strict random allocation would have to be relaxed so that any individual from the control population (usual care) could exercise an option to receive the "special care." In instances where this design has been used, a relatively small number exercised this option, and thus the integrity of the design was maintained. It is clear, however, that this design is only acceptable if a concerted effort is made to fully inform all those involved in the study concerning the benefits of the special care and their rights to obtain such services.

There is no question that this design poses a very difficult set of technical logistic and administrative problems and, as with all intervention studies, it would be very costly; it is equally clear that if the cost and the technical and administrative feasibility issues can be overcome, it would provide answers to many of the questions that have been raised.

CLINICAL TRIAL WITHOUT RANDOM ALLOCATION OF CARE—USUAL PRENATAL MEDICAL CARE COMPARED TO SPECIAL PRENATAL HEALTH SERVICES

The basic difference between this approach and the two above is that random allocation to one or the other kind of care is not used. Basically, however, the same ethical and legal questions are involved as discussed above and could be handled in the same manner. Also, the technical and administrative similarities and the high costs are comparable to the above described design. The sole difference is that the type of care is not allocated on a random basis, but special care, for example, is assigned to one probability population sample within a community while another sample receives usual care. Alternatively, two different communities with comparable demographic and social characteristics could be compared.

This nonrandom allocation design reduces the technical problems and decreases the costs somewhat but retains difficult logistic problems.

NONINTERVENTION (OBSERVATIONAL STUDIES)

The study strategies described below do not involve the delivery of services. Thus, the ethical and legal issues surrounding the delivery of care to some but not to all in need of care are removed. Further, the costs of such studies are greatly reduced. The specific strengths and weaknesses of the three major kinds of nonintervention studies are discussed below.

PROSPECTIVE (LONGITUDINAL)

With this design, populations of pregnant women would be followed through pregnancy and information obtained from their physicians concerning the content of the care delivered. In addition, special social, economic, and behavioral information would be obtained from the patient by interview, and observations would be made regarding attitude. Provided that those who participate are informed of the study objectives and they consent to join, there are no ethical questions raised by this design. However, the logistic and cost problems involved in access to private physicians' offices and obtaining information about delivered services should not be minimized. The design, however, is feasible and would provide a useful body of information.

RETROSPECTIVE

In this type of study, information would be limited to that available in existing medical outpatient and hospital records. It is very unlikely that this approach would provide better information than that already available from the New York study.

RETROSPECTIVE WITH SUPPLEMENTAL PATIENT AND PHYSICIAN INTERVIEWS

By supplementing record data with interviews of the patient and her physician, significantly better information could be obtained than that gathered by the usual retrospective design. This supplemental retrospective study, however, would not produce data as useful as that obtained from a longitudinal study.

In summary, we felt that a nonintervention study combining a prospective design with a retrospective plan supplemented by an interview (to reach women who obtain late or no care) would be feasible and that the cost would be reasonable. Further, this design is devoid of serious ethical or legal issues and is likely to result in information that addresses many but not all of the stated research objectives.